TRANCE
FORMATION OF AMERICA

By Cathy O'Brien with Mark Phillips

TRANCE
FORMATION OF AMERICA

By Cathy O'Brien with Mark Phillips

Published by
Reality Marketing, Incorporated
www.trance-formation.com

TRANCE
FORMATION OF AMERICA

Seventeenth Edition Privately Published in the
United States of America by
Reality Marketing, Incorporated

www.trance-formation.com

Copyright 1995
ISBN
9780966016543
Library of Congress
2001 616223

In loving memory and honor of...

Mark Phillips
1943-2017

US Government Whistle blower who dedicated and ultimately gave his life to empower humanity to peacefully reclaim their inherent right to free thought in light of truths he exposed.

This documented testimony is therefore dedicated to fulfilling his life's mission to:

- Eradicate child abuse, human trafficking, and ultimately mind control
- Arm our military veterans with knowledge to stop the war within
- Peacefully restore individual and national sovereignty by empowering reclamation of innate human values, love, and strength of spirit...

...in light of truth that makes us free!

TABLE OF CONTENTS

BOOK ORDERING INFORMATION
(at the end of book)

PART I

By Mark Phillips

SEVENTEENTH PRINTING

Since the first printing of TRANCE was release in September 1995, many of the hard-to-comprehend details have been verified and miraculously managed to surface through our controlled medias. Please help us any way you can to provide this book to anyone who will further research its contents and thus shine the light of truth on the psychological warfare plan that is being silently waged against humanity.

Please remember, for as long as your thoughts remain free, and consider the psychological annoyance poser of a single mosquito in a room with no light.

This book will remain in print until justice prevails, the technological antidote for Kelly is provided, and unbiased, uncensored mass news media attention is given to the contents of this book. Thank you for your support.

FOREWORD

By Mark Phillips

"…with liberty and justice for all."

Preamble to the United States Constitution

My name is Marquart (Mark) Ewing Phillips, born May 17, 1943 in Nashville, Tennessee. I have no criminal record and I have never been adjudged insane. I am not a scholar, professional writer, or mental health physician. While I lack the official published academic credentials, I am recognized internationally by mental health and law enforcement professionals as an authority on the secret science concerning external control of the mind.

The purpose of Part I of this book is to document how this reputation was gained. This brief and highly condensed contribution is intended to provide an understanding of why, when, and where I embarked on a study of the most secret technology known to man: Trauma-based mind control. Through the publication of declassified United Stated Government documents, our U.S. Department of Defense (DOD) admits that this ancient wizard's mechanism for control is so dangerous that most information pertaining to it must be classified as TOP SECRET. As the employee of a DOD subcontractor with exposure to mind control research, I was required to sign an oath of secrecy. To this day I am restricted by law from revealing certain information that directly pertained to my employment as, among other "sensitive" exposures, a U.S. DOD subcontractor in mind control research.

This super secret technology is an evolved system of remote human physical and psychological manipulation that has only recently been officially recognized by accredited mental health physicians for what it is, absolute mind control.

My first encounter with mind control research began in the late 1960's in Atlanta, Georgia on the Emory University campus at the Yerkes Primate Center. It was there that I learned about primate behavior modification – the basis for human mind control. Part I of this book is my attempt to impart an understanding of how this and other exposures would prepare me for the challenge of a lifetime.

What I witnessed, in terms of technology, at the Yerkes Primate Center and other government sponsored research facilities, combined with years of personal research into this science of mind manipulation, did not adequately prepare me for what I would be exposed to in 1988 through an unexpected chain of events. This exposure came in the form of a personal acquaintance with the human results officially entitled by DOD as, among other cryptic files titles, MK Ultra.[1]

I have outlined this noxious introduction in hopes that the material provided by one MK Ultra survivor, Cathy O'Brien, will incite a legitimate federal investigation of her claims.

1

I was able to liberate MK Ultra victims Cathy O'Brien and her daughter Kelly from the invisible grip of this U.S. government secret weapon of control. In the process, I also helped Cathy recover her mental and physical health. However, I have not been successful in enlisting the cooperation of my government to pursue the justice issue. There is a reason for this failure to obtain justice that you, the reader, NEED TO KNOW. I have been told repeatedly, "Justice is not obtainable, **For Reasons of National Security.**"

This book is primarily the autobiography of Cathy O'Brien, who did not volunteer for service to her country, but was used her entire life against her innate, voluntary will for perpetuating criminal activity by many so-called leaders within the U.S. Government. These "treasonous leaders" did volunteer for political "service" from our country. They must be held accountable for their actions.

Together, Cathy and I have dedicated our lives to the pursuit of justice and rehabilitation for her and Kelly. All avenues for justice and rehabilitative relief have been blocked **For Reasons of National Security.** The question arises, who's security? Cathy O'Brien provides the logical answer. Perhaps after reading this work, you will inspire others to read it. Collectively, as patriots, we can make a positive difference for Cathy and Kelly, our government, and humanity, by having our voices heard. In my opinion, our great *United States Constitution* does not need to be amended, it needs to be enforced.

The grim reality we must all embrace is that there is, in human terms, no justice, and no revenge adequate to equal what these two, and many other victims of this U.S. Government secret weapon experienced. The only remaining remnant of opportunity for justice for these survivors, would derive from a public forum expose` of what they experienced. What these survivors need to witness is the mass dissemination of their story and a radical, positive change in their government's management of secrets. This would be an acceptable, though belated, substitute for justice. Their hope lies in the belief that –

**"Truth lives a wretched life,
but always survives a lie."
Anonymous**

---

[1] Weinstein, Harvey M., M.D., Psychiatry and the CIA: Victims of Mind Control American Psychiatric Press, 1990.

CHAPTER 1

MIND CONTROL BY ANY OTHER NAME

Sometimes words, or groups of words, found in the English language have many definitions or meanings. Within each meaning there may be different logical and literal perceptions of the application of a given word. However, the words mind control usually conjure up a single response. This is most unfortunate due to the vast differences of perception contained within the reference.

For example, if you have access to a late 1980's *Random House* or later *Webster's New Collegiate Dictionary* and reference mind control, you will notice there is a conspicuous absence of a listing. Should you go one step further and secure a college professor's teaching copy of *Oxford's Companion to the Mind* (Oxford Press 1987), you can reference practically anything concerning research of the mind sans a reference to mind control. Perhaps you may now realize that through Random House, Webster and Oxford Press omissions, you are a victim of information control.

Mind control is sometimes loosely defined as information control. This being one of many accepted ways to define the term should immediately raise questions of distrust towards your information sources. Since what we think is based on what we learn, manipulation of a mind, or a nation of minds, can be accomplished through control of information. With thought control being a result of information control, many avid researchers of mind sciences simply label it "soft" mind control.

These days, we live in a world in which the continued existence of multinational businesses and governments depends upon instant communications. However, with consideration to the so-called problem of information overload, it would appear to most people that we hear and see enough to make rational decisions concerning our individual lives. Unfortunately, this is not true. What we don't know, as evidenced by mind control atrocities, is quickly destroying society as we have known it.

The answer to this problem is glaringly apparent. We, as citizens of a supposedly free country, should not permit our government to restrict any information that protects criminal activity under the guise of National Security.

Secret knowledge equals power, with the end result being control. Therefore, despite the deliberate efforts of those persons in control of national media information management (who are not media employees), results of secret mind control projects gone awry have been leaking out for years through the media. People are literally waking up to the mind control reality because there is an obvious lack of logical explanation for certain sensational news events. What really happened at Jim Jones' Jonestown and with Sirhan Sirhan, John Hinkley, and Lee Harvey Oswald? And, more importantly, why did it happen? The simple common denominator existing among these persons has been publicly stated by the media, based on research of their medical histories, to be mind control.

In reality, information control is but one component of mind control. Whereas "brain washing," a term coined by an investigative journalist writing about Korean War P.O.W.'s around 1951, described the results of what the Chinese regarded as thought reform.

The term brainwashing denotes to most people the destruction of a person's memory. This slang term continues to be used by the news media in place of the all encompassing term, mind control. In reality, applied brainwashing techniques are similar to those used in trauma based behavior modification.

During the past three decades, a significant number of religious groups worldwide has been cited by the mainstream news media as <u>destructive</u> cults. An emphasis on the word destructive is necessary in defining these groups as cults. *Random House Dictionary* defines <u>cult</u> as "a particular system of religious worship." By this definition, the word cult would encompass all religions. These so called destructive cults have been publicly denounced by the news media for using brainwashing, thought reform, and mind manipulation tactics on their believers. However, there is an obvious lack of expressed concern by these same media as they fail to address the underlying issues of mind control, the power basis for abuse.

Perhaps the reporting news media cannot, for some reason, publicly open the proverbial Pandora's Box. Is it plausible then to consider that closer scrutiny, by the media and the public, of these destructive cults' leadership could reveal a solid connection to government sponsored mind control research? These are questions that, in themselves properly addressed, would provide important answers to this social epidemic involving physical and psychological abuse. The answers that an in-depth professional investigation would provide could be the first step in resolving the rash of problems that destructive cults, serial killers, and sexual child abuse, thrust upon society.

As consumers of national news media supplied information, we continue to accept half truths which, in this case scenario, is seeing and hearing only what <u>results</u> from mass mind manipulation.

Historians provide us a glimpse into the future through recorded events of the past. It appears that throughout recorded history, man has, towards the end of each millennium, returned to a focus on certain types of bizarre human behavior. For example, there has been in the past 150 years a resurgence of wide spread interest in the occult "black arts," which include Satanism or Lucifarian religions. These Constitutionally protected "religions" use trauma to control the minds of their followers.

Mind control practices within the occult groups (according to survivors adjudged credible and law enforcement officials) have been accredited with bridging the gap between applied science and Shamanism. Occultism as a manner of religious expression has been around for thousands of years. Only in the last 150 years has science aggressively pursued the truths regarding mind manipulation hidden within the occult belief systems themselves.

According to the *Random House Dictionary*, <u>occultism</u> "is the practice of alleged sciences claiming knowledge of supernatural agencies which are beyond the range of ordinary knowledge." Once again, a reminder that secret knowledge equals power.

In 1971, the *New York Times* reported a story on the Central Intelligence Agency (CIA) and occult research, the basis of which was gained through a collection of documents released by the U.S. Government Printing Office under the Freedom of Information Act. This was a report to Congress and clearly showed that the CIA was interested in the cause and effect clinical findings that occult religious practices have on the Black Arts practitioner's and/or the observer's mind. Of particular interest to the CIA were the

4

heightened levels of suggestibility that certain occult rituals produced in the minds of the practitioners. Cannibalism and blood rituals were ranked highest in the order of importance to their research.

Behavioral psychology teaches us that control of human suggestibility is recognized as the fundamental building block for external control of the mind. This suggestibility factor alone potentially creates a human rights legal issue when we consider constructing laws to protect people from overt or covert mind control practices. Consideration to the human suggestibility factor could result in all forms of consumer oriented service and/or product advertising becoming illegal. Advertising and the marketing of services and/or products through communications can be justifiably defined as a type of psychological manipulation, thought reform and/or mind manipulation which results in a form of behavior modification. A patriot friend, Steven Jacobson, published his book entitled *Mind Control in America*[2] in 1985, eloquently exposing the science of mind manipulation through advertising. The basis for successfully modifying human behavior requires mind manipulation techniques that, when expertly applied through advertising media, become a form of "soft" mind control.

Factoring in suggestibility through the tactile senses as the "Achilles heel" of the human race renders everyone vulnerable to becoming, on some level, a victim of soft mind control.

The controversy of what is and what is not mind control rages on among scholars in the schools of law, human rights, and mental health. All the while, the confusion of issues provides a form of legal protection for practitioners of trauma based mind control, the only known form of remote human control that is absolute. All other forms of mind control, including chemical and electronic manipulations, are considered by mind control experts as temporary.

There are laws protecting U.S. citizens' rights to practice their religious beliefs and freedom of speech. There are no laws which specifically protect leaders of destructive cults and/or practitioners of trauma based mind control. However, because of the U.S. Government's use of mind control and the broad diversity of legal opinion concerning the accepted limits of free speech and religious practices, the legal loop holes for criminals employing mind control techniques on their "flocks" for personal gain remain open.

For every problem there exists a solution. The formula for problem solving rests firmly on the quality of the supporting research information concerning the nature of the problem. Legislating laws specifically to protect people from mind control abuses would be futile. Practically every civilized society in existence has some law and/or group of laws which would protect the people and punish the practitioners of mind control. Laws are enforced according to law makers' interpretations of the specific legal language. The lack of enforcement of laws already on the books that could protect us from mind control abuses stems from applied legal interpretations and cover-ups of survivor testimony by the CIA and National Security Agency (NSA) For Reasons of National Security.

Mind control atrocities, if committed by anyone who could be linked to government sponsored projects, are typically ignored and covered up. Access to the courts by these hapless survivors is thus stonewalled by government paid so called legal experts who receive their orders from the National Security Agency.

5

Defining the term "mind control" is akin to defining the limits of the 1947 National Security Act. The basis for the solution to the National   Security controversy is simple. It is known as truth logically applied.

It is an obvious truth that the National Security Act has been interpreted, not to guard the integrity of military secrets, but instead to protect criminal activity of the highest order.

Repeal of this Act and replacement with the established rules of military conduct concerning National Security that do not infringe upon the Constitutional rights of America's citizenry or the rights of its allies would result in compliance with the Constitution.

[2] ISBN # 0-911485-00-7

CHAPTER 2

SALESMAN, AD MAN, MIND MAN, PATRIOT
MY PERSONAL EVOLUTION

"Every revolution, bloody or bloodless, has two phases. The first is the struggle for Freedom; the second the struggle for power. The phase of the struggle for Freedom is divine. He who has participated in it invariably feels, almost physically, that is best and most precious-inner self has come to the surface. We know that being faithful to the TRUTH stands higher than our own participation in governing the country. And that is why we must not have a society that would reject ethical norms in the name of political mirages."[3]

As I was saying to my grandmother Mamaleen Johnson, "My life has turned into a nightmare and I'm wide awake," tears were streaming down my face, dripping off my chin onto her patent leather shoes. She affectionately patted my shoulder as she listened.

The words we exchanged, the room's wallpaper and furnishings, my beloved grandmother Mamaleen, even the taste of my tears combined with a feeling of overwhelming grief -- it is all there etched into my memory.

This was the summer before I was to enter my second year of school in 1950. The first year remains a blur with cause.

Life for me and my family had changed dramatically over the previous year. So radical a change that it had taken almost a year for me to realize life was not becoming any easier to live. My stuttering was getting worse. The rare moments I could speak coherently were limited to short sentences devoid of the word "you" and then only to my mother and grandmother. Occasionally when angry I could speak clearly, or when alone in the woods while talking or singing to trees. Apparently, my frustration with oral communication due to stuttering had been intensified by a trauma I experienced the previous year. Little did I know then that this trauma would positively and negatively influence my future and the lives of others I would know for the rest of my life.

On a hot and sticky Tennessee July day in 1949, my father helped boost first my mother, then me, into the saddle astride our four-year-old high-spirited "gift horse" Wojac. This was to be my first ride on the back of an animal. The excitement of the moment combined with stuttering rendered me, literally, speechless. As I recall and from photographs taken at the time, I was wearing a sweat-soaked pale yellow cotton shirt, dark tan shorts, brown socks, and dirty tennis shoes. At six years old, I was very thin and did not take up the remaining saddle space behind my mother.

With the reins in my mother's hands, the horse responded to her polite command of "Come on, Wojac. Giddyup." He began slowly walking down our driveway to the narrow crushed limestone road beside our property. Upon reaching the gravel road, the horse turned or was guided left, momentarily disappointing me as I knew we were only going for a short ride. It was only about a quarter of a mile to the busy paved intersection that would be dangerous to cross. (Had my mother decided to go in the opposite direction, we could have ridden for a couple of miles before reaching any automobile traffic.)

As quickly as the horse made the turn from our driveway onto the country road, my mother nudged his flanks with her heels. With another command of "let's go," the horse responded with a mild jerk of motion and he began a fast trot down the middle of the road.

The horse's speed, in retrospect, was too fast for safe travel on gravel. Not knowing this then, I was not scared until I saw the crossroads looming closer. I can hear myself half shouting "BBBBBetter slow down. MMMight BBBBe a CCar CCComing." Before I could enunciate the last words, my mother began a slow sideways slide off the saddle. I could not see her face as she disappeared under the horse, and the reins disappeared with her. The horse bolted full speed ahead. In the blink of an eye, my realization of being alone in the saddle with no way to control the horse washed over me. Quickly, I tugged on his mane to no avail. It was in this instant I determined that the runaway horse was not going to stop for the crossroads. I jumped. As I recall, the fall was swift and my abrupt landing in the sharp rocks was not painful, though it seemed that my body would never stop rolling. Panicked and with the dust beginning to settle, I sat up, blinked the dust and sticky blood from my eyes, and looked about for my mother. She lay in a disorganized heap beside the road. I ran to her.

The first mental impression I experienced was that she was just wide-eyed dazed from her fall. Then I noticed her eyes weren't blinking and around her head was a thick puddle of blood. Not wanting to leave her in the road for fear she would be run over, and not strong enough to pick her up, I began screaming in the direction of our home in hopes that my father could hear me. Almost immediately he responded by sprinting to us, all the while shouting, "What happened? What happened?"

For the "life remaining in me" I could not answer for, as usual, I was speechless. As he knelt down to speak to my mother, he stopped mid sentence when he apparently saw her eyes in a fixed gaze and that the back of her skull was crushed inward. Instantly he picked her up, and as we were running back to the house, he commanded my eleven-year-old sister to call an ambulance. To this day I cannot recall how we got to the hospital.

The grisly scenes of this tragedy were not my nightmare. It did not play over and over again in my mind, for I had dissociated from it. I had voluntarily and autogenically created a memory barrier of this trauma. This is a normal human response. Had I been tortured after the trauma, I would not have been able to voluntarily recall either the accident or the torture. Hence the basis of this book.

The nightmare began during the subsequent recovery year when we realized my mother would never be herself again. She had lost over a quarter of her brain when the horse stepped into her skull. Permanently gone was her ability to smell, taste, and hear in one ear. These were the physical handicaps she developed. Her resultant emotional condition would become evident to me many years later. As a child, this new awareness of my mother's condition had minimal impact on me compared to the fear I lived with, moment to moment, due to my father's chronic alcoholism. Years later my sister would follow his lead into a losing battle with the bottle. I was safe, as alcohol made me stutter.

After being told so many times during my developmental years that my mother's condition was attributable to her brain damage, and that my stuttering was because my brain was not working correctly, it occurred to me at some point to learn about the brain. For years after the accident, I overheard adult conversations about my mother's brain. My curiosity peaked about the brain and the resultant invisible mind and had set the course for my life's interest.

Somewhere in this time period, I fantasized I would learn enough about the mind and brain to help my mother and myself.

As a child, my attention span was regarded as abnormal. I was considered very bright, yet my grades in school reflected something different. Although not properly diagnosed, I was most likely suffering from what is now termed Attention Deficit Disorder (ADD). The handicaps of stuttering and ADD were to become my first personal improvement challenges once I was out in the world on my own.

This "on my own" objective came at an early age. I was barely sixteen-years-old when I left home to begin my pursuit of happiness. My first efforts resulted in total failure. However, I could not return to my parents' home because they were now divorced.

Young, broke and rejected, I was able to determine two things. I must learn how to communicate if I was to enjoy any success in life. I went about this task methodically, first by enrolling myself into a local night college. In the classroom I studied speech, business law and psychology. At the library, I studied brain functions and their effect on the mind. I was not degree oriented because I could not earn enough at two jobs to attend the required classes to graduate, but my studies were slowly providing me a usable skill. Somewhere during this period of learning I began to realize I possessed a natural ability to sell. Perhaps this ability to persuade others resulted from my childhood experiencing of having to "read people" through their body language rather than talking with them.

My first real job in sales was so successful that my client base was reduced by my employer. I responded to this action by moving on.

The Viet Nam War was heating up and I was eligible for the draft. No longer in school, I knew that my number would be drawn soon. And it was. Little did I know that my prayers for a deferment would be answered and would afford me an exemption from military duty. I would soon be working for the Ampex Corporation and with the U.S. Department of Defense in a civilian capacity. The defense work closely associated me with top research scientists working in the area of primate and human behavior modification. Ironically, I learned more about the mind from my casual relationships with these scientists than I did working at the various research sites. The sites included teaching hospitals, state mental institutions, military bases, National Aeronautics and Space Administration (NASA) facilities, and the Yerkes Primate Center.

The following years of my corporate employment in national and international sales evolved into sales and marketing management positions in an executive capacity. My personal life, in terms of loving relationships, was again in shambles but my career and ongoing mind, brain, human behavior research was rewarding enough to compensate for my lack of emotional expression. The secrets I had learned so well concerning powers of persuasion, both conscious and subliminal, had long since become a functioning part of my mind's arsenal of defensive and offensive tools of control. I resolved then and there not to become a "control freak." Instead, my fantasy was not to learn what I could control but what was controlling me.

Then, around 1986, a peer friend of mine observed that I had arrived in the proverbial "comfort zone" in terms of presenting profitable ideas for others to act upon, and advised me to go into business for myself. Shortly thereafter, he provided me an excellent example by resigning his six-figure executive marketing directorship and nominating me as a candidate for his replacement. Ironically, for the first time in my life, a nomination was rejected because I did not possess at least a master's degree in business management or communications. His assistant was given the position, and I was subsequently offered the assistant's vacated position with no hope of promotion, which of course I refused. Soon thereafter, my friend, free of his corporate golden handcuffs, established his own firm which became a very successful business. Around this same time, a childhood acquaintance, long since socially separated from my life, reappeared long enough to introduce me to his country music entertainment friend, Alex Houston. From this introduction I learned this acquaintance, Ray Myers and his wife Regina, are alleged pedophiles who reportedly sexually molested Cathy's daughter and their own children. It seemed that Houston was looking for someone with international business negotiating skills who could assist him in putting together a large enough sales deal to finance a manufacturing operation. After spending a few days of complimentary consulting time with him, I had made some rather interesting and intriguing observations about the man and his ideas. First of all, Houston did have a legitimate, potentially profitable idea concerning the manufacture of an electrical capacitor device that could increase energy efficiency for large industrial consumers. Secondly, Houston favorably impressed me as a calculated risk-taker. Thirdly, Houston agreed to finance my production of a marketing plan for presentation to potential foreign buyers. And finally, Houston agreed that I would run the company as President, if and when I sold that plan. I thought, "No problem!"

The intriguing part of this "budding" relationship was my awareness of Houston's propensity for dishonesty. I felt an urgent need for legal advice on how to insure contractual protection from Houston. Within days, Houston and I had conceptually and contractually agreed to start up the business. I designed a logo and assigned the name UniPhayse. The contracts we entered bound both of us to our respective areas of commitment and was iron clad. Houston's willingness to participate in my legal protection maneuver further perplexed me, because of the obvious "honesty type" clauses contained in the agreement. At the time, in my mind, I had determined that if Houston could "keep it clean" and perform his role, we would be able to make this company successful. If not, I owned the company lock, stock, and barrel and could still make it work.

Months later, with business and marketing plans in my briefcase and a demonstration model of the proposed product in hand, Houston and I boarded an airplane to Hong Kong. We were met upon arrival by a tall, well-dressed, Korean gentleman who introduced himself as William Yoon. He owned an international shipping company. His ships carried practically everything from scrap metal to Chinese silkworm missiles all over the world.

Mr. Yoon, as he preferred to be called, in keeping with Far Eastern protocol, was interested in negotiating a joint venture company with his friends in the most populated nation on earth, The People's Republic of China. All arrangements had been made by Mr. Yoon's staff for Houston, myself, and him to fly to Beijing the following day to begin negotiations with the Mining Ministry. After several days of exhausting discussions through an interpreter almost entirely between myself and the deputy director of the Chinese Mining Ministry, it appeared as though we had a workable deal.

An elegant banquet was ordered by our gracious Chinese hosts, and it was there I learned that the Mining Ministry was a part of the Chinese Ministry of Defense. Feelings of patriotism welled up in me for the first time in my life. I was aware that China was engaged in supplying missiles to Libya, a Middle Eastern country with whom the U.S. was in conflict. The Chinese were swapping missiles and other weapons for cheap Libyan light crude oil. The Chinese were about the only country in the world who dared defy the Reagan Administration's trade embargo. These fleeting thoughts of being involved with the Chinese military felt treasonous to me. Although uncomfortable with the idea of a business venture with such potential for political disaster, I reminded myself that hundreds of other U.S. companies were already in China. Houston refused to discuss the subject.

During the return flight from Beijing to Hong Kong, I confided my patriotic concerns to Mr. Yoon knowing that he would soon become my business partner. He eloquently relieved my fears of potential disaster with a complicated explanation that made sense at the time. This man politely informed me that we could not lose money as he and I would have interim control over all product sales revenue generated outside of China. By Chinese law for joint venture companies, 60% of all manufactured product must go outside China.

Houston and I returned to Tennessee and I briefly met his wife, Cathy, for the first time when she greeted us at the gate. She appeared to me to be young, beautiful, very dumb, and dressed like a prostitute. I paced my walk to be several steps away from her as we headed to the baggage claim area.

Within a few weeks of this visit, a delegation of Chinese electrical engineers and finance experts were flown to our Tennessee office for more negotiations and to collect technical production data (we held) for future manufacturing purposes.

Soon after the delegation departed for China, I received a mysterious phone call from someone at the U.S. Department of State, a.k.a. the State Department. It seems someone in my Chinese delegation had earlier been refused entry into this country due to their being identified as an international weapons supplier for terrorists. This telephone voice assured me that there were no problems that would arise and that this information was not to be publicized. I thanked him and assured him the information was secure.

A couple of months later, my new Hong Kong partner, Mr. Yoon, invited me, my wife, Houston and his wife, Cathy, to come to China for the official signing of the Chinese joint venture agreement. When I asked Houston if he and his wife would attend, he flatly replied, "No." He had already booked his "act" and could not cancel. I then offered to escort his wife and mine to China. He responded "no" again, that it was too far and too expensive for a pleasure trip. I was relieved because I had already learned enough of the Chinese language to know our partners did not like or respect him, and Cathy's demeanor embarrassed me. I later learned that Houston's "gig" was to "trance-sport"/transport Cathy and little Kelly to the infamous Bohemian Grove for prostitution.

My trip to China, with all the pomp and circumstance, went well as expected, even though my wife and I were in the process of separating for a divorce. However, just before I was prepared to return to the U.S., I received some extraordinary information from a man who showed me Chinese Ministry of Defense credentials that gained my full and complete attention. This man was in possession of a file on me that could have only been gained through a thorough investigation of my past professional associations. His English skills were only strong enough to roughly, nervously translate some of the file's content. This man had photographic proof of a U.S. Department of Defense security clearance I once held. He acknowledged that the "Chinese knew all about me." Thoughts of blackmail raced across my mind. These thoughts instantly disappeared when he began to voice his government's true concerns. Their concerns were about Alex Houston and his involvement with the CIA, drugs, money laundering, child prostitution, and the big one he saved for last, slavery. No mention of mind control was offered, although he did comment that Houston was a "very bad man" and his crimes were "of the White House." Disbelief was in order but not possible, due to the wide array of "Eyes Only" stamped and initialed (official) CIA letterhead and U.S. Government documents he slowly flashed before my eyes.

My first response to this "officer" was that Houston was too stupid and crooked to be connected to U.S. "intelligence." This comment was quickly countered with a gut wrenching photograph of Houston. He was smiling a demonic grin while apparently having anal sex with a small, very young, frightened black boy. Later he was identified to me as being Haitian.

When confronted with this horrific information and the apparent validity of it, I asked, "What do you (your government) want me to do?"

He replied, "Get rid of him, distance yourself from him and all of his associates."

I responded by asking him how he thought I could accomplish this task. He stated, "Any way you choose." I told him that regardless of what he had seen of American television concerning violence, the only way I knew was to force him out by purchasing his company stock, and I needed money to do it. He said, "Give us the figure and make the arrangements. It is done."

I had returned to Tennessee with a Chinese government contract for products valued at thirty one million dollars. Stapled to it was a telex letter of credit made out to me and the company from Houston's bank connection, the New York branch of the now infamous Bank of Credit and Commerce International (B.C.C.I.). The amount was one million dollars in U.S. funds. The contract was worth approximately ten million dollars in gross profit for Mr. Yoon and me.

Given the charge by the Chinese to immediately discharge Houston of his duties, I knew exactly what my plan of action would have to be. Any other approach to resolving this problem could backfire and all would be lost. And since a former, indirect employer of mine (when I worked for Capital International Airways), the CIA, was implicated, I knew one mistake and it could cost me my life. A comforting thought prevailed and I reminded myself Houston was not only corrupt, but stupid. The CIA must not have respected him either. Otherwise, why would he have had to go outside his circle of powerful perverts to recruit me for an international business deal.

I drove to my office to begin the process of discovering something Houston "must have done" that would breach the performance contract he and I had signed when we started the company. Houston was out of town, supposedly doing one of his entertainment gigs, so I had complete, unobstructed access to all files, his included. As I had mentally predicted during the long flight from Hong Kong, the entire ferreting process took about fifteen minutes. It seemed that Houston and the old acquaintance who had introduced him to me were, as they say, "selling out the back door." I collected the shipping bills and, ironically enough, the bank deposit slip Houston had retained when he cashed and deposited the customer's check. There was even a letter copy where Houston had specifically instructed the customer not to discuss his account with anyone at our company other than Houston himself or his pervert friend, Ray Myers. Upon this discovery, I phoned the local Korean lawyer (whose business card I had been given by Mr. Yoon while in Hong Kong) to begin the stock transfer process. With pleasure, I wrote Houston's letter of resignation.

With this problem in the process of being resolved, I left the office to visit an old, dear friend (now deceased) who had maintained powerful U.S. and foreign intelligence connections. I needed answers I could trust with my life. This "retired" Air Force General from the Intelligence division would be my source.

The word "slavery" delivered in broken English by the Chinese Intelligence officer shouted in my ears during the short drive to a local hotel lobby, a comfortable place my "spook" pal selected for us to talk in private. In the few short minutes of the drive, I had my questions (for him) mentally noted. I wanted so much to gain the most from our meeting. The slavery word had triggered a dark question in my mind, blocking other constructive thought, as I was not comfortable with introducing the term mind control into my presentation. I knew I could speak freely about anything to this trusted friend. I wanted desperately to avoid the words mind control, not for reasons of condemnation, but because they represented a secret I had patriotically maintained for twenty years.

After my arrival and the light chit chat of social niceties had been exchanged between us, the air changed to one of seriousness. I briefed him on my business involvement, and began a methodical line of questions concerning the file the Chinese Intelligence officer had presented on me and, especially, on Houston. Shortly, my friend interrupted me in mid-sentence, smiled a toothy grin, and said, "Flash, you're still the same, and you know damn well what I mean."

"Yes," I replied.

The spook was referring to a '70s rock ballad titled "Still the Same" by singer Bob Segar that was assigned to me years earlier by mutual poker playing buddies who identified with my passion for successful risk-taking. I despised gambling. My passion was "risk management" and poker gave me a recreational outlet for it. Although my friends each paid dearly, they soon learned my poker strategy was not so much "card counting" as it was my ability to read their body language. This included the micromuscle spasm responses around their eyes. Houston also lost to me at cards. The message the General was implying, roughly translated, was that I was once again "lucky as hell" to have survived my brief business relationship with Alex Houston.

The discussion went down hill from that point directly into the dreaded arena of mind control. After several minutes of listening to details concerning a huge, invisible CIA slave trade going on world wide, the talk became more regionalized to Tennessee. I learned that Cathy and her little girl were victims of trauma based mind control. They were slaves and the "soul" property of my Uncle Sam. I learned that everything I knew in theory and application about external control of the mind was fully operational and encroaching on the private sector of society.

I was growing numb. The first words out of my dry mouth were, "How would you spring these people out of it?"

He smiled and said, "I wouldn't! What are you going to do with them if you did get them out?" Before I could answer, he interrupted and said, "Look. You're still the same, but nothing else is with Uncle. Now most of the CIA,

FBI, and the MOB (Mafia) are the same, and they're making their moves on the military."

I responded, "I already know that, but how do I save these two people?" He said, "OK. Get the mother on the phone while her handler is gone. Use the usual hang up code of dial and ring twice, hang up call back, ring once, hang up and call back. Tell her you're God. Give her a Biblical passage. They're all Christian based programmed around here."

Understanding that this procedure would gain Cathy's full attention, the General continued, "She'll do anything, and I mean anything -- except toast Houston -- that you command her to do. Remember, God commands. Find yourself a preacher who knows the Bible and get a double-bind verse. You know what to do -- for God's sake. And, listen, if you do this, you're on your own."

"Mark, this is nuts," he pleaded. Go to China and take them with you. Forget about this Red, White and Blue cesspool. It'll clean up. There's lots of good guys in the inside busting their asses to stop this mess, but you're not going to save the world."

I injected, "No, just my ass and a couple of people who Uncle considers something other than human." Then we briefly chatted about some fine points of the rescue and how to legally stop Houston from taking her back. I never saw this friend again.

Walking back to my car, I listened again in my mind to his haunting words, and my own life suddenly seemed like a scratched phonograph record with the needle following the same groove over and over again. The thoughts in my head were suddenly very unpatriotic -- a far cry from the feelings I had expressed in China concerning Mr. Yoon's involvement in shipping Chinese missiles to Libya.

Now I felt pure rage for what my country had become during the years after I had bowed out of doing defense work. For once, my own mind seemed to be my worst enemy. Hatred for everything consumed me.

I loved what my country had once represented to me, but now I was ashamed to be an American. And unbeknownst to me at the moment, soon I would be ashamed of being a male, based on Cathy and Kelly's memories.

During the long, usually boring drive to my secluded house in the wilderness southwest of Nashville, I distinctly recall considering the inherent risks in the formula I was given for "stealing" two slaves from under the coke filled noses of the CIA. My concerns were not of whether I could do it, but related to my friend's question of, "What are you going to do with them?"

My thoughts went blank as I muttered to myself, "Life is getting complicated again." I then consoled myself with the old adage of "first things first".

Within a few days, I had played God and coordinated the move of Cathy and her 8-year-old daughter Kelly out of Houston's house into a nearby apartment. All of this was totally unbeknownst to Houston. As instructed, I had deliberately placed the powerful coded suggestions into Cathy's mind. These commands partially bridged her own amnestic true perceptions that Alex was going to kill her. Little did I know that the message I was provided to block Houston's former control of her was true.

Cathy and Kelly seemed to me to be very disoriented and somewhat disconnected from reality. In their new, sparsely furnished kitchen, I listened quietly to Cathy excitedly explain that "God had sent me" to her. She "knew" this was true because her hands seemed to automatically open her King James version of the *Holy Bible to Psalms*, Chapter 37, Verse 37, which proclaims for the literal minded, "Mark, the perfect man."

Not only had I placed this Biblical reference by a covert suggestion, in her mind while playing God on the phone, but just now in her home moments earlier, I had broken the spine on her Bible so that it would "magically" open to that page. She said, "See, God did it again for you to see."

Using a deprogrammers' language trick, I replied in a "reversed" response, "Well, I'll be damned. You are right. That's the only explanation left -- that could explain all this." I was anxious to change the subject so as not to risk alerting any one of her observant personalities to my well contained laughter. I had been warned that programmed slaves were hyper-observant.

In retrospect, I could not have had thoughts of being sacrilegious. I was and remain deeply spiritual, but my earlier years of researching religions for life's answers had turned me cynical and cold of man's interpretation of the *Bible, Koran,* and Buddha's teachings. This attitude I privately harbored towards organized religions did nothing to squelch the dread I felt wash over me for that moment.

In my attempt to change the subject from religion, I had remembered the Nazi mind control research performed under Himmler's command on the families of northern European multi-generational Satanists. Christianity, particularly Catholicism, was Himmler's pick of the religions' litter for targeting "Chosen Ones" for his hideous mind control experiments. These Chosen Ones were to be the robotic leaders of Hitler's New World Order. I then asked Cathy what religion she was before she met Houston. She replied, "Mormon, but I was a good Catholic before then."

My mind swirled from that shocking revelation. I again quickly changed the subject and suggested we go out to dinner and discuss her new job as my assistant starting the following day. But tonight we would discuss her divorce plans.

Later that evening, I began my search for a secure phone to find someone from past associations I knew were CIA connected on an officer's level. I needed a get-well-quick formula or a clean mental health referral who could help these two wide-eyed unfortunates. I was informed there were none and that I knew more about "that mind stuff" than anyone who would talk.

I returned home to find my phone ringing with an anxious Alex Houston, who had returned from a "vacation" at Boys Town in Nebraska, on the other end exclaiming that he was looking for his wife. She had "disappeared."

I faked not knowing anything and suggested he come to my house the next afternoon to go over some urgent business. The next morning, I located a lawyer for Cathy, and she had the divorce papers drawn up.

That afternoon, I had Granville Ratclift, a local Sheriff's deputy I partially trusted, who occasionally watched my house when I was out of town, waiting inside my house to witness and legally serve Houston with the divorce papers and his termination notice from the company. My last words to Houston which I recorded on tape were, "You could get hurt if you mess with me or them. Alex, get out!" (Now, I hope Houston lives to be a hundred years of age.)

Getting the legal jump on Houston to protect Cathy reminded me that I needed to attend to my own divorce needs. My wife mutually agreed her life could be more emotionally rewarding without me. She moved to Florida and set up house with her mother. We filed for a non-contested divorce. I agreed to sell the house and what remained of our joint possessions.

Still unable to secure expert help for Cathy and Kelly, I maintained their safety by moving them into my house until it was sold. It was during this time that I was approached by a neighbor who said he had seen someone through his binoculars wearing a gun and taking pictures of my house. Other such intrusive visits by unknown persons followed suit. I was getting real nervous.

I again called on a CIA operative I knew who worked within Nashville's corrupt law enforcement elite who, days later, informed me to "get my ass out of there now -- someone wanted me dead!" When I asked why, he said, "You know damn good and well why!"

The house sold quickly and I had already decided to walk away from my company, my contracts, and the one million dollars on deposit as a letter of credit at B.C.C.I. in New York. Mr. Yoon came to Nashville. He purchased Houston's stock. I returned Mr. Yoon to the airport. My last words to him were, "Farewell, friend." He knew nothing of what was going on and I have never seen or spoken with him again. That afternoon I cleaned out my office, handed the keys to the landlord, closed out my personal and company bank accounts.

I had become angry beyond anything I had ever experienced. In retrospect, this was the birthing process of evolution from man to patriot.

I now only wanted answers to what was going on in my government. We needed to be safe while I searched for these answers. My next stop in this pursuit would be Las Vegas, Nevada. Once there, I met with some powerful, underworld characters I had befriended back in my aviation days at Capital International Airways while "packaging" gambling junkets for these characters. I felt confident that these guys would protect me at least until I could find out what and who Cathy knew. I was reminded by these men that they were a part of the CIA's new funding operations. One of them flippantly remarked while chomping his Cuban cigar, "You can't hide an egg in a hen house, fella."

My contact then coldly informed me that I had become involved in something that affected our National Security. I lied to this "wise guy" and cryptically responded, "Oh, well. I'll take them (Cathy and Kelly) to Alaska and play like a voiceless chameleon." In retrospect, this spontaneous lie must have worked to protect me from "red shirting" myself to become the recipient of a CIA/MOB hit.

Cathy and I continued to stay "parked" in Las Vegas for a few more days waiting to retrieve Kelly from a last minute (suspected CIA) court ordered visit with her biological father, Wayne Cox. Later, I would learn from Kelly's medical reports that she had spent Christmas vacation "in hell."

I was now alone in my mind, scared, and going broke fast. Once again I felt totally alienated from everything and everybody in my life. At this moment, I began constantly reminding myself that I was doing the only thing I knew for sure was right. Realistically, I was astride the proverbial tiger and I could not get off its back and survive.

[3] 1991 Roman Catholic Weekly

CHAPTER 3

THE RECLAMATION OF CATHY'S MIND

"The greatest gift anyone can give
another is a good memory."[4]

It was now the week after Christmas 1988. I was fulfilling half of my pledge to the Vegas mob. With all of our remaining personal belongings containerized and secretly in transit on a different ship, I, my "new family" and pets were ferry bound for Anchorage, Alaska. The sixteen hundred mile trip through ice and snow would take about three days to complete. Unfortunately, it gave me time to think.

Due to our negative cash flow situation, realistically I knew there was no place to run or hide from the CIA. Cathy and Kelly seemed happy and believed they were safe. This was my number one priority! For me, I had to trust that my escape plan would convince interested CIA personnel that we no longer represented a threat to their security. The plan was based on an ancient psychological warfare formula developed by the Romans. I wanted to portray myself as akin to a character in a bad Reagan (western) movie and ride into the sunset never to be heard from again. Thinking to myself that where we were headed geographically, there was no sun to set, at least until spring. Late one night about mid way into our voyage, I sought the solitude that the outside forward deck would afford me. I was thankful for the wind driven sleet and snow that stung and closed my eyes and opened my mind for focused thought. At the time, I was psychologically "strung out" from a combination of rage and unbearable emotional heartache.

To safeguard my precious teenage son, Mason, from being hurt and/or unwittingly used as a pawn to force me to remain silent, I had virtually destroyed our father/son bond. I loved and missed him very much, and still do. The resultant emotional pain from the deception and separation seemed to be compounding within me and was consuming my being.

I had, in the course of rescuing Cathy and Kelly, shunned and insulted my son, collapsed my company, simultaneously orchestrated two divorces and sold all personal treasures. I worried I would never see my elderly mother again. Her health was deteriorating. The tailored clothes I wore no longer fit me, as I had lost over forty pounds and looked skeletal. Chronic insomnia, a symptom of the severe depression I secretly felt, was slowly driving me mad. My own short-term memory was beginning to fail. I had noticed for the first time in over thirty years that I was stuttering when enunciating certain words. I knew this was just the beginning of a long and dangerous expedition in search of answers.

As I stood alone, with eyes closed, on the ship's ice-covered steel deck, a strange feeling of relief washed over me. I had somehow managed to remember from where I could draw "emergency strength." I began silently praying for inner strength and guidance through a meditation technique I'd learned years ago. Immediately, I experienced a feeling of peaceful self-assurance that we would survive to tell our story.

Suddenly, I became aware that the icy wind was freezing my face and hands. I was elated that I could feel again. Apparently, I had repressed my tactile senses along with my emotions. For the first time since I learned of Cathy's and Kelly's mind control existence, I felt functionally alive.

17

I opened my eyes to discover I wasn't alone anymore. A voice was coming from somewhere. I looked around and saw, crouched down and wrapped in a dark green blanket almost beside me, the source of the voice. Again, I heard, "Hey man, you OK?" This good man whom I later came to know and respect was Mark Demont. He was a classic example of what Alaskans term a "sour dough." Roughly defined, a sour dough was anybody from the "lower 48" (states) who was disenchanted with their home and low on money. We were both sour doughs and refugees from a sick society gone mad from CIA drugs, media violence, and uncontrolled greed.

I offered him a cigarette and my hand in friendship, something I had not done voluntarily in almost a year. We agreed to stay in contact after our arrival.

About two days later, we landed safely at the Anchorage docks. We were told by the ferry's Captain that it was the coldest day of the decade. The ship's thermometer read a minus seventy degrees Fahrenheit. For me, this was an anticipated weather condition, and for Cathy and Kelly, a physical challenge.

I had spent about two years in Alaska around 1980. It was then that I helped my former boss from Capital International Airways, George Kamats put a new carrier on line known briefly as Great Northern Airlines. I left Alaska back then, not because of the environment, which I loved, but due to my inability to cope with Kamats' daily tirades. This rigid fellow had a long, colorful history working for other CIA controlled airlines. Among other jobs, he had held top executive positions of authority with the infamous air support section of the U.S. Forestry Service, Air America, and Evergreen (CIA) carriers.

Now, I was back in Alaska, unemployed, and knowing I was being tracked like an animal by the same organization I had previously indirectly worked for, the Central Intelligence Agency. After sleeping the past couple of nights, I was feeling much better and the thoughts of being tracked did not concern me. I recall having more productive things on my mind. I could not allow raw fear to become any part of my daily diet of thought process.

Cathy and I dedicated every possible moment to locate a house we could call home. We finally found a fourplex apartment that was inexpensive, with two bedrooms and a heated garage. We had to have a heated garage for my three beloved pet raccoons and two dogs. Our new home would never have furniture beyond a TV, two beds, and a table and chairs. This inconvenience never was discussed. We were comfortable.

After settling into "our place" in the remote rural town of Chugiak, we immediately began doing normal things. We enrolled Kelly in a great public school, met our new neighbors, and played in the snow. All of this was being enjoyed in a traditional family way -- something Cathy and Kelly had never before known.

Our remaining meager resources were disappearing before my eyes. The cost of asthma medication that Kelly now required to keep her alive was over
$400 per month. I strongly suspected that much of the reason for her declining health resulted from the two weeks "in hell" she had recently spent with alleged serial killer, Wayne Cox. She told me so, by detailing the hideous satanic rituals she and her four-year-old step brother, Jacob, had been subjected to.

Fortunately, I had held onto my expensive Nikon camera, guns, and personal jewelry items. These were the last real assets I had remaining to sell. I sold them and the proceeds paid our living expenses for five more months until Kelly's health needs and circumstances forced us on welfare. During this five-month period, with Kelly in school and no telephone to distract us, I began intensifying my deprogramming efforts with Cathy. Most days, our work started the moment we returned home from taking Kelly to school. As soon as Kelly was in bed at night, after dinner and homework, we resumed our "session." We worked like this day and night, seven days a week, focused intensely on the deprogramming process, until I would pass out from exhaustion around three o'clock in the morning.

The deprogramming formula for putting Cathy's fragmented mind back together was inherently free of problems. The small problems I did experience with the formula stemmed from having to "expertly" apply it based on my educated memory of almost twenty years previous. I had no communication with any recognized authority other than Cory Hammond to guide the initial therapy. My single greatest challenge was to learn how to control Cathy's constant state of trance as she journaled her memories.

In spite of reporting to the FBI that I was a hypnotist, I knew that if the FBI and CIA could prove through my admissions I was using hypnosis on Cathy, her testimony in court would be worthless. Therefore, the threat of reprisal from the CIA was averted. In fact, through my own intensive research of hypnotherapy I learned how to control Cathy's trance states. I regarded it as unhypnotizing her. Eventually I would be regarded by mental health physicians as an "expert" in the application of this little-used clinical tool for recovering memory.

Aside from my learned deprogramming skill, the balance of the formula I used consisted of elements which are actually rules of ethical therapy conduct. These therapy rules were strictly enforced. Cathy understood and agreed that, in order for her to have absolute control of her mind, she must place total trust in me and the therapy regime.

1   I maintained a constant vigil to ensure Cathy's physical and psychological safety from all outside influences.

2   No memories could be verbalized by Cathy until after they were written by her. The only questions I could ask were history oriented and directed to Cathy's presenting personality that was recovering the memory. Those questions could only address the who, what, when, how, and where of the memory. Even if I could have known the answers in advance, I could not inject. Our perceptions would have differed radically and could have created more memory barriers between personality fragments.

3   I fundamentally explained mind control to Cathy and she then understood that what happened to her was not her fault. However, she understood she was becoming responsible for her actions here and now. Through therapy, she was asserting control over her own mind.

4   We devoted many hours to "intellectual discussions" of Cathy's learned religious beliefs and they were "logically" debunked, just as if I were explaining how the illusions of a magician's tricks worked to confuse reality.

5   No expression of emotion by Cathy would be permitted during the memory recovery and journaling process. I never asked her "how does that make you feel?" This is as important as the safety issue for the rapid recovery of memories. I provided Cathy adequate food, vitamins, water, and sleep to restore her failing physical health.

6   I taught Cathy how to view her memories on a "mind movie screen" rather than re?experience them through the mind's "virtual reality" mechanism.

7 I instructed Cathy how to trance herself and control the depth of her trance state through a self-hypnosis technique (some regard as meditation). This was put in place to avoid possible contamination and/or confusion of her memories, which might have happened had I used a hypnotic induction technique known as guided imagery.

8 Cathy was not allowed to read books, newspapers, or magazines, to watch TV, or to discuss with Kelly anything she recalled. Cathy had experienced a lifetime of information control and therefore had minimal contamination of memory to sort through. This rule was also understood and respected by Kelly, whose memories were beginning to surface.

9 All behavior patterns and social habits Cathy exhibited were re-examined through logical discussion between us. All pre-established behavior patterns, including daily routines, were re-scheduled or stopped completely.

10 I required her to wear a wrist watch twenty four hours a day, to alert me of any "lost time" she felt she was experiencing. Losing time, without trauma, is a strong indication that personality switching is occurring. Whereas being able to account for time is an indicator that recovery is occurring.

The memories Cathy was recovering were horrible beyond anything I had ever heard anyone speak about. I often wondered if I had fallen in love with Cathy as a result of my developing the psychological malady known as the Stockholm Syndrome. Those thoughts never bothered me for I knew I had grown to love Cathy. I had heard enough horror from Cathy and Kelly to know I was now suffering from Post Traumatic Stress Disorder (PTSD). The symptoms of this disorder went unnoticed by Cathy and Kelly because they too were PTSDed, and had been all their lives.

My own health began to deteriorate rapidly. My regained body weight began to melt away once again. I was experiencing incredible stomach pain, vomiting, and diarrhea. I was literally living on a patent medicine known to ulcer sufferers as Maalox. A "secure" phone call to a doctor friend in the "lower 48" produced the name of a local internal medicine specialist I could trust. Aware of my predicament, my physician friend made the appointment on my behalf for this doctor to prepare certain in-office tests. One of the tests, using a fiberoptic stomach tube, showed that, as a result of a water borne parasite, there were holes in the walls of my stomach. He recommended emergency surgery. I replied, "No. How much longer can I live with this before surgery?"

He said, "It depends on how well you can follow my instructions."

No problem," I said. Within a few days of feeding myself intravenously and taking the prescribed medications, I began to recover.

It was during this recovery period that I began my telephone search for answers to speed Cathy's recovery process. Again I was told by my former "well connected" associates that I knew it all. I was not convinced. However, my persistence soon paid off as one particular phone call resulted in my striking proverbial "pay dirt."

The medical books on clandestine experimental research for treating dissociative disorders mysteriously appeared "on hold" for me at the Eagle River branch of the Anchorage Public Library. I was covertly alerted to pick them up on a certain day at an exact time. I complied.

As I was leaving the library, a middle aged woman with a grocery sack in her arms approached me. She asked if the library was open. I thought this odd since I was walking out the opened library entrance. My curiosity was short lived when she asked, "Have you read any good books by Dr. Milton Erickson lately?"

I replied, "No, but I am checking one out by (psychiatrist) Dr. William S. Kroger entitled *Clinical and Experimental Hypnosis.*"

"Oh, yes," she said. "I'm a real fan of Dr. Kroger's and he is a real fan of Dr. Erickson who you know is considered the father of subliminal mind control (theory) research. She began walking away and turned, smiled and said, "Enjoy your books and use the book, Mark."

I assumed she was addressing me by name while referring to the book itself. I also concluded from this comment that she was obviously the person responsible for delivering the books to the library. Soon I learned she was referring to a bookmark placed inside one of the books, which provided me a desperately needed communications vehicle. Recorded on the book "mark" was a toll free 800# with a time and date to use it. I used this 800# and many others similarly provided me for a communications vehicle to covertly access the spooks' (spies) subway to information. For two more years, this method provided me with telephonic guidance through a maze of mind work with Cathy.

When I called the bookmark "800" number, it was answered by an electronic voice which said, in part, "Please enter your employee number now." I complied, using a series of numbers that I had been previously "assigned" by someone who must remain anonymous because I do not know their identity. The next sound I heard was that of a phone being rung. After exactly eight rings, my call was answered by someone I did not know. He asked, "What's the problem?" I felt like a vacuum cleaner salesman with his foot in the door, delivering a canned sales presentation, I began nervously emphasizing my desperate need for a quicker therapy regime for Cathy.

The voice asked, "Have you read the books?"

"Yes," I replied. "But many of the clinical terms were foreign to me."

The voice then instructed me to go back to the library and "pick up a psyche reference book on term definitions." I then interrupted his instruction to ask if I could speak with somebody who could make this deprogramming process go faster. He said, "Well, there are only two deprogrammers in this country -- one in Boston [Massachusetts] and the other in Phoenix [Arizona] and neither one could be of much help or be trusted with the kind of information you are getting [from Cathy]." He hesitated, then said, "You're going to need a referral, which I can't provide. But you know how to do it."

I asked, "A referral for what?"

"To have the chance to speak with a doctor who knows about this and might be of some value," he told me.

"OK," I said. "Who's the doctor?"

"Cory Hammond, out of Salt Lake City (Utah)."

"Gees," I said. "That's Mormon headquarters, and that was the last religious trauma base for Cathy."

"Yes!" the voice continued. "But you can trust this doctor if you're careful and don't give up too much (information) on yourself. He's paranoid like all the rest (who know about mind control atrocities) but he could be of some help.

Oh, be alert. Everybody's watching this guy so anything you say they [the bad guys] will know."

"Thank you very much," I replied.

Somewhere in the process of finding a referral professionally acquainted with

Dr. Hammond, I telephoned dissociative disorders specialist, Dr. Bennett Braun, a well-known and published psychiatrist in Chicago, Illinois. I learned from our conversation that he had an entire hospital unit dedicated to therapy for people like Cathy and Kelly. I wondered at the time why his name wasn't previously provided to me for a consultation. As a result of this brief telephone encounter, I learned that Dr. Braun had a number of patients on a long waiting list for a "bed" within this facility. The doctor then provided me the name and telephone number of a "friend" he confided in, *People Magazine* senior investigative reporter Civia Tamarkin.

Contacting this *People/Time Life* magazine reporter was to be my biggest single judgment error in the pursuit of helpful information. I would soon learn she was indirectly responsible for nearly costing me my life and did indirectly cost Kelly her chance for "expert" therapy -- which is another book in itself.

When I first spoke with Civia, she dropped important names like a maple tree drops leaves after a frost. I audio tape recorded practically all conversations with this seemingly well informed source, then and in the years to follow. Civia first provided me the name and phone number of the Boston "deprogrammer," an ex-Moonie programmer by the name of Steve Hassen. Next, she provided the name and phone number to contact Jolyn "Jolly" West at UCLA. Reluctantly, she gave me the referral I needed to communicate with Dr. Cory Hammond. The later contact being the only "briefly helpful" one with whom I would speak.

Maximizing my PTSD impaired judgment, I telephoned programmer Steve Hassen, for advice on how to help Kelly (only), which resulted in his coming to our home in Alaska. Apparently, his agenda was to traumatize Cathy by using a well-known code to trigger her to run for her life -- from me. The method he employed could have been effective, but fortunately for Cathy and Kelly his robotic delivery, like his moral ethics, was very poor. I learned that Hassen's voiced and recorded professional respect for his UCLA psychiatrist friends, Dr. West and Dr. Margaret Singer, derived from sinister reasons. Little did I know that Dr. West had worked for the CIA in Project MK Ultra mind control research for decades. It seems some of Dr. West's CIA supported research had been exposed by a Congressional investigator of the MK Ultra Project in the 1970's. However, he survived the public scrutiny because the U.S. Government had, in essence, halted further investigation of him and his work under the National Security guise. His only reported crime was for killing an elephant with an overdose of LSD in the presence of school children. These facts I would learn after Cathy and I spoke with him by phone and subsequent disaster struck us. This, too, is another story in itself.

The phone calls between myself and Dr. Cory Hammond were informative and supportive. He proved himself to be the single most valuable live information asset I would know in my quest for expert therapy advice. Later, Dr. Hammond delivered to the mental health community, through a symposium presentation in 1991, the whole truth as he knew it on the topic of mind control. His advisory instruction to me on a particular Erickson technique for painless, non abreactive memory recovery, called "revivification", literally saved my precious Cathy from reliving the horrors as she remembered them. This man is my personal hero.

Spring in Alaska was a very different experience from what I was accustomed to in Tennessee. The Alaskans just refer to it as "break-up." In place of hearing the sounds of chirping birds, I listened to the drip noises from the ice melting off everything. The streets had become an ugly brown mush. For spring as normally a welcomed seasonal change, it was depressing to say the least. The only good news was that the days had slowly changed from darkness to warm sunlight. With this seasonal change, a time bomb I did not know existed began its countdown. Kelly's asthma and behavior were radically deteriorating for no apparent reason.

One Friday morning in May, Cathy received a call from Kelly's school principal requesting we pick her up as soon as possible and have her examined by a doctor. The school nurse said Kelly was having a severe asthmatic attack that did not respond to the medication she had with her. We picked her up only to find that her condition seemed to improve miraculously at the sight of us. But this improvement would be short lived.

The following Sunday, Kelly's coughing became almost constant. She had exhausted our supply of an important asthma medication, which she regularly used in her respirator pump. I covertly substituted distilled water and sat with her while she struggled for her breath. Using an Erickson technique of guided imagery, I began telling her a story about a little girl who huffed and puffed and climbed a mountain. The story I told ended with the little girl reaching the top of the mountain only to be so tired that she fell asleep in a bed of wild flowers. Kelly responded by breathing normally and actually falling into a sound asleep for a few hours, only to awaken and repeat her coughing spell. I returned to her bedside and I asked why she coughed.

Kelly, somewhat agitated, responded, "I have asthma." I repeated the water substitution trick and she responded favorably and said, "Dad, Wayne [the father and alleged serial killer Satanist] told me I was gonna' die."

I said, "Well, he's not a doctor."

Kelly continued, "He really did say that over and over and over again." I then asked, "When did he say this?"

"When school's out," she replied. I asked, "What do you mean?"

She robotically repeated, "When school's out."

"Do you remember when Wayne said this to you?" I asked.

"In bed," she continued. "He thought I was asleep and he was talking on the phone to Alex [Houston] and then to me." I knew then Wayne Cox had programmed her to die using a clinical technique known as hypnosleep. Alex Houston was guiding Cox through the program.

I interrupted her (as I saw she was entering a deep state of trance) and responded, "Well, school's not out and tomorrow you will be well enough to go back to school."

As I suggested, Kelly did feel good the next morning and returned to school. This day would be her last day in Birchwood Elementary.

Only a few hours passed before Cathy and I again were called, this time by the nurse who became agitated when Cathy truthfully answered her question, "Didn't you take her to the doctor?"

Cathy said, "No, but we will."

Later that evening, Cathy, Kelly and I would make the last of our emergency
drives to seek medical help for Kelly.

At Anchorage's Humana Hospital, Cathy and I met with the young, very bright and beautiful physician, Dr. Lorrie Shepherd, who seemed perplexed and, perhaps, frightened as to Kelly's unexplainable deteriorating condition. I requested a private meeting and she complied.

After about thirty minutes of my explaining what Cathy and Kelly had been rescued from, I defined mind control for her. Learning this, Dr. Shepherd then consulted with a local female psychiatrist, Dr. Pat Patrick to evaluate Kelly.

The evaluation was completed and Dr. Patrick invited Cathy, and eventually me, to her office for a consultation. This was to be Kelly's first official evaluation that indicated she suffered from Multiple Personality Disorder (MPD),[5] a serious psychological disorder resulting from severe and repeated trauma.

I then asked Dr. Patrick if she could arrange for a sexual abuse specialist to verify if Kelly had been abused. She complied. The results were positive. Dr. Patrick and Cathy seemed almost relieved at this validation. The results sickened me.

Kelly's asthma stabilized at Humana and she was transferred to Charter North Psychiatric Hospital for in-hospital care. Dr. Patrick apparently provided the best care she knew. Unfortunately it was inadequate. Months passed and the State of Alaska welfare authorities began to realize Kelly was not improving and her ineffective care costs were mounting by thousands of dollars weekly.

Dr. Patrick, Cathy, and I, with the cooperation of the Tennessee Violent Crimes Claims Commission, began searching for a hospital that would accept Medicaid insurance. Finally, one was located in Owensboro, Kentucky which advertised a specialty in working with ritually abused children. Kelly was transferred to this facility and the State of Alaska paid all the bills for her move there. Later we would learn that this elegant hospital facility was nothing more than a human warehouse that collected whatever fees the federal and state governments would pay them per child resident. A pretty place to see, but the care for Kelly would prove to be "less than nothing."

During the summer before Kelly was transferred to this Kentucky hospital, and Cathy was recovering satisfactorily, I felt it was safe to leave their side so that I could find work. We desperately needed money to travel, to live, and to return to the "lower 48" with Kelly in the winter.

I quickly secured a job at Alaska Business College as an interviewer of prospective students. My sales "performance" resulted in my being promoted in two weeks from an admissions representative to Director of Admissions. I banked as much money as possible from my earnings over the next five months to provide for our move, to be closer to Kelly. The thought of the separation agony that would exist between Cathy and Kelly served as a reminder of my ongoing separation from my son, whom I had not heard from in almost a year.

Cathy, on ill advice from me, called her father and begged for some financial help for Kelly's sake. Her father wired $500 to confirm our location and commented, "This is America. Unless you come back to Michigan alone, no more money!" It was this statement that triggered Cathy's repressed memories of her own tortured childhood by this alleged pervert and slave salesman, Earl O'Brien.

Soon the FBI telephoned Cathy and told her that she needed to "voluntarily" come to the Anchorage FBI office for questioning. Upon arrival, Cathy was informed that she was under federal investigation for attempting to **extort** money from her father.

Cathy looked strangely relieved when she heard these charges. Later I would learn that she felt better knowing for sure she was not "crazy" or delusional and that her father did in fact do those things to her and her brothers and sisters.

The FBI Agent was openly sympathetic and reportedly the DOJ "inspired" investigation was subsequently dropped upon his recommendation. This agent went on to secure a cash donation through his Mormon church that enabled us to leave his jurisdiction.

It is noteworthy that during this same time, through another special agent at the Anchorage FBI office, I was interrogated for "what I knew" regarding an unrelated crime involving my ex-wife and her lawyer boss in Florida. I knew nothing. I now know that the FBI was, in effect, attempting to destroy my credibility as advocate for Cathy and Kelly through their investigation efforts of me. Their case against my ex-wife and her lawyer was solved, and her lawyer accomplice was convicted of first degree murder. My ex-wife became a state's witness and was acquitted.

However, days later I would "see" my ex-wife being arrested and processed on the popular national television show "Unsolved Mysteries." That unfortunate case involved only one homicide and made the national news for weeks to come. In contrast, Cathy's testimony, with proofs provided FBI officials, was filed and deliberately covered up -- **For Reasons of National Security.**

The fall season in Alaska was now quickly giving in to winter and the "termination dust" (snow) was re-coating the surrounding mountains. The air was definitely becoming nippy. The change of seasons signaled another change within my new family. Kelly was going to soon be transferred to the Kentucky Valley Institute of Psychiatry (V.I.P.).

Cathy and I had been saving every dollar I could earn during my brief tenure at Alaska Business College, in preparation for our move back to the "lower 48."

I realized now that Cathy had gone into a state of recovery known as "fusion." She had long since stopped switching personalities and had become a beautiful, intelligent, and logical lady. She was no longer susceptible to anyone triggering her to go against or away from me. She continued to journal her traumatic memories and was professionally adjudged stable.

The passage on ships and ferries out of Anchorage to Seattle was booked solid for months ahead. They would only accept freight and/or vehicles. I purchased two, one-way tickets on Alaska Airlines and brought our family car, a 1976 AMC Pacer, and remaining belongings to the Anchorage docks for shipment.

Suddenly, as we packed our bags and were ready to board our flight, a nearby volcano erupted and halted all air traffic in or out of Anchorage for the following two weeks. We waited anxiously for the airport to reopen. We would leave first and Kelly and her nurse would soon follow. This would be the first step of what would be an endless journey in our pursuit of justice.

---

[4] Mark Phillips' motto

[5] The term Multiple Personality Disorder (MPD) is now clinically referred to by mental health professionals as Dissociative Identity Disorder (DID).

CHAPTER 4

TRUTH AND CONSEQUENCES
JUST US PURSUED AND JUSTICE DENIED

Our much anticipated arrival into the Seattle (Washington) International Airport terminal heralded a new beginning. Cathy appeared to be openly optimistic that perhaps, at long last, Kelly would soon have her chance for recovery. Privately, I felt much less hopeful. I knew from past personal experiences and through my "insider sources" that mental health physicians from the private sector of society had little acquaintance with secret U.S. Government mind control research. The only mind control information these doctors had access to, for the most part, was from the hysterical comments supplied them by their troubled patients. Hysteria, in this case, as a symptom of misinformation is highly contagious, and therefore spread throughout the mental health profession. Many practitioners displayed symptoms of the "ostrich syndrome" to me, their peers, and patients through fear and chronic denial.

It was 1990, the beginning of the last decade of this century and the millennium, and most mental health physicians remained in a state of denial concerning the existence of mind control. Mental health as a science is barely one hundred years of age. Truly an industry in its infancy in relation to the other recognized healing arts.

Due to mental health's infancy and the fact that it is rooted in the archaic, mystical theories of Jung and Freud, combined with the non availability of government controlled research information, the term "mental health" is viewed by patients and doctors alike as an oxymoron. Patients I have interviewed who suffer from dissociative disorders frequently refer to the profession as "mental hell," and their well-intentioned provider as "the rapist." Unfortunately for all parties concerned, in many reported instances, these cruel labels are consistent with the quality of the care provided. Whereas I strongly support, in concept, the healing arts existing in the fields of mental health that could be applied in the treatment of mind control patients, I cannot foresee their application in meeting the needs of these patients without some radical changes in our National Security Act. Around 1970, I recall witnessing a "mild" case in point. I was overseeing the video taping of a TOP SECRET psychiatric experiment involving a young man who had suffered brain damage resulting from some type of severe head trauma. This patient was ambulatory. He could not remember anything, express himself, or for that matter, think. He was not brain dead. He was mind dead. Through the application of a combination of experimental drugs and hi-tech electronic technology involving harmonics, his brain was being "retrained" to permit constructed thought processes to commence. The brain scar tissue that was inhibiting his ability to think was being chemically and electronically bypassed. I equated this experimental procedure to the "hot wiring" of an ignition switch of an automobile to preclude the use of a key. The extraordinary procedure and subsequent results of this experimental therapy was meticulously recorded. The record, tape, and doctor notes were dropped into a security envelope and were taken by courier to Fort George Meade, Maryland.

What made this case so memorable was the event that immediately followed. I overheard the experiment's attending physician complaining bitterly to his nurse colleague that "his" patient in an adjoining ward, who was not a "DOD guinea pig," through application of this method, could "probably recover." The doctor's complaint addressed his being prohibited from applying state-of-the-art treatment for his patient by virtue of his DOD oath of secrecy. This doctor was frustrated at being forced to serve two masters. The DOD, being one master, held control over his career through his medical license, liability insurance, and the secrecy oath he had signed. The second master was the doctor's own moral and ethical standards, supported by the Hippocratic Oath he had signed upon becoming a physician.

Thus, without benefit of the voluminous DOD research findings and technology developments, the medical field of mental health is in its learning curve for establishing models to provide patients state-of-the-art care. In other words, mental health providers themselves are quickly becoming the second group of mind/information control victims.

The mental health profession is in a state of crisis and has arrived at the proverbial crossroads of failure and success. The road to success through the application of available technologies appears to be blocked **FOR REASONS OF NATIONAL SECURITY**.

As a direct result of DOD management of mind research secrets and the resulting federal information containment practices, mental health providers are on the defensive with their patients, the courts, and more recently with certain special interest action groups. These groups are attacking the mental health professional as a target for destruction. Well-funded organizations with very questionable agendas, such as the False Memory Foundation (FMF) and the Church of Scientology, have publicly denounced mental health as a profession.

The Church of Scientology has emerged as the apparent leader in publicly denouncing the mental health profession. Through the church's Washington,

D.C. based "human rights" lobby group, it has launched a massive negative propaganda campaign accompanied by numerous lawsuits against ethical drug companies and mental health providers.

Scientologists believe their church's founder, L. Ron Hubbard, has discovered a cure-all for mental illness through behavior modification. Hubbard, a successful science fiction writer, allegedly acquired knowledge of subliminal mind control through his military service with U.S. Navy Intelligence. He named his behavioral modification program Dianetics after his first wife, Diane.

The False Memory Foundation is a lobby group which is primarily utilized by persons charged with sexual abuse. The FMF is desperately attempting to develop legislation that restricts therapy for persons suffering from dissociative disorders as a result of trauma. This organization's stated beliefs include that repressed memory is a myth. FMF has found the mental health profession's Achilles heel.

To date, the model for developing an effective therapy regime for dissociative disorders (which are as a result of repeated trauma) has not been published by either the American Psychiatric Association or the American Psychological Association. The difficulty in developing a model is due to a number of factors. The primary factor involves national security secrets concerning classified mind control research.

In the present climate, referring mind control victims to mental health professionals for treatment would be tantamount to subjecting a patient needing delicate surgery to a surgeon who was blind-folded and handcuffed. The knowledge of these conditions produced the private opinion I withheld from Cathy when she professed optimism for Kelly's latest recovery opportunity. Nevertheless, Cathy was nearing complete recovery and we both recognized we were doing all we could at the moment to provide for Kelly's needs.

Perhaps identifying "who" within our government is interested in withholding vital medical research findings and technologies information from the mental health profession could provide a foundation of understanding. From my personal experiences while working for Capital International Airways, I formed a strong opinion that addresses this question. However, the answer that mirrors my perception was later eloquently provided by a Washington, D.C. news correspondent and journalist, Linda Hunt, in her book *Secret Agenda*.[6] The historical basis for this book are the declassified DOD documents identifying Project Paperclip as being the secret importation/relocation of Nazi and Fascist scientist into the United States over a forty year period.

These brilliant criminal scientists were primarily focused on two areas of research, rockets and the mind. They were placed in positions of authority in, among others, prestigious universities, colleges, industries, and NASA. Over the years, these imported criminals have directly influenced our society with advanced rocket technologies and mind control applications through U.S. Government sponsored research. According to "Secret Agenda, Nazism, as a philosophy and form of government, is alive and destroying our country, in part, as a result of Project Paperclip.

I can attest to this statement from personal knowledge gained during my employment at Capital International Airways, which is named as one of the primary transporters for Project Paperclip.

These were background facts for some of the thoughts that rushed my mind on our long drive from Seattle to the Southeastern U.S. I was anxious to discover the end results of my telephone campaign in the pursuit of justice I had waged while in Alaska.

Our first destination would be Huntsville, Alabama. This southern U.S. city is famous for its tourism centerpiece, the NASA owned U.S. Space and Rocket Center. The town also boasts of being home to more Pentagon black budget U.S. dollars per capita than anyplace in America. Cathy harbors a very different opinion of this town, its police force, and the NASA research facility. For Cathy and Kelly, Huntsville had been a place they were regularly taken by Alex Houston for hi-tech torture and the production of child and adult pornography films.

This trip to Huntsville would be different for Cathy, except for one aspect of her previous experiences. Both she and I would receive our first threat to our lives in our pursuit of justice from law enforcement. This was surprising to me and "normal" for Cathy.

The lead-up to this threat began with my phone call to a Huntsville based legal aid group known as the National Association of Child Advocates. This organization publicized that it was formed through the leadership efforts of the local district attorney 'Bud' Crammer, who is known to his constituents as "Gun Ban Bud." After supplying this advocacy center with Cathy's recollections of her past experiences in Huntsville, we were contacted by two Huntsville City

28

Police Department "vice" detectives. Their names were Jeff Bennet and Chuck Crabtree.

Upon our arrival into Huntsville, these two vice cops escorted us and our trailer to a local apartment used for staging drug buys. The place was furnished, complete with audio and video bugs throughout every room. When I asked Bennet if the "place was bugged" he flatly denied it. From this lie I knew with certainty that Cathy and I were there to be specimens for whomever to study. I knew "who," and we gave them our best performance to mislead them. This action probably saved our lives.

After weeks of "delays," the two vice cops sat down with Cathy and me for discussion. She supplied them a myriad of testimony including detailed physical descriptions of two particular perpetrators, their names, and location maps of where they lived and allegedly produced child and adult pornography. The two perpetrators, themselves Huntsville policemen, were also helpful assets in the campaign for electing District Attorney Bud Crammer. Their names were Audie Majors and Sergeant Frank Crowell.

After Cathy had exhausted all of her recollections, Crabtree and Bennet ordered us to "leave Huntsville now while we were still alive, and shut up if we intended to stay that way!"

Later, Cathy and I would learn that Crabtree and Bennet had notified every law enforcement officer in over five states to whom we had provided information. They reported that we were a pair of "professional con artist criminals." Perhaps they were able to accomplish this discrediting tactic as a result of police reports we filed in other states, which included a reference to our "bad experience" with the Huntsville Police Department. In addition, the Nashville office of the FBI was responsible for perpetrating Crabtree's and Bennet's discrediting lies. This FBI action ceased after resident-agent-in-charge Ben Purser was told by a friendly district attorney that I now could prove the identity and prosecute those responsible for the character assassination. The harassment stopped.

It is interesting to note that 'Bud' Crammer would, in less than a year, be elected to Congress. Within months after his election, Bud was rewarded for years of alleged containment practices. Allegedly, Bud has been covering up investigations for the intelligence community, DOD, and of course, his number one financial supporter NASA.

The wife of an Atlanta, Georgia physician, Ms. Faye Yeager, did however survive Bud's wrath in court. Her "crime" was advocating for and protecting a child who had been horribly abused. This courageous lady had her day in court and won. Now she has filed a counter-suit in Federal court. Reeling from Bud's "second hand" threats to our lives, we returned to Nashville. Here we learned that the Kentucky V.I.P. hospital administration had suddenly declared Kelly's State of Alaska medical records "to be in error." V.I.P. said she was "fine!" This statement was supplemented by "you best come here now and pick her up or we'll give her to Kentucky Child Services and they will find adoptive parents."

This was a terrifying development, since Kelly could not function outside a restrictive environment. She had been declared suicidal and homicidal by three attending physicians and/or therapists. Cathy and I were homeless. We brought Kelly back to Tennessee where she, Cathy and I stayed in my mother's tiny two-bedroom home. This living arrangement would not last. Kelly's asthma (program), destined to separate her from her mother, returned within 48hours. We rushed her, gasping for breath, to Vanderbilt hospital in Nashville, for emergency treatment. Again Kelly's condition worsened to the extremely critical point, then returned to normal. Her attending doctor thought he had seen a real miracle until he learned about mind control.

Vanderbilt hospital physicians who reviewed Kelly's past medical and psychiatric records recommended that she be moved to the worst child warehouse we've seen so far, Crocket/Cumberland House, the "home for broken butterflies" (see photo). Because Cathy and I were both unemployed and Kelly only had Medicaid insurance, the State of Tennessee demanded temporary custody. Their demands for custody were legally legitimate and morally equated to extortion, for they had no intentions of seeking expert therapy for Kelly.

Through a lengthy two-year court proceeding, with five lawyers opposing Cathy, we had a partial victory. Kelly was transferred to Charter Hospital in Memphis, Tennessee where again she did not receive MPD/DID therapy, but for the first time did receive genuine empathy from a social worker, Abbott Jordan.

During this period, my life and liberty was threatened by the Nashville Metro Police Department. This verbal death threat was delivered by Metro Homicide Captain Mickey Miller and echoed by his friend and subordinate Lt. Tommy Jacobs. Miller said, "You best forget this woman; walk away from all this now before your health changes. Jacobs said, "There's nothing wrong with that kid that her father [Cox] can't fix. She just has allergies. You'd best forget you ever heard of either one of them." I have all this conversation on audio tape.

Within a few months of these threats came others threatening both our lives and liberty from every branch of law enforcement within the State of Tennessee. This included the Nashville office of the FBI. The latter was in the form of a "clerical mistake" on the part of the FBI that was to be a "frame up" for my supposedly threatening the President of the United States, George Bush. This charge was totally groundless and was subsequently dropped, but only after I secured a lawyer.

It was now 1991, and Cathy and I had determined that we must proceed with "phase two" of our pursuit of justice through a well organized information dissemination campaign. The funding for this project would indirectly come from the assistance of Bill Ross, who also provided constant moral support.

Cathy and I have always felt uncomfortable exposing gentle persons like Bill Ross to such horrific information as pertains to trauma based mind control. However, we have learned over the years through our public speaking engagements and consultations with physicians and others that, generally speaking, people appreciate knowing WHY they are no longer "at the top of the food chain." Bill Ross, like hundreds of others, never gave up hope that we would live to tell our story.

Five years have passed since we returned from Alaska. The lessons learned through this trail blazing effort in our pursuit of justice should never be taught to anyone. No person should have to experience the heartache, desperation, and grinding poverty that Cathy, Kelly, and I have had to live with.

During the winding down portion of our information dissemination campaign, Cathy approached me with an idea she thought could help us win public support. She had repeatedly commented that she wanted to rescue Seidina 'Dina' Reed, daughter of actor/singer Jerry Reed of Smokey and the Bandit fame. According to Cathy, she had been used repeatedly in pornography productions with Seidina over the years and had bonded with this once beautiful woman.

Seidina's husband, David Rorick, a.k.a. Dave Roe, was then her alleged sadistic handler. It is noteworthy that Roe allegedly received his training on how to maintain a slave, using specific tortures, from Alex Houston. Roe lived, and reportedly loved, with Houston before he met Seidina. Cathy and I naively believed at the time that Jerry Reed was not involved in his daughter's enslavement as was Cathy's father. Furthermore, we were convinced that Jerry Reed, with his numerous connections into politics and the entertainment industry could be a powerful ally. This was not to be.

I rescued Seidina and in minutes after the rescue, she began talking, but not until I had discussed my plan in person with her famous father and his agent at a Brentwood, Tennessee restaurant. Reed had more than enough time to warn Roe that I was armed and on my way to his house. All evidences disappeared.

Years later, a U.S. Customs Enforcement officer informed me that I had "somebody" connected to Reed, possibly Reed himself, suggesting "I might be blackmailing him." This "clean" customs officer knew I had rescued Seidina from Roe's enslavement and that I had audio taped all meetings with Seidina, Jerry Reed, and his wife Prissy. He was openly concerned for my safety and that Reed was lying so as to frighten me away.

Within two months after the rescue, Seidina and her mother filed criminal charges, including sexual child abuse (of Seidina's four year old son), against Roe. A "spook informant" working within the Nashville District Attorney's office alerted me to these charges and the anticipated outcome. No action was taken **FOR REASONS OF NATIONAL SECURITY**.

Seidina had been prostituted to, among many others, heads of state, and to the Arabian Ambassador to the U.S., Prince Bandar Bin Sultan. According to non involved witnesses of one of her encounters with Bandar friend of George Bush's) she was one of his favorite slaves. We've never heard from Seidina or any member of her family since the rescue. This trek through hell in our pursuit of justice taught nothing to Cathy that she had not already been told by her abusers. For me, I learned the hard way that our Constitution was only a beautiful plan that had been stolen, plundered, and replaced **FOR REASONS OF NATIONAL SECURITY**.

Today, Cathy, Kelly, I, and all true patriots stand at the proverbial crossroads of revolution or evolution. Through armed revolution, we patriots will perish and the emergence of a totally government controlled society will herald in another period of "dark ages." As a proud gun owner, armed with inside knowledge, I know we are technologically out-gunned. Whereas, if we choose to evolve through the challenges to our psyche that developed communication technologies present we can reinstate our Constitution and set our people free. Revolution or Evolution -- change in life as we know it is inevitable.

Each of us must now take a stand to commit a portion of our individual time and diminishing resources to support the action groups and individuals who are not afraid to work at taking back our government through mass exposure of its crimes. We must seek new leaders who will be committed to doing the most with the least. These leaders share the battle cry that SILENCE DOES (indeed) EQUAL DEATH.

[6] Hunt, Linda, *Secret Agenda: The United States Government, Nazi Scientists, and Operation Paperclip.* St. Martin's Press, 1991.

INSERTS: VARIOUS SUPPORT DOCUMENTS AND PICTURES

Alex Houston

The power of saving energy

Nashville-based Uni-Phayse Inc. has landed a $31 million purchase contract with the People's Republic of China for capacitors, which operate as electronic power factor correction systems.

Founded approximately a year ago, the company will supply the energy managing systems to the Chinese government over the next 15 years, according to Mark Phillips, president.

"Initial applications will be directed toward that country's mining industry," says Phillips. "The Chinese have had to shut factories down on an alternating-day schedule because of power shortages. This device will enable them, in essence, to save enough energy to keep their factories going."

Ranging in size from a computer chip to a small office, the devices primarily affect the energy losses that occur with the use of electric motors, according to Phillips. "There are two types of electrical power," he explains, "and the power factor is the type used to turn a motor on." Although it is not used once the motor is running, it keeps running through the lines, Phillips says. Typically, it is then shot back to the power company and no one benefits.

"However, capacitors, which are installed near the equipment, store the energy almost instantaneously and then release it back to the motor when the motor demands it," Phillips says. Companies can realize a 15-17 percent savings in their energy bills, Phillips claims, in addition to eradicating the "power factor"

penalties charged by the utility companies.

Although the technology has been available in this country for 50 years, according to Phillips, very few efforts have been made to manufacture and market the systems.

"Frankly speaking," he says, "because energy costs have been so low in this country until the last decade, there hasn't been any real interest in conserving energy. Of course, that is changing."

The company is working with TVA to identify industries that are experiencing "power factor" penalties. For now, says Phillips, there are several industries and institutions, such as schools, which can benefit from the technology.

While working with the local market, Phillips is also negotiating with other Pacific Rim and Third World countries, which he says are keenly aware of their need to manage energy.

"The bottom line of what we're doing is developing an educational program on the benefits of energy management for these countries, and we will also be manufacturing other energy-saving devices in the future," the executive says.

Currently manufacturing the systems at full capacity in the company's Florida plant, Uni-Phayse plans to open a second manufacturing operation in Nashville early next year. Phillips is in the process of locating and purchasing equipment for the plant, which he says will employ approximately 30 people.

— *by Bonnie Arnett*

February 5, 1988

Uni-Phayse, Inc.
107 Music City Circle, Suite 310
Nashville, TN 37214

Re: Resignation

Gentlemen:

I hereby tender my resignation as an officer and director of Uni-Phayse, Inc., effective immediately.

W. Alex Houston

34

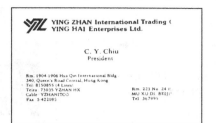

YING ZHAN International Trading (
YING HAI Enterprises Ltd.

C. Y. Chiu
President

Rm. 1904-1906 Hua Qin International Bldg
340, Queen's Road Central, Hong Kong
Tel. 8150855 (4 Lines)
Telex 73035 YZHAN HX
Cable YZHANITCO
Fax 5-422085

Rm 223 No 24 F
MU XU DI, BEIJI'
Tel 367995

JOINT VENTURE CONTRACT

For Establishing

SHENZHEN UNI-PHAYSE CO. LTD.

Party A: Metallurgical Import & Export Corp. Shenzhen
Industry & Trade Co.
Representative:

1987. 10-2

Party B: Metallurgical Equipment Corp of the Ministry of
Metallurgical Industry of China
Representative: 1987.10. 2

Party C. Ying Hai Enterprises Ltd. of Hong Kong
Representative:

Party D: Uni-Phayse Inc. of USA Oct 2'87
Representative:

MEC Ministry of Metallurgical Industry
Metallurgical Equipment Corp.

ZHAI XINTING
President

46 Dongsixi Dajie
Beijing China

Tel: 55,7031—4384
Cable: 3131 Beijing
Telex: 222355 YJMEC C

Section of Economic Information
Economic Information Center
Ministry of Ordnance Industry

868561-
853

LU JUNDA
Bureau Chief

San Li-He
Beijing, China
P.O. Box 84 Beijing

Tel: 86,8441-525
216
Cable: 1105

William S. W. YOC
Managing Director

Tel.: 5-299677 (5 Lines)   Telex: 74889 OCLIN HX
60793 OCLIN HX (A.O.

Oceanlink Limited
Oceanlink Maritime Ltd.
Yinghai Enterprises Ltd.
Rm. 606, Asian House, 1 Hennessy Rd., Wanchai, H.
G. P. O. Box 3312 HKG   FAX: 5-86134

An International Company

Mark E. Phillips
President

Tel. (615) 885-9591
Fax. (615) 885-9590
Tel: 5-299677 (5 Lines)
Fax. 5-6613413

Corporate Headquarters
107 Music City Circle
Suite 310
Nashville, TN 37214

Asian Sales Office
Rm. 606, Asian House
1 Hennessy Rd.
Wanchai, Hong Kong

35

L S E

LASER \ SYSTEMS & ELECTRONICS inc.

MARK E. PHILLIPS
NATIONAL SALES MANAGER
MEDICAL DIVISION

P. O. BOX 858
TULLAHOMA, TENN. 37388
TEL. (615) 455-0686

OUTDOOR RESORTS OF AMERICA INC

Mark E. Phillips
Marketing Operations
Manager

Alaska Business College

907-349-190
800-478-190
FAX 907-349-980

MARK E. PHILLIPS
Director of Admissions

800 East Dimond Blvc
Suite 3-35
Anchorage, Alaska 9951

GNA

MARK E. PHILLIPS
DIRECTOR OF PASSENGER SALES & SERVICES

GREAT NORTHERN AIRLINES

3400 INTL. AIRPORT RD
(907) 243-1414

ANCHORAGE 99502
TELEX 25274

Mark Phillips
President

A PROFESSIONAL ALLIANCE DEDICATED TO VIGILANTLY PROTECTING
HUMANITY'S LAST FREEDOM THOUGHT

P.O. Box 158352 • Nashville, TN 37215

uni phase inc
An International Company

Tel. (615) 885-9591
Fax. (615) 885-9590
Tel: 5-299677 (5 Lines)
Fax. 5-8813413

Mark E. Phillips
President

Corporate Headquarters
107 Music City Circle
Suite 310
Nashville, TN 37214

Asian Sales Office
Rm. 606, Asian House
1 Hennessy Rd.
Wanchai, Hong Kong

BY APPOINTMENT ONLY
Telephone ~~615-000-0000~~

P.O. Box 158352
Nashville, TN 37215

The Affordable / Pleasurable Drug Alternative

MARK E. PHILLIPS, C. HT.

Clinical-Sports Hypnotherapist

Specialty
Neuro-Linguistic Programming
Self Hypnosis Instruction

Purposes
Sports / Athletics Conditioning
Pain Relief / Injury Rehab

U. S. Department of Justice

United States Attorney

Middle District of Tennessee

---

110 9th Avenue South, Suite A-961   615/736-5151
Nashville, Tennessee 37203-3870   FTS/852-5151

September 9, 1991

Mr. Mark Phillips

Dear Mr. Phillips:

This letter will advise you of the following matters pertaining to testimony before the Federal Grand Jury for which you have been subpoenaed.

1. You are a possible subject of an investigation by the Federal Grand Jury. This means that the United States Attorney's Office or the Grand Jury has substantial evidence linking you to the commission of a crime and you are, in the judgment of the United States Attorney's Office, a possible defendant.

2. The Grand Jury is conducting an investigation of possible violations of federal laws including Title 18, U.S.C. Section 871, mailing threatening communications.

3. You may refuse to answer any questions if a truthful answer to the questions would tend to incriminate you.

4. Anything you do say may be used against you by the Grand Jury or in a subsequent legal proceeding.

5. You are entitled to consult with counsel about this matter. If you cannot afford to hire an attorney, one will be appointed for you upon your request to the court.

6. If you have retained counsel. or have been appointed counsel. the Grand Jury will permit you a reasonable opportunity to step outside the grand jury room to consult with counsel before answering questions, if you so desire.

Sincerely,

VAN S. VINCENT
Assistant United States Attorney

/tp

37

AO 110 (Rev. 12/89) Subpoena to Testify Before Grand Jury

United States District Court

MIDDLE   TENNESSEE

_____ DISTRICT OF _____

TO:

MARK PHILLIPS

SUBPOENA TO TESTIFY
BEFORE GRAND JURY

SUBPOENA FOR:
☐ PERSON   ☒ DOCUMENT(S) OR OBJECT(S)

YOU ARE HEREBY COMMANDED to appear and testify before the Grand Jury of the United States District Court at the place, date, and time specified below.

PLACE	COURTROOM
U.S. Courthouse 8th & Broad Nashville, TN 37203	A-825 Grand Jury Room
	DATE AND TIME Sept. 19, 1991 ~~7:00 p.m.~~ 3:30 PM

YOU ARE ALSO COMMANDED to bring with you the following document(s) or object(s): *

You will be asked to provide fingerprints, palmprints, handwriting exemplars, and testimony.

☐ Please see additional information on reverse

This subpoena shall remain in effect until you are granted leave to depart by the court or by an officer acting on behalf of the court.

CLERK	DATE
Juliet Griffin	Sept. 9, 1991
(BY) DEPUTY CLERK _Carolyn Morris_	
This subpoena is issued on application of the United States of America	NAME, ADDRESS AND PHONE NUMBER OF ASSISTANT U.S. ATTORNEY VAN VINCENT, AUSA A-961 U.S. Courthouse Nashville, TN 37203 615/736-5151

38

Mark with pet racoons, 1988   1988 Family Photo: Mark, Cathy, Kelly

Cathy and Mark, 1988 - Las Vegas, Nevada

Cathy and Mark, 1995   Kelly 1984

Cathy in Cozumel,
Mexico prior to
prostitution to
President de la
Madrid, 1986

1987, Cathy and Kelly
drug run in Key West

Cathy during CIA cocaine
operations with Jeff Merritt

St. Thomas, US Virgin Islands

Please Note: Cheney's
"Oz" hour glass used
on Cathy

Cathy on NCL's Stirrup Cay
near CIA communications

-Pierre

40

State-of-Tennessee-run "warehouse," the
"home of broken butterflies," where Kelly's
on-going political prisoner status began

San Francisco protest of
U.S. Army Lt. Col. Aquino's
federal protection and board
position on Childcare
Council

Kelly with biological
father, occult serial
killer Wayne Cox by
court order 1988

Kelly with pedophile Boxcar Willie
Ruland, Vermont 1985

41

Cathy when Gerald Ford knew her

Earl O'Brien
Cathy's pedophile father

Cathy, May 7, 1966
First Communion

The O'Brien family in 1980 Carol, Mike,
Bill, Cathy, Earl, Tom, Kelli Jo, Kim, Tim

Sparky Anderson, who
Kelly named as abuser
and who abused Cathy
as a child

Cathy's brother Tom front of 1966 Ford used
to drive VanderJagt and Ford in local parades

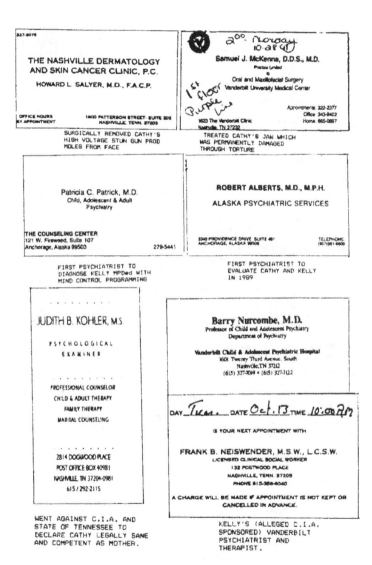

327-3079

**THE NASHVILLE DERMATOLOGY
AND SKIN CANCER CLINIC, P.C.**

HOWARD L. SALYER, M.D., F.A.C.P.

OFFICE HOURS
BY APPOINTMENT

1800 PATTERSON STREET · SUITE 303
NASHVILLE, TENN. 37203

SURGICALLY REMOVED CATHY'S
HIGH VOLTAGE STUN GUN PROD
MOLES FROM FACE

2⁰⁰. monday
10·28 (?)

Samuel J. McKenna, D.D.S., M.D.
Practice Limited
to
Oral and Maxillofacial Surgery
Vanderbilt University Medical Center

1ˢᵗ floor Purple line

Appointments: 322-2377
Office: 343-9402
Home: 665-0897

1620 The Vanderbilt Clinic
Nashville, TN 37232

TREATED CATHY'S JAW WHICH
WAS PERMANENTLY DAMAGED
THROUGH TORTURE

Patricia C. Patrick, M.D.
Child, Adolescent & Adult
Psychiatry

THE COUNSELING CENTER
121 W. Fireweed, Suite 107
Anchorage, Alaska 99503

279-5441

FIRST PSYCHIATRIST TO
DIAGNOSE KELLY MPDed WITH
MIND CONTROL PROGRAMMING

ROBERT ALBERTS, M.D., M.P.H.

ALASKA PSYCHIATRIC SERVICES

3340 PROVIDENCE DRIVE, SUITE 481
ANCHORAGE, ALASKA 99508

TELEPHONE
(907)561-4600

FIRST PSYCHIATRIST TO
EVALUATE CATHY AND KELLY
IN 1989

JUDITH B. KOHLER, M.S.

PSYCHOLOGICAL
EXAMINER

PROFESSIONAL COUNSELOR
CHILD & ADULT THERAPY
FAMILY THERAPY
MARITAL COUNSELING

2814 DOGWOOD PLACE
POST OFFICE BOX 40981
NASHVILLE, TN 37204-0981
615 / 292-2115

WENT AGAINST C.I.A. AND
STATE OF TENNESSEE TO
DECLARE CATHY LEGALLY SANE
AND COMPETENT AS MOTHER.

Barry Nurcombe, M.D.
Professor of Child and Adolescent Psychiatry
Department of Psychiatry

Vanderbilt Child & Adolescent Psychiatric Hospital
1601 Twenty Third Avenue, South
Nashville, TN 37212
(615) 327-7049 · (615) 327-7122

DAY _Tues._ DATE _Oct. 13_ TIME _10:00 AM_

IS YOUR NEXT APPOINTMENT WITH

FRANK B. NEISWENDER, M.S.W., L.C.S.W.
LICENSED CLINICAL SOCIAL WORKER
132 POSTWOOD PLACE
NASHVILLE, TENN. 37205
PHONE 615-356-8040

A CHARGE WILL BE MADE IF APPOINTMENT IS NOT KEPT OR
CANCELLED IN ADVANCE.

KELLY'S (ALLEGED C.I.A.
SPONSORED) VANDERBILT
PSYCHIATRIST AND
THERAPIST.

43

PEDIATRIC CONSULTANTS OF ALASKA, INC.
Clinton B. Lillibridge, M.D. F.A.A.P.

June 22, 1989

Investigator Jack Chapman
Anchorage Police Dept.
4501 S Bragaw
Anchorage, Alaska   99507

RE: KELLY O'BRIEN

Dear Mr. Chapman:

Kelly O'Brien appeared in my office in the company of her mother,
Cathy O'Brien, on 06/12/89. Mother requested evaluation for possible
sexual abuse.

Child appeared somewhat ill at ease but was fully cooperative and had a
good sense of humor - joking during the examination.

PHYSICAL EXAMINATION: HEENT: She was a rather round face child with
prominent cheeks. Otherwise negative. BREASTS: Breasts are Tanner Stage
0 development. CHEST: Fine musical wheezes throughout. GU: The genital
exam is Tanner Stage 0 development. The introitus is intensely red with a
moderate white discharge. Culture for sexually transmitted diseases was
negative. The hymen has a smooth thick edge with a 6 X 8 mm opening. The
vaginal mucosa appeared normal. RECTAL: Anus has no tears, no fissures,
and no scars. EXTREM: Extremities are rather stocky in the proximal
portion.

DIAGNOSIS: Large opening in the hymen indicative of sexual penetration.
Nonspecific vaginitis of childhood. Chronic asthma.

COMMENT: Vaginitis causes some swelling of the hymen tissue. If the
swelling were not present, the opening through the hymen may appear
considerably larger. The size of the opening itself is typical for a child
who has been sexually penetrated with an object the size of an adult
finger. This could not have been caused by an accident because the hymen
is recessed back into the introitus far enough to protect it from damage
occurring from falls, splits, etc.

Lillibridge

CLINTON B. LILLIBRIDGE, M.D.
Pediatrician

CBL/bw
cc: Dr. Bruno Kappes   **JUN 23 1989**

1200 Airport Heights Drive, Suite 230 • Anchorage, Alaska 99508
Telephone (907) 276-5517

PEDIATRIC CONSULTANTS OF ALASKA, INC.
Clinton B. Lillibridge, M.D., F.A.A.P.

September 11, 1989

Dion Roberts, M.D.
4001 Dale St.
Suite 210
Anchorage, Alaska   99508

Dear Dion:

Kelly Cox is a 9 and 1/2-year-old chronic asthmatic that was involved with her parent in a cult which did mind programming. Mother and Kelly are now in rather intensive treatment for this with salutary effect.

She had physical findings of chronic asthma. They have applied for Social Security Disability which requires evaluation and expertise beyond mine. A copy of the paperwork is enclosed.

Clut

CLINTON B. LILLIBRIDGE, M.D.
Pediatric Gastroenterologist

CBL/bw
enclosure

SEP 15 1989

1200 Airport Heights Drive, Suite 230 • Anchorage, Alaska 99508
Telephone (907) 276-5517

CHARTER NORTH HOSPITAL
2530 DE BARR ROAD
ANCHORAGE, ALASKA   99508
(907)-258-7575

COX (O'BRIEN), KELLY
DR. PATRICK
M.R.#: 00-32-75
ADMISSION DATE: 09-19-89
DISCHARGE DATE: 10-16-89
D.O.B.: 02-19-80

DISCHARGE SUMMARY

DISCHARGE DIAGNOSES:
AXIS I: Dissociative Disorder

AXIS II: Post Traumatic Stress Disorder

AXIS III: Bronchial asthma

AXIS IV: Precipitating stress: Severe

AXIS V: Highest level of function: Fair

The patient is a 9½ year old girl who was admitted to the hospital
on transfer from Humana Hospital where she has been a patient for
approximately two weeks. She was admitted there because of an
acute asthmatic episode in which she had deteriorated from a previous
time. Additionally, the patient is a victim of sexual abuse and
ritualized abuse involving hypnosis, mind control, and psychological
programming. The patient had been under the hypnotic control of
her step-father from the age of two and a half until approximately
six months prior to admission. During this time the patient had
been sexually abused and had participated in ritual abuse and had
been programmed to die. Last June, at the end of the school year,
the patient had an acute asthmatic episode requiring intensive
treatment at Humana Hospital. During that time she was on steroids
and has been recently on a course of steroids. The patient is
admitted to Charter North Hospital because of suicidal/homicidal
ideation. The ideation appears to be mostly directed towards herself,
her mother and her step-father.

The patient's mental status examination at the time of admission
indicates an attractive blonde-haired girl with a slightly moon
shaped faces consistent with the use of steroids. She relates
easily to the examiner whom she knows through her outpatient treatment.
She is animated and engaging. She is quite resistant to exploration
of her problems but can fairly easily refer to the sexual abuse
she has experienced. There are no bizarre or unusual behaviors
noted in this examination tonight. She does seem somewhat agitated
and admits that she is apprehensive. She appears to be intellectually
bright.

ADMITTING DIAGNOSIS: Dissociative Disorder OS, Post Traumatic
Stress Syndrome and Bronchial Asthma.

Social history was obtained by the unit social worker. It is his
assessment that she is an engaging and verbal youngster on a superficial
social level. The writer was able to "trigger" the patient's defenses
which consisted of a horse personna and withdrawal. Activity level
was good and eye contact appropriate.

1a. CHILD'S LAST NAME	1b. FIRST NAME	1c. SECOND NAME	2a. DATE MONTH DAY YEAR OF BIRTH
Cox	Kelly	Lynn	Feb. 19, 1980

3. GIRL OR BOY?	4. THIS BIRTH	5. IF THIS BIRTH WAS CHILD BORN		2b. HOUR OF BIRTH
Girl	Single ☒ Twin ☐ Triplet ☐	1st ☐ 2d ☐ 3d ☐		4:15 p.m.

6a. PLACE OF BIRTH (CITY, TOWN OR LOCATION)	6b. PARISH OF BIRTH
West Monroe	Ouachita

6c. NAME OF HOSPITAL OR INSTITUTION	6d. IS PLACE OF BIRTH INSIDE CITY LIMITS?
Glenwood Hospital	Yes ☒ No ☐

7a. USUAL RESIDENCE OF MOTHER (CITY, TOWN OR LOCATION)	7b. PARISH	7c. STATE
Chatham	Jackson	Louisiana

7d. STREET ADDRESS—IF RURAL INDICATE LOCATION	7e. IS RESIDENCE INSIDE CITY LIMITS?
Route 1, Box 84	Yes ☐ No ☒

8a. FULL NAME OF FATHER	8b. CITY AND STATE OF BIRTH IF NOT IN USA NAME COUNTRY	8c. AGE AT TIME OF THIS BIRTH	8d. COLOR OR RACE OF FATHER
Edward Wayne Cox	Hodge, La.	31	White

9a. FULL MAIDEN NAME OF MOTHER	9b. CITY AND STATE OF BIRTH IF NOT IN USA NAME COUNTRY	9c. AGE AT TIME OF THIS BIRTH	9d. COLOR OR RACE OF MOTHER
Cathleen Ann O'Brien	Muskegon, Michigan	22	White

I certify that the above stated information is true and correct to the best of my knowledge *Cathleen Cox*

10. SIGNATURE OF ___ Parent ☐ Other ☐

11. DATE OF SIGNATURE *February 21, 1980*

11. MOTHER'S MAILING ADDRESS

Route 1, Box 84, Chatham, La. 71226

I certify that I attended this birth and that the child was born alive on the date stated above.

13. SIGNATURE OF ATTENDANT _____ m.D.

MD ☐ Midwife ☐ Other ☐

14. DATE OF SIGNATURE 2-21-80

15. DATE ACCEPTED BY LOCAL REGISTRAR	16. SIGNATURE OF LOCAL REGISTRAR	17. DATE FILED BY STATE
MAR 18 1980	*Kate L. Stewart*	MAR 20 1980

CONFIDENTIAL INFORMATION FOR MEDICAL AND HEALTH USE ONLY
(This Section MUST Be Filled Out For Each Birth)

FEB 17 1981

I CERTIFY THAT THE ABOVE IS A TRUE AND CORRECT COPY OF A CERTIFICATE OR DOCUMENT REGISTERED WITH THE DIVISION OF VITAL RECORDS OF THE STATE OF LOUISIANA, PURSUANT TO LSA—R.S. 40:32, ET SEQ.

_____
STATE HEALTH OFFICER

_____
STATE REGISTRAR

47

NAME Cathy O'Brien   DATE 11/26/90

HEIGHT _____ AGE 32   B/P _____

ALLERGIES NKD   MENARCH ___ DAYS

DYSMENORRHEA mild   LMP 11/14/90

PE Br. Aug.   ___

HOS reg.   MEDS Tri Nor 2yrs

PE _____

BREASTS _____

ABD ___

PELVIC CX _____

UT _____

ABD _____

IMP ? _____

PLAN _____

RICHARD E. PRESLEY, M.D.
STEPHEN M. STAGGS, M.D.

From seeing photographs
of reviewing her history & physical ...
... it is my opinion that
Kelly Cox has been sexually
abused.
R E Presley MD

4/15/91 Look at vagina again
... Pt. has been abused.

Certificate

of Birth

This Certifies that _Cathleen Ann O'Brian_

was born to _Mr. and Mrs. Earl M. O'Brian_

in _Mercy Hospital_ _Muskegon, Michigan_

at _6:49_ _.m. this_ _4th_ day of _December_ 19_5_

In Witness Whereof the said Hospital has caused
this Certificate to be signed by its duly authorized
officers and its Corporate Seal to be hereunto affixed.

Sister M. Theodora, R.N. Adm.

49

THE WHITE HOUSE

WASHINGTON

November 20, 1990

Dear Congressman Clement:

Thank you for your recent letter enclosing
correspondence you received from Mark
Phillips of Nashville, Tennessee.

We appreciate your interest in sharing Mr.
Phillips' letter with us. I have taken
the liberty of forwarding a copy of your
correspondence to the appropriate
officials for further attention.

Thank you again for your interest in
writing.

With best regards,

Sincerely,

Frederick D. McClure
Assistant to the President
for Legislative Affairs

The Honorable Bob Clement
House of Representatives
Washington, D.C.   20515

Dear Mr. Phillips:

Congressman Bob Clement has sent us the copies he received of
your November 15, 1990 letters to President Bush and Attorney
General Thornburg. While we have not received your original
letter, we are forwarding these copies to officials at the
Department of Justice for appropriate consideration.

With best wishes,

Sincerely,

Shirley M. Green

Shirley M. Green
Special Assistant to the President
   for Presidential Messages
   and Correspondence

Mr. Mark E. Phillips
Post Office Box 158352
Nashville, TN 37215

BOB CLEMENT
6TH DISTRICT TENNESSEE

COMMITTEE ON
PUBLIC WORKS AND TRANSPORTATION

COMMITTEE ON
MERCHANT MARINE AND FISHERIES

CONGRESSIONAL TRAVEL AND
TOURISM CAUCUS
STEERING COMMITTEE

DEMOCRATIC STEERING AND
POLICY COMMITTEE

DISTRICT OFFICES
552 U.S. COURTHOUSE
NASHVILLE TN 37203
615-736-5295

510 MAIN STREET
SPRINGFIELD TN 37172
615 384-8830

2701 JEFFERSON STREET
SUITE 102
NASHVILLE TN 37208
615 321-1363

WASHINGTON OFFICE
ROOM 325
CANNON HOUSE OFFICE BUILDING
202-225-4311

Congress of the United States
House of Representatives
Washington, DC 20515-4205
November 15, 1990

Mr. Mark Phillips
P.O. Box 158352
Nashville, Tennessee   37215

Dear Mr. Phillips:

As you requested, I have forwarded to the President and Attorney General Thornburgh the packages you delivered to my office.

Should I receive a response, I will be pleased to share it with you. In the meantime, please feel free to call on me if I can be of further assistance.

Thank you, again, for bringing this matter to my attention.

Sincerely,

Bob Clement
Member of Congress

BC/df

52

BOB DOLE
KANSAS
141 SENATE HART BUILDING
(202) 224-8521

COMMITTEE
SPECIAL COMMITTEE ON AGING, NUTRITION AND FORESTRY
FINANCE
RULES

United States Senate

WASHINGTON DC 20510-1601

March 13, 1991

Mr. Mark Phillips
P.O. Box 158352
Nashville, Tennessee 37215

Dear Mr. Phillips:

Thank you for contacting me concerning the Monarch
Program.

The tradition of Congressional courtesy provides that we
allow our colleagues the opportunity to assist their own
constituents. Accordingly, I have referred your letter to
Senator Al Gore. He is in the best position to review the
matter, and I am confident that he will offer all appropriate
suggestions and assistance.

I appreciate the confidence you have shown by contacting
me.

Sincerely,

BOB DOLE
United States Senate

BD/cr

cc: The Honorable Al Gore

Central Intelligence Agency

Washington, D.C. 20505

1 7 JUL 1991

Ms. Cathy O'Brien
P.O. Box 158352
Nashville, Tennessee 37215

Reference: P91-0739

Dear Ms. O'Brien:

This is a final response to your Privacy Act request for
information on yourself. We have searched those Agency systems
that might contain information regarding you and find that we
were unable to identify any information or record filed under
the name or names you have provided.

We appreciate your patience and understanding during the
period required to process your request.

Sincerely,

John H. Wright
Information and Privacy Coordinator

BOB CLEMENT
5TH DISTRICT, TENNESSEE

COMMITTEE ON
PUBLIC WORKS AND TRANSPORTATION

COMMITTEE ON
VETERANS AFFAIRS

CONGRESSIONAL TRAVEL AND
TOURISM CAUCUS
STEERING COMMITTEE

Congress of the United States
House of Representatives
Washington, DC 20515-4205

DISTRICT OFFICES

552 U.S. COURTHOUSE
NASHVILLE, TN 37203
615-736-4296

101 5TH AVENUE EAST
SUITE 201
SPRINGFIELD, TN 37172
615-264-8600

2701 JEFFERSON STREET
SUITE 103
NASHVILLE, TN 37208
615-320-1363

WASHINGTON OFFICE
ROOM 325
CANNON HOUSE OFFICE BUILDING
WASHINGTON, DC 20515-4205
202-225-4311

July 11, 1992

Ms. Cathy O'Brien
P.O. Box 158352
Nashville, Tennessee 37215

Dear Ms. O'Brien:

    Thank you for sharing with me the additional information about your daughter.

    I hope the future looks brighter for you and Kelly. Please keep me informed of any additional progress in this case.

        Sincerely,

        Bob Clement
        Member of Congress

BC/df

55

A WELL KNOWN ALLEGED MIND
CONTROLLED TOP "MOONIE" THAT
THE CIA SENT IN ON MARK AND
CATHY IN 1989 BY U.C.L.A.'S
(C.I.A.) DR. JOLYN WEST, M.D.
AND CULT AWARENESS NETWORK
FOUNDER MARGARET SINGER, M.D.

Steven Hassan M.Ed.

CULT AND MIND CONTROL SPECIALIST
STRATEGIC INTERVENTION THERAPIST

P O BOX 686
BOSTON, MA. 02258   (617) 964-6977

"NULLI VENDEMUS. NULLI NEGABIMUS RECTUM AUT JUSTITIAM"

MARK'S ATTORNEY FOR 9-9-'91   **HENRY A. MARTIN**
FEDERAL SUBPOENA TITLE 18   ATTORNEY AT LAW
U.S. CODE SECTION 871   FEDERAL PUBLIC DEFENDER

                                                      736
808 BROADWAY   615-251-5047
NASHVILLE, TENNESSEE 37203   FTS 852 5047

CATHY'S ATTORNEY FOR MARK'S
FEDERAL SUBPOENA TITLE 18
U.S. CODE SECTION 871

                    MICHAEL E. TERRY
                          LAWYER
                150 SECOND AVENUE N., SUITE 315
                   NASHVILLE, TENNESSEE 37201
                        (615) 256-5555

1 800-527 4529   FAX (615) 256-5652

DICK THORNBURGH'S CHICAGO
CUB-SCOUT FRIEND FROM 1986
N.C.L. CARIBBEAN CRUISE

                    JAMES ZERILLA
                        SCOUT

2115 KING CROSSING S.W.
WINTER HAVEN, FLORIDA 33880   (813) 299-7865

56

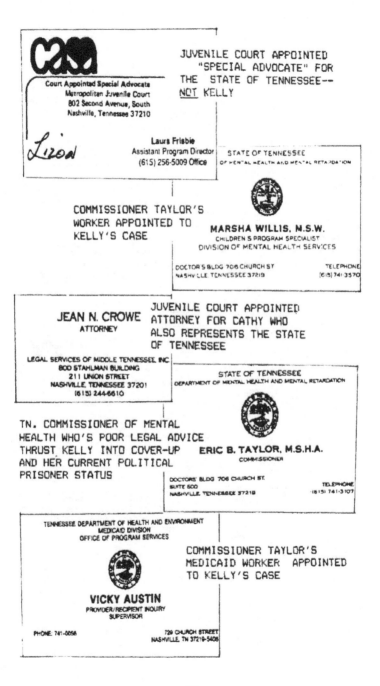

casa

Court Appointed Special Advocate
Metropolitan Juvenile Court
802 Second Avenue, South
Nashville, Tennessee 37210

Lisa

Laura Frisbie
Assistant Program Director
(615) 256-5009 Office

JUVENILE COURT APPOINTED
"SPECIAL ADVOCATE" FOR
THE STATE OF TENNESSEE—
NOT KELLY

STATE OF TENNESSEE
OF MENTAL HEALTH AND MENTAL RETARDATION

MARSHA WILLIS, M.S.W.
CHILDREN'S PROGRAM SPECIALIST
DIVISION OF MENTAL HEALTH SERVICES

DOCTOR'S BLDG 706 CHURCH ST   TELEPHONE
NASHVILLE TENNESSEE 37219   (615) 741-3570

COMMISSIONER TAYLOR'S
WORKER APPOINTED TO
KELLY'S CASE

JEAN N. CROWE
ATTORNEY

LEGAL SERVICES OF MIDDLE TENNESSEE, INC
800 STAHLMAN BUILDING
211 UNION STREET
NASHVILLE, TENNESSEE 37201
(615) 244-6610

JUVENILE COURT APPOINTED
ATTORNEY FOR CATHY WHO
ALSO REPRESENTS THE STATE
OF TENNESSEE

STATE OF TENNESSEE
DEPARTMENT OF MENTAL HEALTH AND MENTAL RETARDATION

ERIC B. TAYLOR, M.S.H.A.
COMMISSIONER

DOCTORS' BLDG 706 CHURCH ST.
SUITE 500   TELEPHONE
NASHVILLE TENNESSEE 37219   (615) 741-3107

TN. COMMISSIONER OF MENTAL
HEALTH WHO'S POOR LEGAL ADVICE
THRUST KELLY INTO COVER-UP
AND HER CURRENT POLITICAL
PRISONER STATUS

TENNESSEE DEPARTMENT OF HEALTH AND ENVIRONMENT
MEDICAID DIVISION
OFFICE OF PROGRAM SERVICES

VICKY AUSTIN
PROVIDER/RECIPIENT INQUIRY
SUPERVISOR

PHONE: 741-0056   729 CHURCH STREET
                               NASHVILLE, TN 37219-5406

COMMISSIONER TAYLOR'S
MEDICAID WORKER APPOINTED
TO KELLY'S CASE

57

301-279-6700
FAX 301-279-2609

SE HABLA ESPAÑOL.

PRUDENTIAL ASSOCIATES, INC.
INVESTIGATIVE AND CONSULTING SERVICES
LICENSED · BONDED · INSURED

THEN-PRESIDENT OF MEXICO
DE LA MADRID'S SPY SENT IN
ON MARK AND CATHY IN 1992

HERBERT QUINDE

212 NORTH ADAMS ST
ROCKVILLE, MD 20850

JOSE OCTAVIO BUSTO
PRESIDENT

IMPERSONATOR OF U.S.
CUSTOMS AND IMMIGRATIONS
OFFICERS WHO WORKED FOR
D.E.A. TO PROTECT C.I.A.
CARIBBEAN DRUG OPERATIONS

P.O. BOX S-2467
400 COMERCIO ST.
SAN JUAN, P.R. 00903

Cable: CONSHIP
Telex RCA (325) 2770
Tel. (809) 725-2632

Tango Bravo International

Investigations, Photographic and Aviation

C.I.A. AERIAL HARASSMENT
PILOT HIRED BY ALEX HOUSTON
IN 1988

Services, Militaria Sales

Jerry Barnes - Owner
909 Rivergate Meadows
Goodlettsville, Tenn. 37072   *(615) 865-5932*

Metropolitan Health Department
Davidson County Community Health Agency
Caring For Children Program

Alicia Lewis
Case Manager

JUVENILE COURT APPOINTED
AGENCY WHO ALSO PROTECTS
AND REPRESENTS THE STATE
OF TENNESSEE

Nashville House, Building A
One Vantage Way
Nashville, Tennessee 37228

Phone 615-862-7950
FAX 615-862-7975

58

STATE AGENCIES TO WHOM MARK AND CATHY PROVIDED DETAILED
TESTIMONY, DOCUMENTATION, AND INFORMATION IN 1991

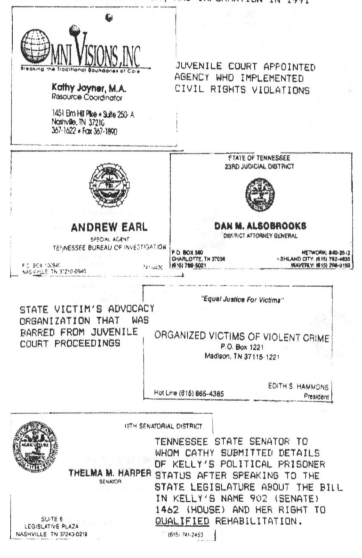

OMNI VISIONS, INC.
Breaking the Traditional Boundaries of Care

Kathy Joyner, M.A.
Resource Coordinator

1451 Elm Hill Pike • Suite 250-A
Nashville, TN 37210
367-1622 • Fax 367-1890

JUVENILE COURT APPOINTED
AGENCY WHO IMPLEMENTED
CIVIL RIGHTS VIOLATIONS

ANDREW EARL
SPECIAL AGENT
TENNESSEE BUREAU OF INVESTIGATION

P.O. BOX 100940
NASHVILLE TN 37210-0940

STATE OF TENNESSEE
23RD JUDICIAL DISTRICT

DAN M. ALSOBROOKS
DISTRICT ATTORNEY GENERAL

P.O. BOX 580
CHARLOTTE, TN 37036
(615) 789-5021

NETWORK: 840-2512
• ASHLAND CITY: (615) 792-4835
WAVERLY: (615) 296-9159

STATE VICTIM'S ADVOCACY
ORGANIZATION THAT WAS
BARRED FROM JUVENILE
COURT PROCEEDINGS

"Equal Justice For Victims"

ORGANIZED VICTIMS OF VIOLENT CRIME
P.O. Box 1221
Madison, TN 37115-1221

Hot Line (615) 865-4385

EDITH S. HAMMONS
President

19TH SENATORIAL DISTRICT

THELMA M. HARPER
SENATOR

SUITE 6
LEGISLATIVE PLAZA
NASHVILLE TN 37243-0219

(615) 741-2453

TENNESSEE STATE SENATOR TO
WHOM CATHY SUBMITTED DETAILS
OF KELLY'S POLITICAL PRISONER
STATUS AFTER SPEAKING TO THE
STATE LEGISLATURE ABOUT THE BILL
IN KELLY'S NAME 902 (SENATE)
1462 (HOUSE) AND HER RIGHT TO
QUALIFIED REHABILITATION.

A FEW OF MANY FEDERAL AGENTS
AND/OR AGENCIES TO WHOM
MARK AND CATHY PROVIDED DETAILED
TESTIMONY AND INFORMATION
FROM 1989 THROUGH 1991

RAYMOND E. EGANEY, JR.
SPECIAL AGENT FBI

FEDERAL BUREAU OF INVESTIGATION

FEDERAL BUILDING
81h & BROADWAY
NASHVILLE. TN 37201   TEL .615. 256 3676

DEPARTMENT OF THE TREASURY
UNITED STATES CUSTOMS SERVICE
OFFICE OF INTERNAL AFFAIRS

KENNETH J. M^cMILLIN
ASSISTANT REGIONAL DIRECTOR (SECURITY)

UNITED STATES CUSTOMS SERVICE
423 CANAL STREET, ROOM 312
NEW ORLEANS, LOUISIANA 70130

FTS 682-2187   (504) 589-2187

KEN MARISCHEN
SPECIAL AGENT

FEDERAL BUREAU OF INVESTIGATION

701 'C' STREET
P.O. BOX 100560
ANCHORAGE, ALASKA 99510   TEL (907) 276-4441

James Max Kitchens
Resident Agent In Charge

907-271-4038

U.S. Customs Service   620 East 10th Ave., Suite 106
Office of Enforcement   Anchorage, AK 99501

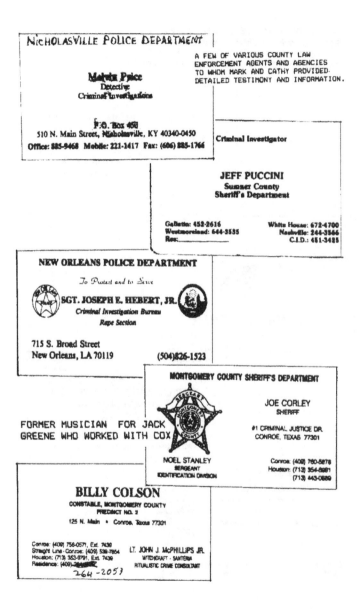

NiCHOLASVILLE POLICE DEPARTMENT

Melvin Price
Detective
Criminal Investigations

A FEW OF VARIOUS COUNTY LAW
ENFORCEMENT AGENTS AND AGENCIES
TO WHOM MARK AND CATHY PROVIDED
DETAILED TESTIMONY AND INFORMATION.

P.O. Box 458
510 N. Main Street, Nicholasville, KY 40340-0450
Office: 885-9468 Mobile: 221-1417 Fax: (606) 885-1766

Criminal Investigator

JEFF PUCCINI
Sumner County
Sheriff's Department

Gallatin: 452-2616   White House: 672-4700
Westmoreland: 644-3535   Nashville: 244-3566
Res: C.I.D.: 451-3425

NEW ORLEANS POLICE DEPARTMENT

To Protect and to Serve

SGT. JOSEPH E. HEBERT, JR.
Criminal Investigation Bureau
Rape Section

715 S. Broad Street
New Orleans, LA 70119   (504)826-1523

MONTGOMERY COUNTY SHERIFFS DEPARTMENT

FORMER MUSICIAN FOR JACK
GREENE WHO WORKED WITH COX

JOE CORLEY
SHERIFF

#1 CRIMINAL JUSTICE DR.
CONROE, TEXAS 77301

NOEL STANLEY
SERGEANT
IDENTIFICATION DIVISION

Conroe: (409) 760-5278
Houston: (713) 354-8981
(713) 443-0889

BILLY COLSON
CONSTABLE, MONTGOMERY COUNTY
PRECINCT NO. 2
125 N. Main • Conroe, Texas 77301

Conroe: (409) 756-0571, Ext. 7439
Straight Line - Conroe: (409) 539-7654
Houston: (713) 353-9791, Ext. 7439
Residence: (409) 264-2057

LT. JOHN J. McPHILLIPS JR.
WITCHCRAFT - SANTERIA
RITUALISTIC CRIME CONSULTANT

264-2057

61

A FEW OF VARIOUS COUNTY LAW
ENFORCEMENT AGENTS AND AGENCIES
TO WHOM MARK AND CATHY PROVIDED
DETAILED TESTIMONY AND INFORMATION.

RONALD J. MILLER
Lieutenant

White House Police Department

P.O. Box 69
White House, TN 37188

Phone
(615) 672-4903

Fred W. Schott

Chief of Police

Goodlettsville

105 So. Main St. ● Goodlettsville, TN 37072 ● (615) 859-3405

P.O. Box 2505
Ft. Lauderdale, FL 33303

Area Code 305
Office 492-1910
Pager 521-3797
1-800-633-0252

DETECTIVE HOWARD RUDOLPH
Organized Crime Division

NICK NAVARRO - Sheriff of Broward County

Nashville Metropolitan Police Department
INTELLIGENCE DIVISION

DETECTIVE
SGT. JAMES A. HICKSON

Office (615) 862-7397
Dispatcher (615) 862-8600

200 James Robertson Pkwy.
Nashville, Tenn. 37201

62

PROJECT MKULTRA, THE CIA'S PROGRAM OF RESEARCH IN BEHAVIORAL MODIFICATION

JOINT HEARING
BEFORE THE
SELECT COMMITTEE ON INTELLIGENCE
AND THE
SUBCOMMITTEE ON HEALTH AND SCIENTIFIC RESEARCH
OF THE
COMMITTEE ON HUMAN RESOURCES
UNITED STATES SENATE
NINETY-FIFTH CONGRESS
FIRST SESSION

AUGUST 3, 1977

Printed for the use of the Select Committee on Intelligence
and Committee on Human Resources

U.S. GOVERNMENT PRINTING OFFICE
96-408 O   WASHINGTON : 1977

For sale by the Superintendent of Documents, U.S. Government Printing Office
Washington, D.C., 20402
Stock No. 052-070-04357-1

BEHAVIOR MODIFICATION PROGRAMS FEDERAL BUREAU OF PRISONS

HEARING

BEFORE THE

SUBCOMMITTEE ON COURTS, CIVIL LIBERTIES, AND THE ADMINISTRATION OF JUSTICE

OF THE

COMMITTEE ON THE JUDICIARY
HOUSE OF REPRESENTATIVES

NINETY-THIRD CONGRESS

SECOND SESSION

ON

OVERSIGHT HEARING
BEHAVIOR MODIFICATION PROGRAMS IN THE
FEDERAL BUREAU OF PRISONS

FEBRUARY 27, 1974

Serial No. 26

Printed for the use of the Committee on the Judiciary

U.S. GOVERNMENT PRINTING OFFICE
WASHINGTON : 1974

BIOLOGICAL TESTING INVOLVING HUMAN SUBJECTS BY THE DEPARTMENT OF DEFENSE, 1977

HEARINGS

BEFORE THE

SUBCOMMITTEE ON HEALTH AND SCIENTIFIC RESEARCH

OF THE

COMMITTEE ON HUMAN RESOURCES UNITED STATES SENATE

NINETY-FIFTH CONGRESS

FIRST SESSION

ON

EXAMINATION OF SERIOUS DEFICIENCIES IN THE DEFENSE DEPARTMENT'S EFFORTS TO PROTECT THE HUMAN SUBJECTS, OF DRUG RESEARCH

MARCH 8 AND MAY 23, 1977

Printed for the use of the Committee on Human Resources

U.S. GOVERNMENT PRINTING OFFICE
87-857 O   WASHINGTON : 1977

BASIC ISSUES IN BIOMEDICAL AND BEHAVIORAL RESEARCH, 1976

HEARINGS

BEFORE THE

SUBCOMMITTEE ON HEALTH

OF THE

COMMITTEE ON LABOR AND PUBLIC WELFARE UNITED STATES SENATE

NINETY-FOURTH CONGRESS

SECOND SESSION

ON

EXAMINATION OF PUBLIC POLICY IN THE AREA OF BIO-
MEDICAL AND BEHAVIORAL RESEARCH

JUNE 16 AND 17, 1976

Printed for the use of the Committee on Labor and Public Welfare

U.S. GOVERNMENT PRINTING OFFICE

74-838 O   WASHINGTON : 1976

HUMAN DRUG TESTING BY THE CIA, 1977

HEARINGS

BEFORE THE

SUBCOMMITTEE ON
HEALTH AND SCIENTIFIC RESEARCH

OF THE

COMMITTEE ON HUMAN RESOURCES
UNITED STATES SENATE

NINETY-FIFTH CONGRESS

FIRST SESSION

ON

S. 1893

TO AMEND THE PUBLIC HEALTH SERVICE ACT TO ESTABLISH
THE PRESIDENT'S COMMISSION FOR THE PROTECTION OF
HUMAN SUBJECTS OF BIOMEDICAL AND BEHAVIORAL RE-
SEARCH, AND FOR OTHER PURPOSES

SEPTEMBER 20 AND 21, 1977

Printed for the use of the Committee on Human Resources

U.S. GOVERNMENT PRINTING OFFICE

96-639 O   WASHINGTON : 1977

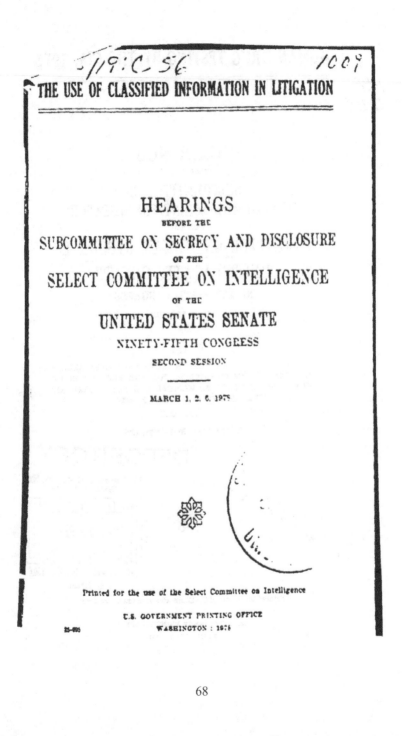

J19:C 56   1009

THE USE OF CLASSIFIED INFORMATION IN LITIGATION

HEARINGS
BEFORE THE
SUBCOMMITTEE ON SECRECY AND DISCLOSURE
OF THE
SELECT COMMITTEE ON INTELLIGENCE
OF THE
UNITED STATES SENATE
NINETY-FIFTH CONGRESS
SECOND SESSION

MARCH 1, 2, 6, 1978

Printed for the use of the Select Committee on Intelligence

U.S. GOVERNMENT PRINTING OFFICE
25-695   WASHINGTON : 1978

68

LEGISLATION TO MODIFY THE APPLICATION OF THE FREEDOM OF INFORMATION ACT TO THE CENTRAL INTELLIGENCE AGENCY

HEARING

BEFORE THE

SUBCOMMITTEE ON LEGISLATION

OF THE

PERMANENT
SELECT COMMITTEE ON INTELLIGENCE
HOUSE OF REPRESENTATIVES

NINETY-EIGHTH CONGRESS

SECOND SESSION

FEBRUARY 8, 1984

Printed for the use of the Permanent Select Committee on Intelligence

U.S. GOVERNMENT PRINTING OFFICE

E-780   WASHINGTON : 1984

Y4.In 8/19.F96

WHETHER DISCLOSURE OF FUNDS AUTHORIZED FOR INTELLIGENCE ACTIVITIES IS IN THE PUBLIC INTEREST

HEARINGS

BEFORE THE

SELECT COMMITTEE ON INTELLIGENCE

OF THE

UNITED STATES SENATE

NINETY-FIFTH CONGRESS

FIRST SESSION

APRIL 27 AND 28, 1977

Printed for the use of the Select Committee on Intelligence

U.S. GOVERNMENT PRINTING OFFICE

94-794 WASHINGTON : 1977

For sale by the Superintendent of Documents, U.S. Government Printing Office
Washington, D.C. 20402

ABUSE OF PSYCHIATRY FOR POLITICAL REPRESSION IN THE SOVIET UNION
VOLUME II

HEARING

TESTIMONY OF DR. NORMAN B. HIRT

SUBMITTED

TO THE

SUBCOMMITTEE TO INVESTIGATE THE
ADMINISTRATION OF THE INTERNAL SECURITY
ACT AND OTHER INTERNAL SECURITY LAWS

OF THE

COMMITTEE ON THE JUDICIARY
UNITED STATES SENATE

NINETY-FOURTH CONGRESS

FIRST SESSION

STAFF INTERVIEW OF OCTOBER 27, 1973,
COVERED BY JURAT OF MARCH 12, 1974

Printed for the use of the Committee on the Judiciary

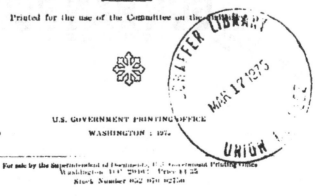

U.S. GOVERNMENT PRINTING OFFICE
WASHINGTON : 1975

For sale by the Superintendent of Documents, U.S. Government Printing Office
Washington, D.C. 20402 - Price $1.35
Stock Number 052-070-10730

Cramer on 'top-secret' panel

By BRETT DAVIS
Times Washington Correspondent

WASHINGTON — Rep. Bud Cramer, D-Huntsville, has been on the Permanent Select Committee on Intelligence for a little over a year now, but there's not much he can say about it.

Or rather, to use the old joke, he could tell you about it but then he'd have to kill you.

"It's a remarkable committee," Cramer said in an interview with *The Huntsville Times*. "There's a lot I can't tell you."

The committee has oversight on the intelligence budgets and activities of the CIA, the National Security Agency (which used to describe itself as "No Such Agency,") and the Defense Intelligence Agency, which includes Redstone Arsenal's Missile and Space Intelligence

> The panel also has oversight of the Pentagon's "black" budget of secret programs.

Command. It also has oversight of the Pentagon's "black" budget of secret programs.

It's the only committee that both writes budget authorizations and approves actual spending for the programs it oversees, two functions that are usually kept separate in Congress.

Cramer is one of 19 members on the committee and is one of the youngest in terms of congressional seniority. Freshman members can't get on the panel at all, and Cramer made it a lot sooner than most.

"I think I've done some things to get the attention of the Speaker, including taking him down to my district, and I'm a regional whip," Cramer said.

He was appointed to the committee by Speaker of the House Tom Foley, D-Wash., at the beginning of his second term in Congress. Cramer said he had started lobbying for the spot shortly after being re-elected.

"To me, it's one of the most invigorating committees that I'm on," Cramer said.

He didn't have to undergo a background security check or take any special oaths or learn any secret handshakes, but he does learn top-secret information.

He has visited intelligence offices in the Pentagon, the CIA, the DIA and others, has "got to see some hardware and

See CRAMER, page 8J

DEFEAT
GUN BAN BUD
CRAMER

POPULAR LOCAL BUMPER STICKER

72

PART II

By Cathy O'Brien

AN OPEN LETTER

Mind control is absolute. Under MK-Ultra Project Monarch trauma-based mind control, I lost control over my own free will thoughts-I could not think to question, reason, or consciously comprehend-I could only do exactly what I was driven to do. Those who controlled my mind, and ultimately my actions, claimed to be "aliens," "demons," and "gods". But it was my experience that these perpe-TRAITORS of New World Order controls were/are bound by earthly, human confines, despite their terror-tactic claims and illusions. The same laws of nature, and the same laws of man do, indeed, apply to them. While they manipulated me by my religion, my maternal instincts, and my genuine concern for humanity-they never "possessed" my innate being. They could not make me one of them. They never took into consideration the strength of the human spirit. They did not even know it existed. Ask why.

DEDICATION

This book is for Kelly, in order that she is understood and granted her right to qualified rehabilitation for the MK-Ultra Project Monarch Mind-Control abuses she endured at the hands of our country's so-called leaders.

This book is dedicated, as am I, to Mark Phillips for rescuing Kelly and me from our mind-controlled existence and clearing the way to recovery for Kelly by lovingly assisting me in the restoration of my mind, memory, and ultimately my free will.

<u>ACKNOWLEDGEMENTS</u>

A special thanks to these unseen, whose presence have been evident. And a special thanks to those unsung-you know who you are.

TRANCE-FORMATION OF AMERICA

My name is Cathleen (Cathy) Ann O'Brien, born 12/4/57 in Muskegon, Michigan. I have prepared this book for your review and edification concerning a little known tool that "our" United States government is covertly, illegally, and unconstitutionally using to implement the New World Order (one world government). This well documented tool is a sophisticated and advanced form of behavior modification (brainwashing) most commonly known as MIND-CONTROL. My first hand knowledge of this TOP SECRET U.S. Government Psychological Warfare technique is drawn from my personal experience as a White House "Presidential Model" mind-control slave.

Much of the information enclosed herein has been corroborated and validated through brave and courageous "clean" members of the law enforcement, scientific, and Intelligence communities familiar with this case. These individuals' efforts helped me to understand and corroborate what happened after a lifetime of systematic physical and psychological torture orchestrated to modify my behavior through totally controlling my mind. Some of these courageous individuals are employed by the very system that controlled me and live in fear of losing their jobs, their families, or their lives. They have gone as far as they dare towards publicly exposing this tool of the engineers of the New World Order-to no avail. This book is a grassroots effort to solicit and enlist the public and private support of Human Rights advocates, the recognized, respected doers in America to expose this invisible personal and social menace. This can be done by well organized, cooperative citizens with a passion for justice, who have expressed interest in restoring our Constitution and taking back America. This copy you hold is for your edification and action.

While these pages have been condensed for your quick perusal, there are literally thousands of files of documentation that support much of what I am reporting. Thanks to those dedicated individuals who found a means of manipulating the system more cleverly than the perpetrators, the documents referred to were declassified for release right at the source!

It is my patriotic respect for the principals of truth, justice, and ultimately that freedom on which America was founded that compels me to expose the world domination motivations of those in control of our government, commonly referred to as the Shadow Government. By taking back America NOW, we can maintain the integrity of our country's history and future by detouring its destined course of being recognized world wide for the mind control atrocities unleashed on humanity that literally begin where Adolph Hitler left off. Hitler's version of world domination that he termed in 1939 the "New World Order" is currently being implemented through advanced technologies in, among others, genetic mind control engineering by those in control of America.

Senator Daniel Inouye, (D. HI) commented about the operations of this secret government before a Senate Subcommittee well when he described it as "...a shadowy government with its own Air Force, its own Navy, its own fund raising mechanism, and the ability to pursue its own ideas of 'national interest', free from all checks and balances and free from the law itself."

The expertise of my primary advocate and skilled deprogrammer, Mark Phillips, developed through his U.S. Defense Department gained knowledge of "Top Secret" mind control research and researchers, was responsible for the restoration of my mind to normal functioning. As a

77

result, I have recovered the memories related in this text, and having survived the ordeal, have reached this point of enormous frustration. In 1988, through a series of brilliantly orchestrated events, Mark Phillips rescued my then 8-year-old daughter, Kelly, and me from our mind-controlled existence and took us to the safety of Alaska for rehabilitation. It was there that we began the tedious process of untangling my amnesic mind to consciously recall what I was supposed to forget.

Many U.S. and foreign government secrets and personal reputation were staked on the belief that I could not be deprogrammed and rehabilitated to accurately reveal the criminal covert activities and perversions Kelly and I were forced to participate in, particularly during the Reagan/Bush administrations. Now that I have gained control of my own mind, I view it as my duty as a mother and American patriot to exercise my gained free will to expose the mind control atrocities that my daughter and I endured at the hands of those in control of our government. This personal view of inside Pandora's Box includes a keen perception of how mind control is being used to apparently implement the New World Order, and a personal knowledge of WHO some of the so-called "masterminds" are behind this world and mind dominance effort.

Most Americans old enough to remember recall exactly where they were and what they were doing when President John F. Kennedy was shot. His assassination traumatized the nation and provides an example of how the human mind photographically records events surrounding trauma. The traumas I routinely endured during my mind controlled victimization provided me the latitude to recover my memory in the photographic detail in which it was recorded. The direct quotes I have included in the following pages depicting carefully selected events, are verbatim. I apologize for any obscenities quoted, but this was necessary to maintain integrity of the statements and accurately reflect the character of the speaker(s).

While I am free to speak my mind, Kelly, now 14, is not so fortunate. Kelly has yet to receive rehabilitation for her shattered personality and programmed young mind. The high tech sophistication of the Project Monarch trauma based mind-control procedures she endured, literally since birth, reportedly requires highly specialized, qualified care to aid her in eventually gaining control of her mind and life. Due to the political affluence of our abusers, all efforts to obtain her inalienable right to rehabilitation and seek justice have been blocked under the guise of so-called "National Security." As a result, Kelly remains warehoused in a mental institution in the custody of the state of Tennessee--a victim of the system-a system controlled and manipulated by our abusive government "leaders" a system where State Forms make no allowances to report military TOP SECRET abuses--a system that exists on federal funding directed by our perverse, corrupt abusers in Washington, D.C. She remains a political prisoner in a mental institution to this moment, waiting and hurting!

Violations of laws and rights, Psychological Warfare intimidation tactics, threats to our lives, and various other forms of CIA Damage Containment practices thus far have remained unhindered and unchecked due to the National Security Act of 1947 AND the 1986 Reagan Amendment to same which allows those in control of our government to censor and/or cover up anything they choose. Now, with our country free from outside threats, since the fall of the Soviet Union, our "free press" is reportedly no longer encumbered by censorship. This fact alone should free us to pursue justice, but it has not. Please ask why.

Hence the purpose of releasing this book at this time. After five long years of being unjustly and painfully separated from my daughter, while our abusers have had full access to her through a corrupt and manipulated system, it is my fervent hope and intent to solicit help from you in the form of advise, expertise, and public outcry concerning this very solvable problem.

I could not prevent the traumatic mind control abuses Kelly endured due to my own victimization, but she is depending on me now to expose the truth and enlist the help that the Juvenile Court has restrained her from seeking. I dedicate this book to Kelly, and all others like her, and to every American unaware of the mind control atrocities prevailing in this country. What Americans don't know is destroying them from the inside out. Knowledge is our only defense against mind control. It is time to WAKE UP and arm ourselves with the truth, restore the Constitutional values of freedom and justice for all, to retroactively enforce the 13th Amendment, and take back America!

CHAPTER 1

MY INTRODUCTION TO HUMANITY

My pedophile father, Earl O'Brien, brags that he began substituting his penis for my mother's nipple soon after I was born. My multigenerational incest-abused mother, Carol Tanis, did not protest his perverse actions due to (reportedly) having similar abuse as a child which caused her to acquire Multiple Personality Disorder.[1] My earliest recovered memory was that I could not breathe with my father's penis jammed into my little throat. Yet I could not discern his semen from my mother's milk. I do not recall thinking, but I am aware through education that this early sexual abuse distorted my primitive concepts of feeding, breathing, sexuality, and parental perceptions.

I recall as a toddler being unable to run (I could barely walk) to my mother for help as my instincts demanded. Through my gulping sobs, my terror rose as I tried to clear my throat of my father's semen and draw a breath of air. My mother finally arrived at my side. Rather than comfort me, she accused me of throwing a temper tantrum and "holding my breath." She responded only by throwing a glass of cold water in my face. I was shocked! As the water splashed my face, I knew she would not help, and it was up to me to save myself. I automatically Multiple Personality Disordered. I was, of course, too young to logically understand that what my father was doing to me was wrong. I accepted his strangling sexual abuse as a normal and natural part of my home life and split off a personality to deal with the pain and suffocation to satisfy his perversions. Therefore as a child, I was dissociative of my father's abuse. I was totally unable to recall his sexual abuse, even in his presence, until I saw and felt his penis. Then the terror, which was my conditioned response, triggered access to that part of my brain that previously endured the trauma. I was remembering the abuse and how to deal with it. This part of my brain developed into a personality of its own -- which belonged to my father -- which he rented out and later sold to the U.S. Government as will be explained and detailed in the following pages.

Other parts of my conditioned mind dealt with other abusers, abuses and circumstances. My father was (as revealed by my own investigations) apparently a multigenerational incest child from a large, poor, and horribly dysfunctional family. His mother earned a living as a prostitute for local lumbermen after his father died when he was two years old. My father's brothers and sister were all sexually and (occult) ritually abused just as he was. They grew up to be drug addicts, prostitutes, street derelicts, and pedophiles who also sexually abused me and my brothers and sisters. I developed more personality splits to deal with the traumas of these torturous relationships.

My mother's dysfunctional family also appears to be multigenerational, but of a slightly higher socio-economic class. Her father owned the building occupied by a Masonic Blue lodge he led and managed a local beer distribution business with her mother after completing his military career. Together they sexually abused my mother and her three brothers, who in turn sexually abused me.

My family often went camping on the vast wilderness acreage surrounding my grandfather's Masonic Lodge in Newaygo, Michigan. Large bluffs referred to as "The High Banks" overlooked the White River flowing through his property, which is where we pitched our tents. My mother's brothers, Uncle Ted and Uncle Arthur "Bomber" Tanis, often accompanied us and sexually abused my brother and me.

It was deer hunting season in or around November, 1961, when my father took the family camping on The High Banks to hunt with my Uncles. That night, as my brother and I were being sexually passed around the campfire to satisfy pedophile perversions, a lost hunter stumbled into our camp. My father shot him when he attempted to run; the rifle's blasts piercing my brain and further fragmenting my mind. I sat dazed in a dissociative trance while my mother methodically picked up the campsite and my father and uncles disposed of the body.

As my father drove us away from the crime scene, we were stopped by several hunters who had the road blocked in a desperate attempt to locate their missing companion. They described the man I saw my father kill, and said they heard gunshots. Reality intruded on my dissociative trance, and I screamed and cried hysterically until I no longer knew why I was crying.

My Uncle Ted[2] soon became a street derelict. Uncle Bomber died a few years later from alcoholism in his early forties. And my father became more financially and politically connected.

My mother's oldest brother, Uncle Bob, was a pilot in Air Force Intelligence and often boasted that he worked for the Vatican. Uncle Bob was also a commercial pornographer, producing kiddie porn for the local Michigan Mafia, which looped back to Mafia porn king and U.S. Representative Jerry Ford.[3] I split off more personalities just to deal with my Uncle Bob, his "friends," and the perverse business he shared with my father.

My father's sixth grade education had earned him a job as a worm digger for local sport fishermen. By the time I was six years old, however, his pornographic exploitation of my older brother Bill and me had provided enough income to move us into a bigger house nestled in the Michigan sand dunes. My father was right at home there. The tourists and drug dealers who littered the eastern shore of Lake Michigan further supplemented his income by paying for perverse sex with us children. My father also became involved in illicit drug sales.

Soon after we moved, my father was reportedly caught sending kiddie porn through the U.S. Mail. It was a bestiality film of me with my Uncle Sam O'Brien's Boxer dog, Buster. My Uncle Bob, also implicated in manufacturing the porn, out of apparent desperation informed my father of a U.S. Government Defense Intelligence Agency TOP SECRET Project to which he was privy. This was Project Monarch. Project Monarch was a mind control operation which was "recruiting" multigenerational incest abused children with Multiple Personality Disorder for its "genetic mind control studieso. I was a prime "candidate," a "chosen one." My father seized the opportunity as it would provide him immunity from prosecution. In the midst of the pandemonium that ensued, Jerry Ford arrived at our house with the evidence in hand for a meeting with my father.

"Is Earl home?" he called to my mother, who nervously stood behind the screen door, hesitating to let him in.

"Not yet," my mother replied, her voice shaking.[4] "He should have been home from work by now -- I know he's expecting you."

"That's OK." Ford turned his attention to me. I was standing outside on the front porch, and he crouched down to my level. Patting the large, brown envelope containing the confiscated porn tucked under his arm he said, "You like doggies, huh?"

"Buster is a nice doggy," I replied. "He's funny." Not understanding why the dog had been whisked away when the porn was confiscated, I complained, "Buster's gone."

"Buster's gone?" Ford asked.

"Yeah. My Uncle Sam took him away," I told him.

Ford laughed loudly at the irony of my statement. In my limited view, I thought he found it humorous that Buster was gone. My father pulled into the driveway, honking the horn of his new tan convertible. Ford stood up. With his fly eye level to me, I noticed his penis was erect and reached for it as conditioned.

"Not now, honey," he said. "I have business to tend..." Ford went inside with my parents to officially seal my fate.

Not long after that my father was flown to Boston for a two-week course at Harvard on how to raise me for this off-shoot of MK Ultra, Project Monarch.

When he returned from Boston, my father was smiling and pleased with his new knowledge of what he termed "reverse psychology." This equates to "satanic reversals," and involves such play-on-words as puns and phrases that stuck in my mind like, "You earn your keep, and I'll keep what you earn." He presented me with a commemorative charm bracelet of dogs, and my mother with the news that they "would be having more children" to raise in the project. (I now have two sisters and four brothers ranging from age 16 to 37 that are still under mind control.) My mother complied with my father's suggestions, mastering the art of language manipulation. For example, when I could not snap my own pajama top to the bottoms in a childish effort to keep my father out of them, I asked my mother, "please snap me." She did. She would snap her forefingers against my skin in a stinging manner. The pain I felt was psychological as this proved to me once again that she had no intention of protecting me from my father's sexual abuse.

Also in keeping with his government provided instructions, my father began working me like the legendary Cinderella. I shoveled fireplace ashes, hauled and stacked firewood, raked leaves, shoveled snow, chopped ice, and swept -- "because," my father said, "your little hands fit so nicely around the rake, mop, shovel, and broom handles."

By this time, my father's sexual exploitation of me included prostitution to his friends, local mobsters and Masons, relatives, Satanists, strangers, and police officers. When I wasn't being worked to physical exhaustion, filmed pornographically, prostituted, or engaged in incest abuse, I dissociated into books. I had learned to read at the young age of four due to my photographic memory which was a natural result of MPD/DID.

Government researchers involved in MK Ultra Project Monarch knew about the photographic memory aspect of MPD/DID, of course, as well as other resultant "super human" characteristics. Visual acuity of an MPD/DID is 44 times greater than that of the average person. My developed unusually high pain threshold, plus compartmentalization of memory were "necessary" for military and covert operations applications. Additionally, my sexuality was primitively twisted from infancy. This programming was appealing and useful to perverse politicians who believed they could hide their actions deep within my memory compartments, which clinicians refer to as personalities.

Immediately after my father's return from Boston, I was routinely prostituted to then Michigan State Senator Guy VanderJagt. VanderJagt later became a U.S. Congressman and eventually chairman of the Republican National Congressional Committee that put George Bush in the office of President. I was prostituted to VanderJagt after numerous local parades which he always participated in, at the Mackinac Island Political Retreat, and in my home state of Michigan, among other places.

My Uncle Bob helped my father decorate my bedroom in red, white, and blue paneling and American flags. He provided assistance in scrambling my mind according to Project Monarch methodologies. Fairy tale themes were used to confuse fantasy with reality, particularly Disney stories and the Wizard of Oz, which provided the base for future programming.

I had personalities for pornography, a personality for bestiality, a personality for incest, a personality for withstanding the horrendous psychological abuse of my mother, a personality for prostitution, and the rest of "me" functioned somewhat "normally" at school. My "normal" personality provided a cover for the abuse I was enduring, but best of all it had hope -- hope that there was somewhere in the world where people did not hurt each other. This same personality also attended Catechism, a weekly class at our Catholic church, St. Francis de Sales in Muskegon, Michigan.

My Catechism teacher was a Nun, or "Sister." Although I could not consciously think to protect myself from abuse, I had decided that becoming a Nun would provide me with the kind of life I sought. I could not rely upon my family, the police, or politicians to protect me. The church appeared to be my answer, and I listened diligently in class and prayed religiously. I learned all about the political structure of the church, and was prepared for my first Confession.

The Catholic beliefs I was taught include the idea that man is not fit to talk to God (the Father) directly, but must have a priest intercede instead. This is the purpose of going to Confession. I was instructed to tell my sins to the priest (also referred to as Father), who would relay the message to God. He would then supposedly tell me how many "Hail Marys" and "Our Father" prayers to say as my penance, or punishment. My Cathecism teacher gave the class several examples of "sins," which included "sex outside of marriage." When the Priest, Father James Thaylen, slid open the little screened partition in the closet sized confessional, I began as I had been instructed, "Forgive me Father, for I have sinned...." I then proceeded to tell him that I had sex with my father and brother, to which he responded that I should "say three Hail Marys and one Our Father and Io would be forgiven?!"

I knew then that I had to either believe that this Confession thing was a hoax, or that God condoned sexual child abuse. That night, my father had a talk with me. Apparently he was the "Father" that the priest had interceded to. My father instructed me that "from now on," I was to simply say "I disobeyed my parents" when I went to Confession and nothing more!

The next time I went to Confession, I did exactly as I was told. The veiled screen came off the Confessional partition between me and the priest, and a penis was stuck through the window. "God said that your penance is to "treato me as you would your father. And remember, 'whatsoever you do to the least of your brothers, that you do unto me'." After performing oral sex on Father Thaylen, I emerged from the Confessional where all the other kids were waiting very impatiently for their turn. My teacher scolded me for taking so long and told me to add a few extra "Our Fathers" to my penance. When I told her I already did my penance, she told me again the "order of things" to the Confessional ritual -- which did not fit anything I had just experienced! Without ever consciously knowing why, I abandoned the idea of becoming a Nun as that part of me, too, split off from what was left of my "normal" base personality.

I continued to maintain an illusion of normalcy for school,[5] excelling in my studies due to my photographic memory and in spite of my chronic "day- dreaming." I had plenty of friends and played enthusiastically at recess, expending large amounts of energy in my subconscious effort to escape my own mind. And I lost myself in the books my father suggested I read: *The Wizard of Oz, Alice in Wonderland, Island of the Blue Dolphins, Disney Classics*, and *Cinderella* -- all of which were used in conditioning my mind for what soon would become mind control programming.[6]

My television viewing was restricted and monitored in keeping with my father's gained knowledge. I was, however, permitted to watch the "best" of movies: *The Wizard of Oz, Disney Classics, Alice in Wonderland*, and *Cinderella* -- over and over and over again.

When I was in second grade, my Brownie Troop marched in the Memorial Day Parade in which then Michigan State Senator VanderJagt also participated. At the end of the parade, he took me into a nearby motel and had me perform oral sex on him before sending me back to where my Brownie Troop was waiting. My Brownie leader and peers thought it commendable that VanderJagt took me with him. They gathered around to hear all about it. I noticed a white splash of semen on my sash, and hurriedly explained that he had "taken me for a milkshake" as I wiped it away. Having to cover for his perversion to my Brownie Troop infringed on my school personality, and the "normal" remainder became even smaller.

With the memory of this incident compartmentalized in my mind, I made no conscious association to VanderJagt when my third grade teacher announced that we were taking a field trip to the State Capital in Lansing, Michigan where he was in session. Once at the Capital, I was ushered away from my classmates and taken to VanderJagt's office where he was waiting along with his friend and mentor (soon to be President) Gerald Ford. VanderJagt lifted my skirt, pulled down my panties, and placed me on his desk for sex with him and Ford. Afterward they laughed as VanderJagt placed a small American flag in my rectum and instructed me to wave it. He then presented me with a Kennedy pen inscribed with the motto that would lead me for the rest of my mind controlled existence, "Ask not what your country can do for you, Ask what you can do for your country."

VanderJagt then escorted me back to the balcony of the Legislature where my classmates were gathered. He put his arm around me in front of all my classmates and presented me with the American flag he had just had me wave for him and Ford with my rectum. My school personality split off again, but I still maintained the hope that somewhere, someday, I would find a place where people didn't...what? I could not remember what I was seeking to escape.

[1] Multiple Personality Disorder (MPD), now known among mental health professionals as Dissociative Identity Disorder (DID) is the mind's sane defense to an insane situation. It is a way of dealing with trauma that is literally too horrible to comprehend. Incestuous rape violates primitive instinct and surpasses pain tolerance. By compartmentalizing the memory of such horrendous abuse, the rest of the mind can function "normally" as though nothing had happened. This compartmentalization is created by the brain actually shutting down neuron pathways to a specific part of the brain. These neuron pathways are triggered open again when the abuse recurs. The same part of the brain that is already conditioned to the trauma deals with it again and again as needed.

[2] Uncle Ted had also cried hysterically the night of the murder. Several years later, he almost killed himself when he drove his car into the White River near the place of the murder.

[3] Gerald Ford, a.k.a. Leslie Lynch King, Jr., served on the appropriations subcommittee for the CIA and was appointed to the Warren Commission to investigate the assassination of President John F. Kennedy while I knew him only as a porn boss!

[4] My mother often voiced complaints that she "could not see faces," which personal experience has taught me indicated that she was suffering from on going physical and psychological traumas, and therefore was not in control of her senses.

[5] Had my teachers been educated in the obvious signs of child abuse, my "illusion of normalcy" would have been interpreted as a cry for help. Dissociative trance daydreaming, tones of helplessness and sexuality in drawings, and the electric prod marks on my face should have been recognized.

[6] These same themes were routinely used in creating Project Monarch slaves. This fact emerged through years of networking with mental health professionals.

CHAPTER 2

THE RITE TO REMAIN SILENT

On May 7, 1966, I was dressed in white from my Catholic veil to my white patent leather shoes as was mandatory for making my first holy communion. I was standing outside the newly built twisted concrete structure of Muskegon's St. Francis de Sales church waiting for the ceremony to commence when Guy VanderJagt, who was affiliated with the church, strode across the lawn towards me.

Crouching down on one knee, VanderJagt said, "You look beautiful today. You are as beautiful as your name. Cathleen is Gaelic for "the pure," and it is clear to me that you are flawless in your purity. Ann means "grace." It is by the grace of God, not your actions, that you are pure. Pure at heart. You are covered by the blood of our Lord and Savior, just like the cross on which he hung. This is for you." He opened a black velvet box, revealing a rosy cross necklace. Like the Kennedy inscribed pen, he had presented me with at the state Capital, the meaning behind the rosy cross necklace would lead me through the rest of my mind-controlled existence.

VanderJagt's pedophile comrade in Project Monarch, Father Don, joined us, reaching deep into the pocket of his robes to present me with a delicate blue charm of the Holy Mother. It was to be worn in conjunction with the rosy cross "to symbolize your service to the holy Catholic church," Father Don told me, which I would "promise to serve and obey."

As VanderJagt fastened the rosy cross and blue virgin around my neck, he told me I was now dressed appropriately for the ceremony in red, white, and blue. I could feel his breath on my neck as he fastened the necklace and instructed, "When Father says 'Body of Christ' and you say 'Ahhh men'... you acknowledge that Christ is God made man, and that you know what men are for. When Father gives you the host, it will stick to the roof of your mouth unless you suck it off his thumb."

I hurried to line up with my Catechism classmates for the procession into the church for our holy communion mass.

"Body of Christ," Father Don said, holding up the host.

"Ahhh... men," I responded as instructed, sucking the wafer off his thumb.

After services, VanderJagt and Father Don talked with me briefly while my parents congregated with other parishioners. Father was telling me, "...God has chosen you for work within his holy church. You are a Chosen One,[1] my child..."

Later that evening, VanderJagt attended the reception that my parents were holding for me at our house. He talked with my father awhile but spent most of his time talking with my Uncle Bob, who had recently flown in from "a mission over seas." My Uncle Bob and VanderJagt were friends and remained so throughout the years. As the party dispersed, VanderJagt drove me back to church for a "special evening service with Father Don."

VanderJagt unlocked the rectory door of the old church across the street from the new St. Francis structure, explaining that we had to "have a very important talk now that I had eaten the body of Christ." The talk, blood trauma, and sexual abuse that ensued conditioned my mind to readily accept programming throughout the years that deliberately merged both U.S. Government and Jesuit mind control efforts for New World Order controls.

"I work for the Vatican, and now, so do you," VanderJagt told me. "You have just entered into a covenant with the holy Catholic church. You must never break that covenant."

Still capable of questioning at that time, I asked, "What is a covenant?" VanderJagt answered, "A covenant is a promise to keep secrets, the secret that the church knew all along. The Pope has all the secrets locked away at the Vatican. Your Uncle Bob and I have been to the Vatican. It is time you entered into the holy covenant and learned the secrets of the church that were written long before Christ even came into being. The Dominican monks kept the covenant that Noah carried into the new world. They kept the secret with them. It was written on parchment and kept in a secret place in the Vatican. They took a Vow of Silence to never reveal its location, or its content. You must enter into the covenant. You must carry the secret to your grave. Keep it secret from your mom, dad, everybody."

VanderJagt proceeded to fill my suggestible young mind with biblical interpretation that laid the groundwork for future "inter/inner dimensional" programming themes utilized by Project Monarch programmers to control the compartmentalization of memory synonymous with MPD/DID.

"Christ saw them all," VanderJagt was telling me. "They are dimensions, places you can see on your way to death.[2] That's why they're called die- mentions. You must remember that Christ died and came back to tell us everything he saw while he was on his way to heaven. He was gone three days, but it was much longer than that where he was because time isn't the same in other dimensions. Purgatory is one other dimension. Hell is one. And there are lots of others in between. Oz is another dimension. The sky is not the limit to all the worlds out there waiting to be explored. You can travel in and out of all these dimensions, learning the secrets of the universe. You have been chosen to explore these other worlds for the church. Listen in the stillness and you will hear his voice guiding you[3] on your missions. The rosy cross is like Dorothy's ruby slippers. Never take your rosy cross off, Cathy, when traveling other dimensions and you will always be able to return home."

Father Don joined VanderJagt in a ritual which bathed me in the blood of a slaughtered lamb, and subsequently, through this hideous blood trauma, locked their stated perceptions and a basis for mind control programming deep in my mind. This basis for programming was anchored in the Vow of Silence which the Jesuit monks take "not only to keep secrets, but so they can still their mind and hear their inner guidance." Certain that the "Rite to Remain Silent" which they had performed would ensure that I keep their secrets, Father Don and Guy VanderJagt subjected me to their pedophile perversions. The two joked that I had become "a good Cathy-lick."

After the Rite to Remain Silent was installed, the voices of my multiple personalities that I had previously heard in my head ceased. In the silence of deliberately created memory compartments, I could only hear the voices of my abusers who created them... commanding my silence.

Silence for who and what I knew was involved in Project Monarch mind control.

My family routinely vacationed at Mackinac Island, Michigan which is a small island positioned in the Great Lakes close to the Canadian border. Mackinac Island, with the Governor's Mansion and historical Grand Hotel, was a political playground where I was prostituted by my father to, among others, pedophiles Jerry Ford, Guy VanderJagt, and later U.S. Senator Robert C. Byrd. The mind controlled part of me that was prostituted there perceived Mackinac as another dimension, the timelessness of which was enhanced by the island's antiquated styling. Automobiles were forbidden on the tiny island, which relied on horse drawn buggies or bicycles for transportation. Once when Lee Iaccoca was attending a cocktail party at then Governor Romney's Mansion, I overheard him comment, "What better place for auto execs to get away from it all than on an island with no cars?"

Mackinac Island, due to its geographic location, provided an air of friendliness between the U.S. and Canada that formed my childish perception that our countries knew no boundaries. This political view was further enhanced by my father always taking the family to Niagara Falls where my mind was to be symbolically "washed of all memory" of what had occurred in Mackinac. Niagara Falls' numerous, powerful waterfalls were in reasonably close proximity to Mackinac Island, and shared the border between the U.S. and Canada.

When Pierre Trudeau was elected Prime Minister of Canada in 1968, I often heard it said, "Pierre Trudeau is one of Ours, you know." I first heard this phrase cryptically referring to Trudeau's loyalty to the Vatican when Father Don was discussing him with my father one Sunday after mass. This fact circulated quickly among those I knew who were involved in the Catholic/Jesuit aspect of Project Monarch.

The summer after Trudeau was elected, my father took the family to Mackinac Island as usual. Climbing on a large statue on the grounds of the Governor's Mansion, I could see across the field to the Grand Hotel. I noticed Canadian flags flying amongst the American flags that lined the front of the old hotel. As I slid down off the statue, Guy VanderJagt approached with a drink and a cigarette in his hand. Patting my hair into place he said, "Straighten your shirt, I've got someone important for you to meet."

"I knew someone important was here because of those flags," I said, tucking my shirt in my pink shorts.

"When I was at the Vatican," VanderJagt began, "I was told that Prime Minister Trudeau is a friend of the Pope. He thinks like one of us. A true Catholic. He likes Cathy-licks."

VanderJagt led me upstairs in the mansion, where Pierre Trudeau was lowering the window shades in a dimly lit bedroom crowded with antiques. VanderJagt closed the door behind me. Trudeau's tuxedo coat was neatly draped over a chair, which left him in his formal pants, white shirt, and a bright red cummerbund which caught my eye. "I like your sash," I said.

"Hasn't anyone taught you Silence yet?" His somber, gruff attitude was softened by his smooth, silky voice.

Triggered into the part of me that endured the Rite to Remain Silent, I assumed Trudeau knew all about interdimensions according to my deliberately formed perceptions. I could not/did not understand that interdimensions actually equated to the inner-dimensions of my own compartmentalized mind. Likewise, I did not understand that "Keys to the Kingdom" referred to knowing the codes, keys, and triggers to my controlled mind. "Guy said you like Cathy- licks," I said, repeating what VanderJagt had told me. "Are you the Keeper of the Keys?"

Trudeau seemingly bore his cold, dark eyes right through me. "You can learn more from the school of thought than you can by asking precocious questions. Haven't you learned that children are to be seen and not heard?"

"Is that a precocious question?" I asked. "What is a precocious question?"

Trudeau sighed with impatience. "That is irrelevant. What matters is that you shut your mouth, still your mind, and enter the school of thought. Silence is a virtue. Listen to the silence in the stillness of your mind. Go deep inside your mind," he slowly led. "Deeper and deeper where it's quiet and still..."

Trudeau expertly manipulated my mind with sophisticated hypnotic language. Not only did he enlist my Silence for the pedophile perversions he indulged in, but he instructed my "school of thought" in a manner that equated to programming. He laid a foundation for Air-Water programs that is a mirror- dimensional theme often used by NASA and others involved in Project Monarch. Playing off his own name "Pee-Air," he added a perverse twist to the theme that he accessed each time I was prostituted to him.

Had I been capable of fear, I would have been afraid of Pierre Trudeau. Trudeau's slow, deliberate movements masked the brutal power of his body much the way his smooth, soft voice pierced my mind and intruded on my thoughts. The icy cold touch of his effeminate, manicured long fingers contrasted with the heat of his perversion... a perversion for which he blamed me and my "temptuous, contemptuous ways".

In my childish ignorance, I believed Trudeau's demeanor and forward combed hair were characteristic of his French descent. "I know all about the French," I had bragged to my new "Grandpa" Van while visiting his home in Milwaukee, Wisconsin.

My mother's father had died shortly before Kennedy was assassinated, and my Grandmother quickly latched onto a wealthy, highly political businessman from Milwaukee. She met Grandpa Van Vandenburg on the passenger/cargo ship that traveled the waters of the Great Lakes, the Milwaukee Clipper. The Clipper transported cargo including Cadillacs from Vandenburg Motors to Canada, as well as the drugs sanctioned by the local Coast Guard via the U.S. Government that my father distributed. Sometimes I accompanied my father to the docks in Muskegon to pick up the drug shipment, which usually involved prostitution. Jerry Ford and Guy VanderJagt combined business with pleasure in the ship's casinos on occasion, which is where the connection between my Grandma and Grandpa Van was reportedly made. Grandpa Van knew Jerry Ford, and subsequently was acquainted with Pierre Trudeau.

"What do you know about the French?" Grandpa Van asked me as I sat on his living room floor petting the dog he just brought home. Improperly cued and dumfounded by his question I remained silent. "I know you've met Pierre Trudeau," he prompted. "I also know you love doggies. So I bought this dog, for your grandma now, so you could enjoy him, too. His name is Pepe. He's a French Poodle."

"I know all about the French," I said, mentally comparing the large French Poodle in front of me to Trudeau. "They have pretty nails..." I stroked Pepe's painted toenails. "They have funny hair..." I petted Pepe's clipped fur. "And they pee a lot," I giggled.

"You'd better take him outside, then," Grandpa Van told me, attaching Pepe's leash. After walking the dog past what felt like every tree in the neighborhood, I   announced that I would call him "Pee-pee."

Uncle Bob filmed Pepe and I pornographically on numerous occasions, producing bestiality films that I would later learn Pierre Trudeau was privy to. Pepe remained a part of my experience long after Grandpa Van divorced himself from my Grandma, and long after I developed beyond Trudeau's perversion for little children.

I was slow to grow into adolescence. By the time I was thirteen years old, my breasts were tender and beginning to swell, which made me "too old" for VanderJagt's pedophile perversions. When my father brought me to Mackinac Island for routine prostitution at the Political Retreat, VanderJagt introduced me to a new friend he had made now that he was in Washington, D.C. as a U.S. Congressman -- U.S. Senator Robert C. Byrd, Democrat from West Virginia. Byrd had been a U.S. Senator as long as I had been alive, serving as Senate Whip and later as President Pro Tempore of the Senate and as the all powerful Senate Appropriations leader. Byrd commanded attention and respect from all who came in contact with him, particularly from my father. When we were left alone in his room, he loomed over me in a threatening stance. His cold, blue slitty eyes locked onto mine. I undressed and climbed into his bed as ordered. I was momentarily relieved to find that his penis was abnormally tiny -- so small it didn't even hurt! And I could breathe with it in my mouth! Then he began to indulge himself in his brutal perversions, talking on and on about how I was "made just for him" due to the vast amounts of pain I could withstand. The spankings and police handcuffs I had previously endured were child's play compared to Senator Byrd's near death tortures. The hundreds of scars on my body still show today. With VanderJagt, sex was a matter of "how much I could give," whereas with Byrd it was "how much I could take." And I was forced to take more pain than any human could logically withstand. I was dedicated to Byrd at age thirteen, which meant he would be directing my future in Project Monarch, and my father would raise me according to his specifications.

My MPD/DID existence became more regimented from that point on. I was kept physically worn down to the point of exhaustion in order that I be sufficiently receptive to my father's limited hypnotic programming capabilities to condition my mind for mind control. The pornography I was forced to participate in became much more violent immediately after Byrd, switching me from predominantly pedophile and bestiality themes to torturous versions of sadomasochism (S&M). My father and mother worked in tandem daily to "break my spirit," destroying any remnants left of my self-confidence, tearing down my self-esteem, and thus annihilating my free will urges. They conditioned/taught me my dreams were reality and my reality were dreams, that black is white and up is down. "Good night, sleep tight, dream about your mommy and daddy" is what I heard every night. This was intended to confuse my mind to believe incest in the middle of the night was "just a bad dream."

My television, books, and music became even more strictly controlled and monitored than before. This was not only to infringe on my last minuscule freedom of choice, but for total mind control conditioning purposes.

For example, the annual televising of Judy Garland's *Wizard of Oz* was celebrated as a grand holiday around my house. This was to prepare my mind for future base programming on the theme that I, like Dorothy, could "spin" into another dimension "Over the Rainbow." After all, "Birds (Byrds) fly over the Rainbow..." was a theme that became a part of my life.

My father insisted I watch the Walt Disney movie *Cinderella* with him, paralleling my existence to Cinderella's -- "magically trance-forming from a dirty little slave to a beautiful Princess." In typical "reverse psychology" humor, he referred to pornographic photos when singing "Someday my Prince (prints) will come," or by placing literal sexual emphasis on "will come."

My brother, Bill, who was often featured in kiddie porn with me, was not a "chosen one" for Project Monarch (beyond supplying more children to be dedicated in later years). Yet my father figured that "what was good for me would be good for my brother." He took us to see Walt Disney's Pinocchio, explaining that my brother and I were his puppets still in the carving stage. The distortions of reality that these and other Disney theme movies provided when coupled with my father's government trained conscious and subconscious controlling influence, began to further erode our ability to discern fantasy from reality. My brother, two years older than me, remains psychologically locked in to those traumatic childhood years and is obsessed with Disney themes and productions to this day. His house is decorated in Disney memorabilia, he wears Disney clothes, listens to my father's instructions on his Disney telephone, and maintains "When You Wish Upon a Star" as his favorite song, which has locked his children into the same theme.

My father also instructed me to watch Alfred Hitchcock's horrifying movie The Birds with him. This reinforced in my mind the movie's theme that there is "no place to hide from the birds/Byrd".

I was quickly beginning to lose all ability to question anything but my own judgment. It was easy to believe that there was indeed "no place to run, no place to hide," which is a necessary and primary psychological basis for government/military mind control. In later years, "who ya' gonna call?" and Ronald Reagan's quip "you can run, but you can't hide" echoed deep within my mind. After all, even if I could think to seek help, who would help me? The police? The church? My parents? Relative? Politicians? School? There was no one left that would help me, I sensed.

My television programming was then expanded to include the shows that every Project Monarch mind control slave I knew had to watch I Dream of Jeannie, The Brady Bunch, Gumby And Pokey, and Bewitched. I could relate to the Genie pleasing her master, who was a Major for the Air Force in I Dream of Jeannie. This served to confuse the reality of my own experiences with the fantasy of television production. I told all outsiders that my family was "just like the Bradys." Through Gumby And Pokey I was led to believe that I was as flexible as these animated clay performers. Therefore, I was capable of being physically maneuvered into any sexual position. The mirrors depicted a doorways to other dimensions and adventures interlocked with my Catholic conditioning and Alice in Wonderland and Wizard of Oz theme programming. In Bewitched, it is the normal next door neighbor that is considered crazy rather than the witches. This is another reversal that was applied to my bizarre existence. I was one of the only kids in my school that listened to country music. But then, Senator Byrd fancied himself a country music fiddler and it was "my duty to love what he did." I was ordered to listen to country music or no music at all. Music was my psychological avenue for escape, a dissociative tool. But this, too, was used in setting the stage for my future as a Project Monarch "Presidential Model" mind-controlled slave.

As suggested, I read the Boxcar Children Series over and over again. I empathized with the trials, traumas, and tribulations the children endured while they fended for themselves from their boxcar home along the railroad tracks. My father often made train sounds at me in passing to subconsciously remind me that I was currently "in Train-ing" on the undeterable track of the "Freedom Train.[4]" This term, taken from Harriet Tubman's underground railroad for slaves, reversed the meaning of the word "freedom" to confuse one's "one track mind" and instill the belief "I

91

am free to be a slave." This also reinforced my training to stay on track -- the plan (track) laid our for me. My father would often quip, "When God passed out brains, you thought he said 'trains' and got in the wrong line." Convicted (capital crime) career criminal, country music entertainer, and CIA operative Merle Haggard often used well documented cryptic language in his songs pertaining to government mind-control slave operations. He released songs including "Freedom Train" and "Over the Rainbow." My father told me repeatedly that Merle Haggard was my "favorite" singer, and his songs reinforced my programming.

Of course, Senator Byrd remained my "favorite" fiddler as ordered. He played train songs like "Orange Blossom Special" while making train sounds on his fiddle. Sometimes I was his captive audience, bound and gagged, while he played his fiddle. Other times he instructed me to spin round and round like a music box dancer in order to add "new dimensions to our sex." These new dimensions included more and more physical pain through "kinky" torture.

My father took advantage of his new political connections and advanced himself occupationally, manufacturing camshaft auto parts a t a local factory. Soon he was promoted to a sales management position due to his connections within the Pentagon Procurement Office and General Services Administration, coupled with what he had learned about double bind hypnotic persuasion. He continued to supplement his income by sexually exploiting us children. This now included brazenly prostituting me to Muskegon Coast Guard officials while on cocaine runs to and from the base. Meanwhile, my father took us all to church every Sunday, and my mother stayed busy having babies to raise in the Project. In true pedophile fashion, he surrounded himself with children by coaching little league sports, chaperoning school and Catechism activities, and becoming involved with the Boy Scouts. All of this made him appear to be a model citizen and "pillar of the community." The illusion was formed. The parts of me that knew otherwise had no choice but to remain Silent.

---

[1] Project Monarch slaves were referred to as "Chosen Ones".

[2] Torture to the point just before death, such as with Death's Door programming, was jointly used by the Catholic Jesuits and CIA in Project Monarch.

[3] It was the voices of my mind control programmers and handlers that I later heard guiding me.

[4] "Freedom Train" is the internationally recognized cryptic code term for Project Monarch slave operations that I heard repeatedly throughout my victimization.

CHAPTER 3

MY FIRST PRESIDENT

Muskegon, Michigan is a coastal tourist attraction, and home of the annual Seaway and Coast Guard festivals which bring people to the town from all over Michigan. VanderJagt remained publicly visible through opportunities such as these. My father often could be seen with VanderJagt and was photographed at his side while judging festival events like the kiddie parades, sand sculpturing contests, and so on -- all of which I entered and won. In later years, my father polished and shined the red paint of his 1966 Ford convertible to chauffeur VanderJagt through the local parades. This only served to reinforce the illusion that my father was a "pillar of the community."

In 1973, Senator Byrd instructed my father to send me to Muskegon Catholic Central High School, which was overseen by the director of St. Francis de Sales church, Father Lepres. The Catholic church, of course, has its own political structure, with the Pope presiding over all. The strong political ties between the Catholic church and the U.S. Government was overtly evidenced by the much publicized relationship between the President and the Pope during the Reagan Administration. Of course, I had been privy to this political relationship ever since my First Communion -- a relationship that the Rite to Remain Silent was intended to cover. My experience with Catholic Central's direct involvement in Project Monarch's physical and psychological conditioning further confirmed the union between the U.S. Government and the Catholic church.

When Senator Byrd changed my school from public to Parochial, he also destroyed through dissociation my school personality. I no longer viewed school as my haven from abuse, as it was controlled by the church and, as I later learned, monitored by a corrupt segment of the C.I.A.

By the time I enrolled in Catholic Central, the cliques and groups had already been formed. I had a personality to fit in with the "good" kids and one that interfaced with the "bad." It did not take long for the "good" kids to notice I also got along with the "bad." I soon found the only kids that could relate to me were the other known Project victims. We clung together in a close knit group, herded around like the proverbial sheep by those in the school who knew we were MPD/DIDed and under mind control. We each switched personalities as circumstance demanded, most often in unison. We were ritually traumatized, constantly tranced, and then programmed during school hours. Since I no longer had my singular "school personality" and was constantly switching instead, the compartment of my brain that held school memory was no longer consciously retrievable. Therefore, I had no basis for continued learning aside from what I could photographically memorize from class. My grades appeared erratic, ranging from A's to failing. And some A's received I did not earn academically.

In my required religion class, Sister Ann Marie had been leading us in study on the topic of Confession. This was to prepare us for the kind of Confessions we were to be giving Father Vesbit, who was also our school principal. The day Sister ordered us to Confession, I refused to go. I unconsciously feared I would be sexually assaulted again in the Confessional, this time while my teenage peers waited impatiently outside the door. Sister made an example out of me to the class, saying I was a "Satanist" and that I was "going to hell." With seemingly no escape from the occultism that proliferated at the school, I could no longer differentiate between Catholicism and Satanism. Whatever Senator Byrd's purposes in sending me to Catholic school, no one seemed to notice that I had no reason to religiously adhere to Catholic principles. Therefore, the applied reversal of Satanism held no "spiritual magic" to it either. The wedge of anti-superstition that the Catholic school was inadvertently driving into me only served to discount the occult principles and superstitious traumas that they were attempting to use to control me.

Satanism is often used as an extreme pain/violence trauma base in Project Monarch mind control, reportedly due to the previous German Nazi Himler Research. I did not adhere to the desired helplessness attitude that this was "spiritual warfare" and out of the realm of mankind's ability to stop. Regardless of my religious beliefs or disbeliefs, I experienced the "results" just the same. Being subjected to and witnessing trauma so horrible, while my body was raped, tortured, and ravaged by men literally drove me out of my mind.

Catholic Central did increase my endurance capabilities as planned, however. I signed up for the two mile run in the girls' track team as ordered. Muskegon Catholic Central led the state of Michigan in high school athletics, using mind control technique to "modify" their star athletes and cause them to excel beyond pre-established records. The school gained national recognition for its contribution to professional leagues with their manufactured programmed athletes. But, like Tommy LaSorda's Dodgers, Catholic Central's consistent victories began to raise suspicions and questions. This created a public scandal for the school that threatened to close its doors in 1975.

The girls' and guys' track teams converged after school for practice. I was among the few females singled out for coaching by Coach Cheverini and his hypnotic mind control methodisms due to my Project Monarch victimization. I was instructed to run 13 miles per day (another corny satanic ploy) to get in shape for my two-mile race. I often ran with a male friend who was the record holder for the two mile in guys' track. He and I were friends, sharing much due to our similar Project Monarch victimizations. Together we learned how to shut out pain and fatigue when we ran. We tranced into a fast pace set in our minds by Coach Cheverini with no comprehension of time or distance. We perceived the track as our "Yellow Brick Road" in accordance with the Oz theme programming. Senator Byrd's plan for building my physical endurance through Catholic Central's coaching methods proved successful for allowing me to survive his intensely torturous sexual perversions.

In addition to routine trips to Mackinac Island and Niagara Falls, my family often took camping trips to "get away from it all." In reality, I was taken to key places for ritual abuse, prostitution, and pornography. In the fall of 1974, my father announced we were going to go camping "back in time" to an old fashioned festival in the small remote town of Cedar Springs, Michigan for their annual Red Flannel Days celebration. My mother told me to pack my jeans and sweaters and my Catholic school uniform which she had washed and pressed for the occasion.

Cedar Springs was quiet, with the festival events including dilapidated amusement rides set up in a small parking lot, and contests where local farmers pitted their mules and horses against each other to see whose could pull the most weight. The main (and only) street of town was lined with the few local businesses, including the town's red flannel underwear "long

94

johns" factory. In the center of town, a mock single jail cell had been erected to hold any and all parade participants who failed to wear the required red flannel underwear. The jail was guarded by quasi Keystone cops. I was amused when the townsfolk began lining up to march in the parade, with very few remaining to watch it. A mentally retarded man carried the baton to lead the parade, followed by kids on bicycles, haywagons of old folks, a grade school band and people walking -- all in their red flannel underwear. The grand finale' of the parade, the town firetruck, was approaching, surrounded by numerous motorcycle police. I heard folks whispering, "the President is coming." I assumed they meant the President of the underwear factory. I was wrong. I watched in horror as the firetruck rolled to a stop, and Secret Service helped then President Gerald Ford as he stepped down to the pavement.

My father was excitedly tugging on my arm, half dragging me through the wall of Secret Service agents, to talk with President Ford. I looked around nervously as my father made the necessary arrangements with Ford to prostitute me to him later that evening. VanderJagt, who never missed a parade it seemed, was signing autographs. As he smiled at me, someone roughly grabbed my arm. Nervous and startled, I screamed. The crowd laughed as a Keystone Cop threw me in the jail, scolding me for not wearing my red flannel underwear when I was talking to the President. I was trying to be inconspicuous in hopes no one would see me with the likes of Ford, but then, they did not know him as I did. The Keystone Cop rattled on and on about "how lucky" I was until my father paid my bail and I was released from the cell.

That night, I wore my Catholic uniform as instructed and went into a dissociative trance as my father drove me to the local National Guard Armory where I was prostituted to Ford. Ford took me into an empty room, pushed me down on the wooden floor as he unzipped his pants and said, "Pray on this." Then he brutally sexually assaulted me. Afterward, my memory was compartmentalized through use of high voltage. I was then carried out to the car where I lay in the back seat, muscles contracted, stunned, in pain, and unable to move.

When we got back to Muskegon, my father sent me to the beach as always, to let the repetition of crashing waves against the beach "wash my mind free of memory" while I watched the sun set. I was totally locked in to the belief that truly there was "no place to run," not even to the President of the United States.

I remember that the "sane" part of "me" -- my innate personality -- seemed to die after seeing Ford as President. I recall walking up the steps of Catholic Central High School one morning, reaching for the door, and crying uncontrollably. I cried myself into a heap at the top of the stairs. I did not even know why I was crying. As an MPD, I rarely cried at all. But I was still sobbing hours later when school let out. Someone found me, but I do not recall to this day ever leaving the school steps. I never really experienced "emotion" after that day until I was rescued, deprogrammed and reintegrated in 1988. Now all of my brain was functioning through a wide variety of memory compartments, also known as multiple personalities, with no part of me left "free" of abuse. Now it was as though I had "no place to run," not even in my brain. This drove me out of my mind, which is exactly what my abusers needed for total control.

95

CHAPTER 4

THE MOST DANGEROUS GAME

When I learned of a pending rendezvous with Senator Byrd in Traverse City, Michigan (VanderJagt's headquarters), I stole some candy at a local convenience market hoping to go to jail and escape my encounter with Byrd. I was caught, and the police were even called. But, of course, my politically powerful abusers would not allow for me to have a police record. The entire matter was not-so-mysteriously and suddenly dropped. My only "punishment" was to have a conference with the school principal, Father Vesbit.

Father Vesbit knew I was part of Project Monarch and handled the matter accordingly. He raped me in the school's private chapel after school while holding a satanic ritual involving several of my project friends. Kids often attached nicknames to their teachers, and there was only a few of us who knew the reason why Father Vesbit was called Father "Fuzzbutt." His backside was covered with thick black hair. He "counseled" me on several occasions, once remarking, "I thought kids in your situation were all part of the Exchange Student program."

My Uncle Bob Tanis was visiting our house soon after that. He had flown in from what he claimed was a "black ops" Air Force Intelligence operation. I know now that in typical CIA mode of operations, he was relating a story of lies salted with some truth. His point was to inform me that the Catholic Church is "justified" in its involvement with our government due to the Priests' "hearing confessions from mobsters and spies." He also explained that Exchange Students were "spies in the making" that Priests found, through Confession, were problems. Thus they were considered expendable and transferred out of the country. He then suggested to my father that I see the school guidance counselor, CIA Operative Dennis DeLaney, immediately. My father enthusiastically told me that DeLaney was a long time friend of his from St. Francis who "knew how to handle kids like me." Arrangements were made for me to see him after school.

DeLaney began by informing me that he was "aware of "everything" and that he knew just what I needed "to put me back on track." He said that my family needed to take a trip to the Teton Mountains of Wyoming. He even provided maps and information in an envelope for my father. He turned off the lights in his office and turned on a slide projector. He showed me scenes of the numerous waterfalls of the Tetons, all of which were to "wash my brain" of the reality that I was performing oral sex on him as ordered while the slides ran. Then he scheduled a follow up appointment for further "counseling."

This trip to the Tetons would provide a change of scenery from the usual Mackinac/Niagara Falls trip, but I could no longer hope for a change in the direction life was leading me. I was told my life was "predestined," and all I had to do was follow the road stretched out before me, i.e. the "Yellow Brick Road." I was destined for Wyoming but would not know why until I arrived.

I confirmed the family trip to the Tetons when I saw DeLaney for my follow up "counseling." He informed me that he had already talked to my father about the trip, as well as our upcoming trip to Disney World in Florida. I was not surprised to learn of an additional trip. Nor did I have the capacity to become excited, suspicious, or apprehensive. I was aware that DeLaney was heavily involved in Project Monarch, not only because he was accessing my sexual personalities again, but because he was helping to pave the way toward my destiny of total mind control.

During Christmas vacation of 1974, my father flew us all to Disney World by route of Tampa, Florida. Ignorant of geography, it did not occur to me that Tampa was out of the way to Disney World until my father drove the rented van to the gates of MacDill Air Force Base. Military personnel met me there and escorted me into the base TOP SECRET high tech mind control conditioning facility for "behavioral modification" programming. This was the first in what became a routine series of mind control testing and/or programming sessions on government installations that I would endure throughout my Project Monarch victimization.

Whether I was in a military, NASA, or government building, the procedure for maintaining me under total mind control remained consistent with Project Monarch requirements. This included prior physical and/or psychological trauma; sleep, food, and water deprivation; high voltage electric shock; and hypnotic and/or harmonic programming of specific memory compartments/ personalities. The high tech equipment and methodisms I endured from that time on gave the U.S. government absolute control of my mind and life. I had been literally driven out of my conscious mind and existed only through my programmed subconscious. I lost my free will, ability to reason, and could not think to question anything that was happening to me. I could only do as I was told.

After the MacDill Air Force Base experience, my home life worsened. The controls and conditioning that my father and mother executed on me tightened even more. I was no longer permitted to have any contact with my own brothers and sister (I only had one younger sister at that time). This stopped me in my subconscious efforts to protect them from my father's abuse, and left me with a desperate, empty aching for the loving relationships I previously shared with them. Of course, I never was able to protect them any more than I could defend myself or later protect my own daughter. However, until government programming began, I had routinely "baby sat" them every evening and took them for long walks that lasted for hours in my feeble attempt to keep them out of my parents' range. Subconsciously I believed I was making a difference. The day my youngest brother told my mother he much preferred my company over hers was the day I could no longer be near him or my other brothers and sister. Apparently, I was making enough of a difference that my parents were compelled to separate me from them. I was ordered to my closet-sized bedroom in the garage as soon as I got home from school or work. I could not speak to, look at, or hug my brothers and sister. I was not permitted to eat dinner with my family, although they let me out of my room to set the table, wash dishes, and do other chores. If I ventured from my bedroom to use the bathroom and was caught by my mother, she said, "nobody rattled your cage" and ordered me back to my room in the garage.

In the summer of 1975, my family drove all the way from Michigan to the Teton Mountains of Wyoming. I was ordered to ride in the back storage area of the family Chevy Suburban since I was forbidden to associate or communicate with my brothers and sister. So I dissociated into books, or into the metaphorical, hypnotic suggestions from my father and tranced deeper as I watched the prairie's seemingly endless sea of "amber waves of grain" streak past my window. Once when we stopped at a gas station, my father took me inside to show me a stuffed "jackalope" mounted on the wall. Due to my tranced, dissociative state and high suggestibility level, I believed it was indeed a cross between a jack rabbit and antelope. It was 100+ degrees in the Badlands when it cooled down at night. The intense heat of the day accentuated my ever increasing thirst. My father was physically preparing me though water deprivation for the intense tortures and programming I would endure in Wyoming

Dick Cheney, then White House Chief of Staff to President Ford, later Secretary of Defense to President George Bush, documented member of the Council on Foreign relations (CFR), and Presidential hopeful for 1996, was originally Wyoming's only Congressman. Dick Cheney was the reason my family had traveled to Wyoming where I endured yet another form of brutality

-- his version of "A Most Dangerous Game," or human hunting.

It is my understanding now that A Most Dangerous Game was devised to condition military personnel in survival and combat maneuvers. Yet it was used on me and other slaves known to me as a means of further conditioning the mind to the realization there was "no place to hide," as well as traumatize the victim for ensuing programming. It was my experience over the years that A Most Dangerous Game had numerous variations on the primary theme of being stripped naked and turned loose in the wilderness while being hunted by men and dogs. In reality, all "wilderness" areas were enclosed in secure military fencing whereby it was only a matter of time until I was caught, repeatedly raped, and tortured.

Dick Cheney had an apparent addiction to the "thrill of the sport." He appeared obsessed with playing A Most Dangerous Game as a means of traumatizing mind control victims, as well as to satisfy his own perverse sexual kinks. My introduction to the game occurred upon arrival at the hunting lodge near Greybull, Wyoming, and it physically and psychologically devastated me. I was sufficiently traumatized for Cheney's programming as I stood naked in his hunting lodge office after being hunted down and caught. Cheney was talking as he paced around me, "I could stuff you and mount you like a jackalope and call you a two legged dear. Or I could stuff you with this (he unzipped his pants to reveal his oversized penis) right down your throat, and then mount you. Which do you prefer?

Blood and sweat became mixed with the dirt on my body and slid like mud down my legs and shoulder. I throbbed with exhaustion and pain as I stood unable to think to answer such a question. "Make up your mind," Cheney coaxed. Unable to speak, I remained silent. "You don't get a choice, anyway. I make up your mind for you. That's why you're here. For me to make you a mind, and make you mine/mind. You lost your mind a long time ago. Now I'm going to give you one. Just like the Wizard (of Oz) gave Scarecrow a brain, the Yellow Brick Road led you here to me. You've 'come such a long, long way' for your brain, and I will give you one."

The blood reached my shoes and caught my attention. Had I been further along in my programming, I perhaps would never have noticed such a thing or had the capability to think to wipe it away. But so far, I had only been to MacDill and Disney World for government/military programming. At last, when I could speak, I begged, "If you don't mind, can I please use your bathroom?"

Cheney's face turned red with rage. He was on me in an instant, slamming my back into the wall with one arm across my chest and his hand on my throat, choking me while applying pressure to the carotid artery in my neck with his thumb. His eyes bulged and he spit as he growled, "If you don't mind me, I will kill you. I could kill you -- Kill you -- with my bare hands. You're not the first and you won't be the last. I'll kill you any time I goddamn well please." He flung me on the cot-type bed that as behind me. There he finished taking his rage out on me sexually.

On the long trip back to Michigan, I lay in a heap behind the seats of the Suburban, nauseated and hurting from Cheney's brutality and high voltage tortures, plus the whole Wyoming experience. My father stopped by the waterfalls flowing through the Tetons to "wash my brain" of the memory of Cheney. I could barely walk through the woods to the falls for the process as instructed, despite having learned my lessons well from Cheney on following orders.

The next year when our "annual" trip to Disney World rolled around, my father drove, pulling his new Holiday Rambler Royale International trailer. (I slept outside in a tent because I was not permitted inside it since "I wasn't family.") My father dropped me off en route at the Kennedy Space Center in Titusville, Florida where I was subjected to my first NASA programming. From then on, I was "obsessed" with following the "Yellow Brick Road" to Nashville, Tennessee. Moving to Nashville was all I could talk about. If anyone asked me the question I could not think to ask myself "Why?", I would respond by reiterating it was something "I had to do."

I had gone through the motions of my senior year in a dissociative trance. I became further distanced from religious values by my religion class teacher, Brother Emmett. This was due to his promotion of cannibalism via Pier Paul Reed's book Alive, and by his teachings at a religious 'corseal' retreat I attended that included occult ritual at St. Francis church. I graduated from Muskegon Catholic Central High School in our bicentennial year of 1976. I was led by Senator Byrd to revise my plan to attend Hope College like I had promised VanderJagt as a child. This new plan was for me to temporarily attend Muskegon Community College, because my "real education" was to come through mind control programming -- not school. In order to be exhausted, as was necessary for my "real education," I worked three menial jobs in addition to attending college.

During my first semester of college in 1976, I made plans to take a trip to Nashville with my Project Monarch friend from Catholic Central. (She remains an expendable victim to date, and therefore her identity must be protected from public release for her safety.) My father explained that I was to stay at the Fiddler's Inn in Nashville, see the World Famous Printer's Alley row of sleazy country music nightclubs, and attend the Grand Ole Opry on Friday night, as ticket arrangements had been made through a "friend," in spite of their scarcity during the Thanksgiving holiday.

I never thought to associate Fiddler's Inn with Senator Byrd's fiddle playing when my friend and I arrived in Music City, U.S.A. Nor did I find it odd when a country music "star" entertaining at the Black Poodle nightclub in Printer's Alley began directing my activities. My friend and I were provided with free passes to the Black Poodle to encourage us to return each night where entertainer and CIA operative Jack Greene and his Desperado band were playing. During breaks between sets, Greene and his band would sit with my friend and me to manipulate our suggestible minds. I was told it was "my destiny" to have met band member, Wayne Cox, who had been trained for paramilitary mercenary operations under Louisiana's U.S. Senator J. Bennett Johnston. I soon learned that everyone associated

99

with Greene was involved in his CIA "Freedom Train" operations. When I told Greene that my friend and I would not be returning on Friday night due to attending the Grand Ole Opry, he told us that he would be working the Opry that night. He made arrangements for us to come back stage and see him immediately following his segment. He explained that the "security" guard at the Opry, Nashville Metro Police Lt. Bob Ezell, was a good friend of his and would let us in.

At the Opry, my friend and I sat in the audience watching as Jack Greene introduced his "special guest," U.S. Senator Robert C. Byrd. At the sight of Byrd, I went into a pre-conditioned deep trance and robotically went through the motions of following Greene's instructions. Once backstage, Greene pointed out his dressing room, which he was sharing with senator Byrd, and ordered me in. The personality that had been sitting in the audience had perceived Byrd as an entertainer and could not, or would not, think further. But as I walked into the dressing room and saw Byrd perched on the edge of the mirrored vanity in his boxer shorts, I switched into the child personality that had known him as a U.S. Senator on Mackinac Island since age 13, and responded sexually. Afterward, Byrd was claiming me as "his," excitedly telling me that he had "always wanted his own little witch." I soon learned the enormity of this statement.

Jack Greene's band member, Wayne Cox, later told me that playing music behind Senator Byrd at the Opry was not the only way he "backed him." He also backed him politically and in Freedom Train operations. Cox then made arrangements for my friend and me to stay the remainder of our trip at his trailer in Hendersonville, Tennessee. There was no choice but to comply. The following night, after Jack Greene completed his show at the Black Poodle, he drove my friend and me to a nearby participating after-hours club, the Demon's Den. There, Cox was to pick us up and take us to Hendersonville. Instead, we were slipped a drug and taken "on a tour" of Union Station, Nashville's then abandoned train station, where supposedly the only train still running through there was the Freedom Train.

Senator Byrd's attempted cultivation of superstition through my Catholic schooling should have maximized the impact of the occult ritual I was subjected to in the tower of the old stone and slate turn-of-the-century train depot. But the pain and horror was sufficiently effective in itself -- even without my adhering to superstition -- to produce the intended mind shattering results. Cox took my friend and me on a "flashlight tour" through the rubble of Union Station, until we came to a homeless man sleeping on the ground. Cox ordered me to "kiss the railroad bum good-bye," then shot him between the eyes while I was still only inches away.[1] He then used a machete to chop off the man's hands, which he put in a zip lock bag. He then led us up the rickety stairs into the tower of the old depot. There Jack Greene, his band members, and others dressed in black robes were gathered around a black leather alter in a room lit by candles and draped in red velvet. In total shock, I was laid on the alter and subjected to rape and torture while the participants indulged in sex, blood, and cannibalism ritual.

The next day I woke up on Cox's couch, vaguely aware that I had suffered a "bad nightmare." When I stood up, I passed out from blood loss. I was bleeding profusely from the vagina. It was all I could do to prepare to drive back to Michigan, and my friend was certainly not in a stable frame of mind to help. I did not know what happened to me, nor was I able to question it. I had a new "obsession" on my mind. I had been programmed at the ritual to move to Nashville and marry Cox, as ordered by Senator Byrd.

Back in Michigan, I made the announcement to my parents that I was moving to Nashville to marry Cox, as it was "predestination." What they would not tell me was that my father had just literally SOLD me to Senator Byrd in exchange for lucrative military contracts that made him a millionaire overnight -- a millionaire on a sixth grade education -- a perverse, child exploiting criminal, immune from prosecution, working as a CIA operative for the U.S. government! That mind shattering occult ritual I endured in Nashville marked a new life of wealth and prestige for my father while thrusting me into a new phase of my torturous existence -- and I had no choice in any of it!

---

[1] Nashville Metropolitan Police Lieutenant Bob Ezell, who also acted in the capacity of Grand Ol' Opry security guard, covered up the murder.

CHAPTER 5

TINKERING WITH THE MIND

It was 1977. I was a 19-year-old mind-controlled programmed slave in the CIA/DIA Project Monarch Freedom Train operation, literally owned by U.S. Senate Majority Leader Robert C. Byrd, who was then a 20-year incumbent and on the Senate Appropriations Committee. As Byrd's "own little witch" (sex slave), I would also become involved in covert government operations. I now understand that this required more memory compartments/ personalities than I had developed. Hence one more reason for the mind shattering occult ritual, and my "predestined" marriage to Cox. In typical Project Monarch structure, Byrd was my "owner" and in control of my life, while Cox became my primary "handler" and followed Byrd's orders to ensure that I was at key locations and events at appointed times and to maintain me under mind control. Cox reportedly was not paid cash for his role like my father was. Instead, he either followed orders or would be prosecuted for distributing drugs and being the occult serial killer that he was and is to date. Cox's primary role was to shatter my mind further through repeated occult trauma as well as father my daughter, Kelly, to be raised in the genetic mind control studies of Project Monarch.

I moved to Nashville as ordered to marry Cox, who took me to the backwoods of his hometown swamp in Chatham, Louisiana for months at a time for occult traumatization. Cox had been brought up in witchcraft by his mother, and admittedly longed for her sexually and ritually. Together they subjected me to their beliefs, which included what equates to a weakened version of mind control used by witches for centuries, anchored in superstition rather than scientific fact. These superstitious beliefs seemingly conflicted with Cox's mercenary training to the point that his killing raged out of control. For example, Cox would murder a human through repeated stabbing with a knife, believing that the "departing spirit" and splattered blood gave him power to control my mind. In truth, it was my aversion and subsequent traumatization by the event that caused me to dissociate and trance, leaving my subconscious open to his suggestions and those of others. During the three years I was with Cox, he ritually impregnated and aborted me six times, consuming several of his own offspring and preserving the others shaped in ceramic for sale in his interstate occult body parts business. Cox's M.O. for murdering always included removing the hands with a machete, the so-called "Hands of Glory" he kiln- dried in the ceramic shop of his and his mother's house were in demand and thus distributed throughout the occult underground supply network. Cox's protected cocaine and body parts distribution routes included Texas, Arkansas, Mississippi, Tennessee, and Florida.

Cox and I traveled to Florida on several occasions as his mother's parents lived in Mims, which is only minutes away from the NASA Kennedy Space Center in Titusville. Cox, like my father, made sure I was there for mind control testing and programming as ordered. Cox perceived me as a "Chosen One," and often used this CIA Project Monarch term when referring to me and for proudly "justifying" his leaving me at the NASA installation.

Cox had a variety of belief systems that he applied to various situations, all of which were superstition based. He believed in spirit communication or "divine guidance" through nature spirits and demons, that Satan must be appeased, that Jesus is an alien, that the Bermuda Triangle is a door to another dimension, and that the end of the world is near. He 'religiously' carried a Bible with him everywhere -- including to occult rituals -- quoting scripture like a theologian. He justified "eating the body and drinking the blood," "being washed in the blood," and even "murdering children" according to the story of God testing Abraham by ordering him to murder his son Isaac by knife on an altar. Jim Jones was one of Cox's idols, as was Charlie Manson, and he touted the Jonestown massacre as a prime example of the "power of [CIA] mind control."

Cox demanded I become a Mormon in the Church of Jesus Christ of Latter Day Saints. This was to "prove" that Satan was everywhere -- particularly in the Monroe, Louisiana Mormon church where he led occult ritual, and in the Hendersonville, Tennessee church that the so called Freedom Train rolled through.[1]

Cox's determination to instill his religious superstitious beliefs in me was side-tracked by J. Bennett Johnston in his Shreveport, Louisiana office early in the summer of 1978.

Cox's mother, Mary, had driven us to Johnston's office near Barksdale Air Force Base as ordered. As she knocked boldly on the obscure metal door, I read the attached metal sign: "General Dynamics Research and Development." A smaller sign near the doorknob read: "Unlawful to enter premises without prior authorization. All violators will be prosecuted under penalty of federal law."

Johnston, wearing a light blue leisure suit and smelling strongly of body odor, opened the door. "Well, hey Senator," Mary drawled in her backwoods Louisiana dialect. "I brought the children to see you like you said."

Johnston looked at her with annoyed disgust. "I see that," he said matter- of-factly. He then proceeded to instruct Mary to wait outside a moment while he talked with Cox, then to take him on to her home in Monroe where I could be picked up at the Airport a few days later.

Cox and I were ushered into Johnston's barren military-style furnished office. Several Presidential and military photographs hung on the wall and served as the only decor. Johnston sat on the front of his military issue desk and talked to Cox's subconscious mind using cryptic, hypnotic Disney Peter Pan theme language,[2] as he apparently had done in the past when Cox had a mind left to control.

"As long as your ticker's running, that crock-a-dial you've been feeding over the years will be running right behind you. (Peter) Pan knew how to stay a step ahead of the game and stop the inevitable process of becoming gator bait himself by offering to give him a hand now and then."

Cox dismembered his murdered victims and distributed the "Hands of Glory" to fellow Satanists and occult traumatized/ Peter Pan theme programmed mercenaries, while feeding "left over" body part to an alligator that lived in the swamp behind his house. This was indicative of Cox's twisted, murderous response to Johnston's traumatic Peter Pan theme programming... a programming them I was about to experience "first hand."

Cryptically instructing Cox on Senator Byrd's orders, Johnston continued, "I've got to hand it to that Pan. His livelihood of creating hookers for the Captain (Hook) was indeed lucrative. And speaking of creating hookers, a little Byrd told me that a shift from routine hand-ling to a theme that is alien could prove lucrative to you." Revealing his intent to ensure my military mind-control programming,

Johnston told him, "I'll lay a little groundwork and set the patten for countdown. Then I'll send her out to launch for you, and its your job to man the craft from there..."

Cox was ordered out of Johnston's office, and he turned his full attention to me. When alone with the Senator, Johnston manipulated my mind, and ultimately my beliefs and perceptions, for future programming. He referred to a picture of himself shaking hands with unknown Navy brass as he dramatically told me, "I was there that fateful day in 1943 when a hole was ripped in the fabric of time through what later became known as the Philadelphia experiment. All those fine boys vanished along with their ship in a bizarre twist of events that parallels the Atlantis disappearances. A vortex was created in an effort to slip dimensions and become invisible to the enemy. It was a success beyond the highest expectations and launched us all into universal travel. It is no wonder at all that we have had a man on the moon. Traveling to distant planets and galaxies is Mickey Mouse stuff in comparison to the high tech wizardry of trans-dimensional travel. Trans-dimensional travel circumvents all measures of time, including distance and speed. When the fabric of time was torn, we opened ourselves up to intergalactic travel -- both in and out of this dimension -- and in and out of the future, as well as the past. We can alter the course of history by traveling back in time to alter events, or we can blast off into the future and gain wisdom and knowledge of events yet to come. We can control the future by controlling the past. At present, this is a relatively easy task according to the theory of relativity and abilities gained through the Philadelphia experiment. I came back an ET (extraterrestrial) myself. And our ship returned to this earth as a space ship.[3] I gained the keys to the universe on that fateful day, and I carry them with me now, sharing only a Key or two at a time with those who are Chosen. You are a Chosen One (Johnston was deliberately interfacing with Rite to Remain Silent conditioning), and therefore must learn the ins and outs of interplanetary travel. Your mission is trans-dimensional. You can span infinite dimensions by learning from me. Take it from me, you're going places, kid. And I'll teach you to get there by riding the light. I'll teach you the groundwork, and you do the light work. The key to the universe lies in the speed of light. The only way to travel is by beam of light. You will learn to go to the light... Your mission is to learn how to Tinker with time. I'm going to take you on that journey myself. Come with me now. It's time we were leaving this plane and boarding another."

Johnston took me the short distance from his General Dynamics Corporation provided office to the Barksdale Air Force Base airfield. He was apparently well known at Barksdale, and a small cargo plane was ready to take us to our destination -- Tinker Air Force Base in Oklahoma.

Once we were airborne, Johnston accessed my sex programmed personalities for his own aggressive perversion. His use of cocaine further accentuated his hyperactive demeanor as he brutally slung me around the back of the small plane while he had sex with me. At one point the pilot hollered from the cockpit, "Hey, you're creating turbulence. Knock it off, will you."

Johnston laughed and responded, "What the fuck do you think I'm doing?"

By the time we arrived at Tinker A.F.B., my arm was beginning to show a dark bruise that extended from my shoulder to my elbow. A uniformed man greeted us as we walked across the airfield. Johnston apparently knew him quite well, and referred to him as "Cap'n" (which tied in with the Peter Pan theme

Johnston told him, "I'll lay a little groundwork and set the patten for countdown. Then I'll send her out to launch for you, and it's your job to man the craft from there..."

"Yeah, I know. Take care of it for me. Here..." Johnston took the straps of my tank top and pulled them down around my forearms (which still could not cover the bruise.) "There, that just about covers it." He smiled and continued, "You look like a Southern belle that way rather than a damned ol' Yankee anyway."

Cap'n said, "She'll be a Tinker-belle by the time we're through here today." Then, referring to Johnston's primary purpose in actually escorting me to Tinker he asked, "How are your South American operations progressing?"

"I've got to talk to you about that," Johnston answered. The two talked as though they had worked in tandem on given mercenary operations/assignments in the past. "I may need a few of your boys to back me on something."

"Back you or cover you?" the Cap'n retorted. Johnston laughed, "Both if you'll front the operation."

Johnston had previously "justified" his use of Tinker (Peter Pan theme) programmed mind controlled mercenaries to me by saying, "Mercenaries are missionaries who follow their inner guidance system rather than their old Uncle Sam. Politics hinder the route to freedom, and these boys slip under international laws, undetected, to carry out the work the military boys only dream of doing..."

I was escorted away from the two by a nurse, who purported to be tending to my injured arm. In fact, she was preparing me for the "Tinker-belle cage"[4] -- an electrified metal cage with an electrified grid bottom. Locked inside, I was subjected to high direct current voltage to compartmentalize the Peter Pan theme mind control programming that I endured. Like Peter Pan's Tinkerbelle, I learned to "ride the light" as a means of travel.[5] Additionally, my instilled Tinker-belle theme mind manipulation included a sense of Never-Never-land timelessness that was rooted in my "natural" inability to comprehend time due to my MPD/DID.

Back in Louisiana, Cox and I shared a subconscious understanding of Peter Pan themes and "riding the light." The difference between us was that Cox consciously activated Tinker Air Force base programming within Johnston's band of mercenaries, while my trance was perpetual whereby I could "Never- Never-Land."[6]

I was with Cox on numerous occasions when he was running guns and/or cocaine, and activating specified mercenaries for operations as instructed by Johnston. In the course of these travels I saw numerous underground arsenals and stockpiled weapons that were known to Senator Johnston, but were not on military installations. I was also privy to government sanctioned cocaine operations.

On one such cocaine run in 1979, I traveled with Cox to a remote area in the Ouachita National Forest near Hot Springs, Arkansas to "watch for fairies like Tinker-belle" and "ride the light."

We sat in the brush near a railroad track until we saw a light approaching from the Eastern sky. At the time I thought I would be "riding the light" as I was led to believe, but in retrospect I recall my personalities being deliberately switched and a helicopter landing in a nearby clearing.

Cox and I unloaded approximately 200-400 pounds of cocaine from the van he had driven, and stacked it in the helicopter. We were then flown to a small airport that appeared to be no more than a dark, fenced in clearing where I saw a row of metal buildings that looked like mini-warehouses. While the cocaine was unloaded into a warehouse, Cox and I were taken by car to a nearby gray stone hotel. The driver led us upstairs and knocked on the Penthouse door.

"Yeah," a voice answered.

"I got a Tinker-belle and a Peter Pan here to see you, Sir," the driver called. "Send 'em in." Cox and I walked into the suite where then Governor of Arkansas Bill Clinton was shuffling through a briefcase. Clinton and Johnston were cohorts in illegal covert operations that emanated from Tinker Air Force Base.

Cox spoke up. "Senator Johnston said a little (Senator) Byrd told him that you are one of Ours."[7]

"So what does that make you?" Clinton asked impatiently. "A Chosen One." Cox nodded his head toward me.

Clinton asked me, "Chosen by who's order?"

I cryptically delivered the proper coded response, which cued Clinton to proceed. "What brings you here?" he demanded.

Interpreting his question literally as is "natural" for programmed MPD/DID slaves, I answered, "I rode the light, Sir."

Clinton rolled his eyes, and looked back over at Cox who was nervously rocking back and forth as he so often did. "State your business," Clinton ordered.

"Uh," Cox cleared his throat, habitually picked his nose as he rocked back and forth and said, "Well, uh..." Clinton looked disgusted.

"Get him the fuck out of here!" he ordered the driver. Cox was immediately escorted out.

"That's better," Clinton said. Using standard Jesuit hand signals and cryptic language, he triggered/switched me and accessed a previously programmed message.

"Senator Johnston sent me to give this to you." I handed Clinton a thin, large brown envelope. "And I have some fairy dust guaranteed to make you fly high." I took the personal stash of cocaine that Johnston was sharing with Clinton from my pocket.

Clinton snorted two lines of the coke immediately. He smiled. "Tell Ben I'm impressed." He showed me to the door.

The severe torture and mind control programming that I was enduring at Tinker Air Force Base had prepared me for this simple "mission" and many others. Although Cox's out-of-control occult serial killings polyfragmented my multiple personalities as intended by Byrd, it was Johnston's alien theme mind conditioning that locked me into absolute robotic helplessness. After all, had I been capable of rationalizing, I would have found that the thought of interdimensional travel and aliens was no more bizarre to me than Cox's murderous actions or having found out pornography king Jerry Ford held the office of President.

When my daughter, Kelly, was born in February of 1980, Cox's former employer, Jack Greene, traveled to Louisiana to meet with me in keeping with his role as Nashville's CIA Freedom Train "conductor." He took me aside and explained that since Cox had fulfilled his (genetic) role in producing Kelly, Senator Byrd had ordered me back to Nashville. Greene talked at length, hypnotically reviving my original programmed "obsession" to move to Nashville. He told me that Cox had proven too insane to follow orders anymore as was evidenced by my extremely poor health (much of my hair had fallen out) and by the stench of decaying human flesh that permeated the area surrounding his remote Chatham, Louisiana swamp house.

If I had had a mind of my own, I know in retrospect I would have felt as though I had been released from a prison dungeon. But I could only respond by telling Cox matter-of-factly that I had received "divine guidance" to move to Nashville at once to a home that awaited me. Cox had no choice but to comply with Byrd's orders. Kelly and I moved to Tennessee when she was only three months old, and Cox temporarily moved with us in order to apprise our new handler of the latest details of our victimization. Within weeks, Cox moved back to Chatham, Louisiana to live with his mother (even to this date). Now he reportedly raises goats for sacrifice and carries on his occult serial killing activities unhindered due to his immunity from prosecution because of whom and what he and his mother know.

---

[1] Substantial information regarding the saturation of occultism in the Mormon church is a published fact, circulated among the Bishopric, then released by Bishop Pace in an effort to restore morality and freedom of thought to church members.

[2] Senator Johnston's duel and triple cryptic language perplexed me at the time. In retrospect, I understand how this component of mind control allowed for undetected proliferation of criminal covert activity, even when overheard by strangers, to the extent that I believed it must be occurring in "another dimension" as I was told.

[3] Johnston "validated" his ploy in my mind by arranging for me to see his "space-ship" -- a then TOP SECRET experimental aircraft which would eventually be known as a Stealth fighter -- at a military installation near Baton Rouge. The classified triangular Stealth was so alien to me at the time that it looked more like a spaceship than the U.S. fighter plane it actually is. This, in combination with his inhumane demeanor and my previously instilled belief in transdimensional travel, convinced me he was the "ET" he purported to be.

[4] I understand this is referred to as a Woodpecker grid.

[5] "Riding the Light" scrambled my future experience of being transported by military helicopter or airplane to robotically carry out some program for the government. This "trance- dimensional" travel caused my earthly experiences to be perceived as having occurred in another dimension.

[6] I remained in a Post Traumatic Stress Disordered (PTSD) trance.

[7] Same Jesuit reference used to describe Pierre Trudeau.

CHAPTER 6

UNITED STATES MILITARY
& NASA MIND CONTROL TRAINING

Soon after moving to Tennessee, I learned that Senator Byrd had simply exchanged one living hell for another for me. My new mind control handler, CIA operative and country music ventriloquist/ stage hypnotist Alex Houston, seemed only to pick up where Cox had left off. As "destined," Kelly and I moved into a run-down old trailer on Houston's property, which adjoined Jack Greene's farm in Goodlettsville, Tennessee. I was subjected to further occult ritual on Greene's farm, and was ritually impregnated and aborted again, this time by Houston. A difference between Cox and Houston was the superstition factor; Houston knew exactly what he was doing and why he was doing it, in accordance with tried and proven scientific U.S. government mind control research and development. I gleaned this knowledge from conversations I overheard between him and "those in the know."

Alex Houston was 26 years older than I and claimed to have gained his knowledge of stage hypnosis and government mind control methods from the military while entertaining overseas in Bob Hope's USO tours. After the tour, Houston reportedly moved to Washington, D.C. where he and his alter-ego dummy, Elemer, were regulars on the *Jimmy Dean* television show in the '60s.[1] According to Houston, he was regularly booked to entertain in officers' clubs on military bases due to his involvement in covert government operations.

During the brief interim period that Cox resided on Houston's farm with us, he played music behind government mind controlled slave Louise Mandrell and her husband/handler R.C. Bannon. Cox had previously worked with Louise's sister, Barbara Mandrell, at the onset of her government sponsored career in the 1960's, traveling overseas with her in the same U.S.O. tours that launched Houston's career. Irby Mandrell, the Mandrells' father and manager, reportedly sexually abused all three of his daughters and eagerly thrust them into their mind controlled existence much the same way my father had sold me. His daughters, too, were owned by U.S. Senator Robert C. Byrd.

Cox was soon fired from his position with Louise due to his insanity. Once when Houston was traveling with the Mandrells as he so often did throughout the years, Irby Mandrell relayed the events that prompted his firing of Cox. He told Houston and I that Cox had become an embarrassment to him while traveling.

"I knew he was weird," Irby Mandrell said. "That's OK. I can live with that. But when he pitched a tent behind the hotel so he could hear the trumpets sound, signaling him to march to Missouri,[2] I said, 'Start marching, son. You're done. You're through in Nashville. Don't ever come back.' That's it, he was done."

Houston reminisced with Mandrell about the U.S.O. days and inquired as to how he had tolerated Cox back when he played music behind Barbara.

"Oh, yeah. I remember he [Cox] had somewhat of a brain back then." Irby Mandrell continued, "Barbara was just a kid back then with the talent of a full blown star. I thought she had what it takes to make it in the industry. Then the Byrd came along and introduced us to the latest in technology."

108

Houston interrupted, "Are you talking about [music] equipment or the kind they've got in Huntsville [Alabama's NASA mind control training center]?"

"Both," Mandrell replied. "But it was Huntsville that launched her to the stars. The doors opened wide after that. Byrd took a lot of pride in Barbara, and the doors just kept opening. With my baby's talent and the Byrd's influence on her mind and career, there was no way we could loose."

When Houston became my appointed mind control handler in 1980, Byrd's influence on my mind boosted Houston's "entertainment" career. His travels had expanded to accommodate covert drug and money laundering operations across the U.S., in Mexico, in Canada, and throughout the Caribbean.

Houston had, and has, a great deal of "no show" money, but I was never permitted access to it. Poverty was one more means of control I endured, as slaves like myself were not afforded the freedoms that having money allows. When I was working three menial jobs during college, all of my money was taken from me by my parents. All money earned by Cox's cocaine and body parts enterprises was reinvested in the coven and drugs, leaving us dependent on charities for our basic necessities. With Houston, I had to "earn" every penny I spent on groceries and necessities over and over again, which made "earning my keep" a deliberately impossible cycle. This kept me financially dependent and further hindered my ability to escape, even if I had known enough to attempt it.

My innate protective maternal instincts as a mother may have been accentuated due to my past unsuccessful attempts to protect my brothers and sisters (I now had two sisters). It was my desperate need to keep Kelly safe that drove me to the point of "fight or flight" when I was transferred to Houston. I had long ago lost my ability to "fight," but my new maternal instincts compelled me to "flight." I did all I could to save Kelly and myself from Houston and her fate in Project Monarch. Since I had no ability to reason and was amnesic, I "fled" to my parents' new house in affluent Grand haven, Michigan. I had no concept of what I was running from or to. I arrived with my baby daughter in my arms, the tattered clothes on our backs, and what few donated belongings I had acquired for Kelly. Within a few days, my parents received and followed Senator Byrd's instructions, and turned me back over to Houston -- who, in turn, sent me back to Louisiana for further conditioning.

After three more months of intense, nonstop tortures by Cox, I could not think to follow maternal instincts and barely knew my own name. I had no idea how old I was, where I was, how long I had been there, and what had happened to Kelly during that time. Kelly's own testimony and current programmed polyfragmented Multiple Personality/Dissociative Identity Disorder reflects the high tech, sophisticated conditioning and torturous trauma she endured during this and numerous ensuing times that we were separated. When I was returned to Houston as orchestrated by Byrd, my brain contained a series of new compartments ready to be programmed and led.

Intensive mind control behavior programming began at once, and Houston ensured that I was taken to my appointed destinations under the guise of his travels in the country music industry. In the early 1980's, my base programming was instilled at Fort Campbell, Kentucky by U.S. Army Lt. Colonel Michael Aquino. Aquino holds a TOP SECRET clearance in the Defense Intelligence Agency's Psychological Warfare Division (Psy Ops). He is a professed Neo-Nazi, the founder of the Himler inspired

109

satanic Temple of Set, and has been charged with child ritual and sexual abuse at the Presidio Day Care in San Francisco, California. But like my father and Cox, Aquino remains "above the law" while he continues to traumatize, and program CIA destined young minds in a quest to reportedly create the "superior race" of Project Monarch mind controlled slaves. I quickly learned that Aquino did not adhere to his profoundly professed occult superstition any more than I did. His "satanic power" was in the form of numerous variations of high voltage stun guns,[3] which he used on me regularly. Although Aquino used occultism (blood trauma) as a trauma base, his programming was high tech and "clean" -- not muddled in a proverbial witches brew of ignorance. He quickly dispelled the Cox influence and began programming me according to Byrd's specifications as his "own little witch" for sadistic sex, covert CIA drug muling, black mail, and prostitution operations.

During the three months I was back with Cox, a muscle in my upper vaginal wall was cut and dropped in preparation for Houston to flesh carve a hideous witch's face[4] for Senator Byrd's perversion. Aquino provided the ancient instructions on how to mutilate me, and Houston used silver nitrate and hot exacto knives to carve the details of the face without any form of anesthesia. By flexing the muscle downward, the face protruded out of my vagina. Not only did this surgery give Byrd a vagina suited to his minute, underdeveloped penis, it also provided an equitable "curiosity" to be displayed over and over again in both commercial and non-commercial pornography and prostitution.

On the 1981 anniversary of John F. Kennedy's assassination, I was forced to "marry" Alex Houston for appearance sake. Earlier that month when I had been taken to Washington, D.C. for prostitution purposes, Byrd informed me that I would actually be "marrying" him when I "pledged my vows" to Houston.

"It is a covenant between the two of us," Byrd had said. "It is me that you will honor and obey 'til death do us part." Byrd then instructed me to pick up my wedding dress from a nearby D.C. store. Throughout the years, Houston often joked about the significance of my Washington, D.C. wedding dress -- which was depicted in pornographic photos and a commercial video to "commemorate our wedding night."

Alex Houston's "best man," Jimmy Walker, was also a photographer for Larry Flynt's sexually graphic commercial pornography magazine, *Hustler*. When I met Byrd after the ceremony at Nashville's Opryland Hotel as ordered, he presented me with a "wedding gift" -- a rose patterned crystal crucifix deliberately designed to anchor "our wedding" in my Catholic/Vatican instilled beliefs. The Larry Flynt photos depicting me in my wedding dress with the crystal crucifix to "commemorate our wedding night," was standard lock-in procedure for all mind controlled slaves I knew who were forced to "marry" their handlers/owners.

Houston's booking agent, Reggie Mac (MacLaughlin), of United Talent and later of MacFadden Agency in Nashville, Tennessee, had been booking CIA involved country music acts into key locations to aid the execution of covert government operations. For example, Houston's ventriloquist act "Alex and Elemer" would be scheduled to perform at a county or state fair near Washington, D.C., where I would be picked up by car or helicopter and escorted to the White House or the Pentagon. The ensuing activities would be compartmentalized in my memory in a manner that caused me to believe I had simply been traveling in the country music industry, and no one "back home" would be suspect of my absence.

Another example would be that Houston "entertained" at Byrd's West Virginia State Fair every year, which gave a legitimate appearance to my presence there when in fact I was being prostituted to the Senator I had "married."

During the early '80s, Reggie MacLaughlin primarily booked Houston into areas that were conducive to my mind control programming with Aquino. I was first subjected to Aquino's tortures and programming in Fort Campbell, Kentucky; Fort McClellen in Anniston, Alabama; and most frequently, at Redstone Arsenal and Marshall Space Flight Center in Huntsville, Alabama. Military mind control was fast, effective, and highly technological, but it was the NASA programming that launched me as a "Presidential Model." Even though Aquino instilled my programming on both military and NASA installations, he had access to the latest technological advancements and techniques through NASA. These included mind foolers such as sensory deprivation tanks, virtual reality, flight simulators, and harmonics. By the age of two, Kelly had already been subjected to Aquino and his programming through these latest technological advancements, which shattered her fragile young mind before her base personality had a chance to form. Rather than use occultism on Kelly, Aquino traumatized her through sexual assault and high voltage tortures of the mind and body. She, like I, to this day carries numerous scars from this "non satanic" abuse base. I know, from years of research, NASA technology and Aquino's programming, combined with the Project Monarch standard sleep, food, and water deprivation and high voltage, made Kelly a subject of state of the art genetically multigenerational MPD/DID psychological mind control engineering.

In 1981, Byrd personally joined Aquino in Huntsville, Alabama during one of our programming sessions. NASA cooperated fully with Byrd on any and everything, since it was Byrd's Senate Appropriations Committee that determined how much and/or whether NASA received government funding. I lay naked on the cold metal table, tranced and photographically recording every word and detail of my programming and every word that Byrd and Aquino not so privately discussed. Byrd was providing Aquino with specific details of certain perversions he wanted me equipped to fulfill or perform. Additionally, they talked about scrambling my immediate memory with two private porn films they were arranging to have produced locally. These were titled *How To Divide a Personality* and *How To Create a Sex Slave*. These films are the kind NASA became involved in producing for the dual purpose of "scrambling" memory and documenting their mind control procedures. The resident Huntsville, Alabama pornographers were two local cops, one of which was (and is) a Sergeant.[5] This served NASA and the CIA well when cover-up was necessary.

The *How To Create a Sex Slave* film depicts the common "spin" programming, which in essence is the combination to unlocking or accessing a specific programmed act. For example, the compartment of the mind that holds memory of incest is stimulated to open when the original abuse is eminent. Seeing my father's penis would "trigger" a specific response, supposedly opening the neuron pathways of my brain to allow the part of my brain that dealt with his actions before to deal with them again. With "spin" programming, the trigger of seeing my father's penis is replaced with a combination of specific verbal commands and a specific number of physical spins so that anyone with the "combination" could access that particular part of my brain. The part of my mind containing "knowledge" of the original abuse by my father learned to "like" painful, sadistic sex. Senator Byrd wanted me programmed in such a way that he could decide if he wanted me to scream and cry when he whipped me, or if he wanted me to become sexually aroused and "beg" for more. After programming, when I met with Byrd, I would "dance" like a music box dancer, twirling round and round until Byrd's fiddle music stopped. My mind precisely calculated how many revolutions I had made whether I was capable of conscious counting or not (much like a normal person wakes up at a particular time without an alarm clock), and the desired results were produced as accessed.

This is but one simplified example of sex programming, and I was programmed for more than sex. But this particular incident of programming at the U.S. Army Redstone Arsenal would change my existence entirely and set the stage for my role in covert government black budget type operations as a "Presidential Model."

Seeing and/or knowing that Kelly was being tortured and programmed proved to be a detriment to my own mind control programming, such that the common "cross programming" of mother and daughter was rarely viable. In the fall of 1982, Houston was scheduled to perform at the State Fair in Senator Byrd's home state of West Virginia. Byrd arrived at our hotel with Lt. Col. Aquino, who took Kelly with him, supposedly for programming purposes. I was left alone in the hotel room with Byrd, whose KKK affiliation fueled his rage over my having been recently prostituted to black entertainer and CIA operative Charlie Pride. Although I had had no control over the situation to begin with, Byrd expended his fury on me rather than on Houston who was ultimately responsible for the incident. He took out his whip and began beating me as he had so many times before. Only this time, it seemed to last forever.

Byrd was still whipping me when Aquino returned with my tranced and traumatized daughter. I regained consciousness enough to pull myself up off the floor when I heard Kelly's hysterical cries. Byrd ordered me to the bathroom for a cold shower to stop the bleeding. My body could not carry out his orders, and I collapsed again in the bathroom, smearing blood all over the floor. Kelly's cries again revived me, and I crawled to the door to find Byrd sexually assaulting her and Aquino disrobing to join them. One small window in the bathroom appeared to be a possible means of escape to obtain help, but Byrd caught me and knocked me to the floor. The whole bathroom was smeared in blood by the time he threw me into the shower and turned the cold water on to slow the bleeding.

Later that afternoon, Kelly and I stood hand in hand in the afternoon sun at the State Fair where Senator Byrd was about to make a speech to his constituents. My blouse stuck to my freshly whipped skin as Byrd walked onto the stage, and the crowd cheered. Although Byrd periodically sexually abused Kelly throughout her Project Monarch victimization, the horrific incident in West Virginia was the last time I was able to instinctively think to respond at all. Aquino's mind control programming further insured it, as did Byrd's access to high tech mind control equipment via West Virginia's Jesuit College, where he claimed the role of "Head Friar".[6]

Kelly has reported enduring much sexual abuse by both Byrd and Aquino. Aquino apparently incorporated sexual abuse with his mind control programming and sex training of her and shared more such events with Byrd. It was also my experience that Byrd's sexual perversions were heightened when Aquino shared in the assault. Traumatic events such as this one in West Virginia reinforced my own programming through conditioning, and further locked me in to Byrd's seemingly inescapable control.

112

The majority of my programming, as well as a large part of Kelly's, was again Oz theme based. This means the combination of codes, keys and triggers to access me were related to L. Frank Baum's story, *The Wizard of Oz*. Whether or not it was Baum's intention (or for that matter Walt Disney's, Lewis Carol's, etc.), it is evident that his psychologically intense story was used for manipulating minds. Much of *The Wizard of Oz* lends itself to themes commonly used by perpetrators. For example, nearly all MPD/DIDs have suffered the loss of pets during ritualized torture. And all of Baum's primary character Dorothy's nightmarish experiences "over the rainbow in Oz" stemmed from her desire to risk her own life to protect her threatened pet. Abusers use this lesson to condition the victim to drop all resistance and cooperate or "I'll get you, my pretty, and your little dog (or child) too." The "over the rainbow" scramble of dreams vs. reality provides abusers a theme by which to manipulate an MPD's subconscious perception of switching personalities. Oftentimes this theme is transdimensional as is Oz, or that which was just experienced was "just a bad dream" like Dorothy was told upon her awakening in her own bed back in Kansas.

CIA cryptic language is manipulation of the English language such that words have a double meaning (aka 'double binds' in mental health terminology.) It works much the way as communication through "inside jokes", among people familiar with each other. Perhaps this is a reason for the government's use of professional comedians as slave handlers. Since mind controlled slaves' minds function consciously through their subconscious, which has no way of discerning fantasy from reality or intended meaning from literal meaning, cryptic dual level language is especially effective. Many CIA covert operations I was involved in occurred in public. Anyone who overheard the conversation would have discerned something very different from what actually "trance-spired." For example, one of my Washington, D.C. Secret Service escorts linked arms with me like Dorothy did with her companions when walking the Yellow Brick Road. This would have appeared to be normal behavior, or even romantic, to outsiders. But to me it was a signal to "stay the course" (Bush's quote) and follow directions. Arm in arm we walked through the crowded Air and Space Museum of the Smithsonian to the nearby NASA headquarters. There he read the "Service Entrance" sign on the door accentuating syllables ever so slightly so that I heard him cryptically command, "Serve-us, En-Trance".

---

[1] Jimmy Dean is knowledgeable of, and a willing participant in, criminal covert activity including the use of mind-controlled slaves.

[2] "Marching to Missouri" is a Mormon based belief that interfaced with the CIA's faction of the country music industry being transferred to Branson, Missouri in the mid 1980's.

[3] 120,000-volt stun guns leave two indented prod marks or moles two inches apart, while the cylindrical stun gun used primarily in the vagina and rectum leaves prod marks/moles 3/4 of an inch apart. A look into trash-magazine publisher Larry Flint's *Hustler* will show prod marks on the mind controlled slaves he photographs, particularly on the throat, near the lips, and on the back.

[4] The "witch's face" has also been referred to as that of a baphomet and Jesuit monk.

[5] I photo identified the Sergeant and his (jailer) officer in 1990, and Mark's and my lives were threatened through then-District Attorney, now U.S. Representative, Bud Cramer (D. Huntsville, Alabama) of the Congressional Permanent Intelligence Committee as a result of this revelation!

[6] To a literal mind controlled MPD/DID slave, the term "Head Friar" equates to "head fryer," meaning high voltage to the brain.

CHAPTER 7

CHARM SCHOOL

After Aquino instilled my base sex programming, I was often taken by Houston to Youngstown, Ohio to attend the sex slave training camp hell hole referred to as "Charm School." Houston often performed in the Youngstown area at county fairs, Fraternal Order of Police shows, or any little country music entertainment gigs that would bring us in the proximity of the dreaded Charm School. On occasion, Kelly would go through the torture process with me. But usually Houston delivered me to the door for training with other CIA and Mafia slaves my age, and then left taking Kelly with him. When Charm School was in session, there were several girls being tortured and trained at once. I have seen and known numerous girls to go through Charm School, but, understandably, few are reported to have survived or recovered their minds enough to talk about it.

Charm School was reportedly operated by an identified member of the Mellon Banking family (Byrd's endowment for the Arts largest contributor). The operator took the name and role of "Governor" from the movie *My Fair Lady*, in an attempt to confuse my torturous reality with movie fantasy. In the movie, Governor is the cockney title given the professor who transformed a female street urchin into a functioning high society lady. Additionally, Mellon's use of the title Governor was intended to create scramble for the real Governor who frequented the school as though it were only a whore house. I am referring to then Governor of Pennsylvania (and later U.S. Attorney General, now secretary for the United Nations) Dick Thornburgh.[1] Aquino provided some of the programming at Charm School and everyone I knew in government operations was at least aware of it. Then Youngstown Sheriff, now U.S. Representative Jim Traficant, was usually present. He capitalized on his ability to portray himself as "Lurch" by slowly opening the door and saying, "Walk this way." To a literal slave in training, this means walk like he is walking -- like Lurch, Egor, a street whore, Scarecrow, and so on.

Once the door closed behind me, Charm School meant I would be charmed, mesmerized (hypnotized), and programmed to be a high class prostitute for select politicians. I did learn their way to walk. I learned when to talk, how to dress, how to sit, stand, and all the rest. Table manners were not taught as they were not needed since slaves endured food and water deprivation when working. Above all, we were taught how to gratify any sexual perversion. Just as Traficant opened the door to Charm School for slaves, he oftentimes was the one to "test" their newly learned sexual skills to determine when or if slaves could leave.

A typical three-day course at Charm School included the usual factors of sleep, food, and water deprivation; trauma; high voltage; and programming. Often times experimental or tried and proven CIA manufactured "designer" drugs were administered which produced specific brain wave activity to maximize and/or compartmentalize programs. I usually spent the first day hanging in the dungeon. Charm School is housed in an identified stone historical railroad barron's former residence, and the basement was in fact a wine cellar dungeon. It was dark, damp, and musty and was decorated in classic torture chamber fashion. It was complete with various hanging chains, a stretching rack, whips, and alters including one specially designed for bestiality sex. As I hung by my wrists, I could hear and smell the animals in the next cells -- a black Nubian goat called Satan, a small donkey named Nester, sometimes a small white pony referred to as Trigger, and various dogs, cats, snakes, and others. All Charm School animals were trained to sexually respond to the smell of urine. When someone, such as Dick Thornburgh who particularly enjoyed this kind of kink, entered my cell and urinated on me, I knew I would soon be released from my chains and led to the animal alter for bestiality lessons, pornography, or to please a perverse onlooker. I was hung by my ankles, stretched on a rack, burned, and tortured repeatedly. My feet and hands were chained to a wall for what was termed "off the wall sex." I was taught "Silence" in Oz fashion since screaming did not produce results anyway unless they wanted it for pornography. This was implemented with an electronic canine bark collar normally used to train a dog not to bark.

I was repeatedly filmed pornographically, and always taken upstairs to the "Master's Chambers" for prostitution to participants, including the real "Governor" of Charm School, then Pennsylvania Governor Dick Thornburgh, Congressman Jim Traficant,[2] Lt. Col. Michael Aquino, and others. When Kelly was with me, she endured the same and we were forced to see each other physically tortured as further psychological trauma. This was to ensure I could never remember the who, what, when, or where of our bizarre enslavement. This is what is sometimes referred to as cross programming.

In spite of the deliberately created amnesic blocks, I developed a subconscious sympathetic understanding for other Charm School slaves that extended outside the walls of this man made hell. This understanding emanated from the depths of my being, creating a compassion for other mind control victims that compels me to give voice to their silent pleas for help to this day.

I became close friends with one such victim, who must remain anonymous in order to survive to eventually recover. This beautiful blonde and I had numerous opportunities to be together throughout the years, as Houston's government sponsored travels routinely took him into her home state of Pennsylvania while Dick Thornburgh was Governor.

My friend and I were photographed together for Larry Flynt's commercial pornography publications, and featured in the illicit films that contributed to funding CIA covert operations. In addition to this, she and I were able to spend two weeks together when her husband/handler traveled to Houston's farm in Tennessee for instructions on handling his new "bride."

I was "made of honor" for my friend's "wedding," which was no more a marriage than mine to Houston. As was customary with Project Monarch slaves, her marriage to her handler equated to marriage to her mind control owner, U.S. Senator Arlen Spector.

The "wedding" I was forced to participate in was for pornography purposes only, and it took place in Arlen Spector's Conneaut Lake house in Pennsylvania. Spector's stone house was located in a wooded, remote setting and was masculine in decor. Side rooms were either designated for perverse sex or were furnished with antiquated NASA virtual reality and programming equipment. The musty smell of Spector's playhouse was overpowered by the scent of roses, which he symbolically presented to his slave on their "wedding" day.

My friend's "wedding" photos included Catholic themes, and the crucifix featured was rose cut crystal similar to the one I received from Byrd. Regardless of how this girl was depicted, her innate morality was apparent to me. She and I were referred to as "mirror/mere cats," due to the similarity of our victimizations. Like me, she was controlled through manipulation of her religious beliefs and maternal instincts. The delicate rose tattooed on her left wrist signifying her role in government operations did not detract from her high class projection any more than Spector's immorality could mar her innate goodness. Once Arlen Spector officially became this slave's owner, her Charm School status rose to "Presidential Model".

In addition to Charm School, I endured extensive programming to prepare me for future operations. Houston was often booked into Oklahoma fairs, Masonic Lodges, F.O.P. Conventions, and so on, in order that I be back in the vicinity of Tinker Air Force Base for further programming. My Tinker-Belle conditioning further enhanced my photographic memory through direct control for receiving and delivering government messages which amounted to a computerized compartmentalization of my brain, so to speak. I was also trained in covert criminal operations, such as international drug mule transactions for funding the Pentagon's and CIA's Black Ops Budgets.

Houston's CIA orchestrated travels in the country music industry led me to a TOP SECRET military/NASA installation at Offit Air Force Base in Nebraska. The "you can run, but you can't hide"[3] conditioning was deeply ingrained in my mind there through a technique that was later used on Kelly, as well as on other mind control slaves. I was taken underground to a so-called 'secret' circular room where the walls were covered with numerous screens showing satellite pictures from around the world. These satellites are referred to as the "Eye in the Sky." An Air Force official explained to me that my every move "could be monitored via satellite." On a separate four-screen viewer, he demonstrated what in retrospect was a contrived pre-recorded slide show, with the scenes changing as rapidly as he spoke and typed it into the computer.

"Where will you run?" he asked me. "To the Arctic? The Antarctic? Brazil? The mountains? The desert? The prairies? The hills of Afghanistan? The city of Kabul? Devils Tower [Wyoming]? Would you try to run to Cuba and live among our enemies? We can find you there. There is truly no place to run and no place to hide. The U.S. Senate [the picture was of Byrd]? The White House? Or to your own backyard? [My father was depicted waving from his front door, cupping his hands over his mouth saying, "come back" just like Aunt Em in *The Wizard of Oz*.] The moon? We got you covered. You can run, but you can't hide." This had been sufficient to convince me in my suggestible state that my every move could be monitored.

During the course of my training/conditioning, I was routinely prostituted to Senator Byrd in Washington, D.C., at the West Virginia State Fair, NASA in Huntsville, Alabama, and at the Opryland Hotel in Nashville, Tennessee. One such night when I was to be prostituted to Byrd at Opryland Hotel, was scheduled to join him in perversely assaulting me. Much to my horror, Aquino arrived early, in full army dress uniform, backstage at the Grand Ol' Opry. When I saw Aquino talking with the Vatican based Project Monarch slave runner, Kris Kristopherson,[4] whom I had known since 1979, my personality programmed for Opry events "short circuited." Under circumstances such as this, a multiple without programming would have switched personalities autogenically, whereas I could only switch upon command. I backed away, dazed, right into a soft drink machine. Kristopherson saw me as I backed further, between the wall and the machine. "What are you doing in there, little lady?" Kristopherson asked. "The Colonel wants to see you."

Aquino had walked over and sarcastically asked, "What are you doing in those machine wires? That could very well be a shocking experience for you." All experiences with Aquino or Kristopherson resulted in high voltage electric shock torture, and apparently neither had any regard for human life.[5] Aquino used the opportunity to reinforce his belief that I "had no where to run, no where to hide" from his "power" -- his stun gun.

While I untangled myself from the wires, Kristopherson and Aquino continued their banter at my expense. Kristopherson held up his key ring and jingled it, catching my undivided attention as conditioned, while he told Aquino, "You're gonna need the Keys to the Kingdom to work with this one right here."

"Keys to the Kingdom," of course, referred to my previously instilled (Enter/Inter) "Inner-dimensional" Catholic programmed personalities. Since Aquino was my primary mind control programmer at the time, Kristopherson was informing Aquino of programs previously instilled in childhood via the "Rite to Remain Silent." By jingling the keys, he was demonstrating his control over me and his momentary edge on Aquino.

"I got 'em," Kristopherson was saying as he jingled the keys. "She's mine unless you wanna play ball. Besides, you have to. The Byrd sent me."

"I've been expecting you," Aquino said with a smile. Events later that night proved that Aquino had been supplied the keys to my previously established Jesuit based programming, which he and Byrd used and altered to suit their own perversions.

Byrd monitored all of my programming "progress," and often tortured me with his whip and pocket knife. He picked up where my mother left off, to destroy any self-esteem I might have inadvertently developed. He said, "There is no place for you to turn because if you could think to talk no one would ever believe I would have anything to do with the likes of you." He often threatened me that I was considered "disposable" because, after all, "The first Presidential Model, Marilyn Monroe, was killed right in front of the public eye and no one knew what happened."

Byrd's threats and cruelty were unnecessary as I could no longer think to seek help anyway, but he loved to hear himself talk and would often drone on and on and on in his infamous long-winded recitations, while I was photographically recording every word he said. He detailed the inner operational structure of the world domination effort, including psychological warfare strategies, and explained how he had and would utilize his "expert" knowledge of the Constitution to manipulate it and the so-called U.S. Justice System, and more. His loose lips provided me yet another means of surviving and staying a step ahead of "the game" once Kelly and I were rescued from our mind controlled existence.

Senator Byrd revealed his "justifications" for criminal activity to me as well. He used me as a sounding board even though he knew I was incapable of input or response. He rehearsed in keeping with his motto "The only way we can fail, is to fail to think of an excuse."

Byrd "justified" mind control atrocities as a means of thrusting mankind into accelerated evolution, according to the Neo-Nazi principals to which he adhered. He "justified" manipulating mankind's religion to bring about the prophesied biblical "world peace" through the "only means available" -- total mind control in

the New World Order. "After all," he proclaimed, "even the Pope and Mormon Prophet know this is the only way to peace and they cooperate fully with The Project."

Byrd also "justified" my victimization by saying, "You lost your mind anyway, and at least you have destiny and purpose now that it's mine." Our country's involvement in drug distribution, pornography, and white slavery was "justified" as a means of "gaining control of all illegal activities world wide" to fund Black Budget covert activity that would "bring about world peace through world dominance and total control." He adhered to the belief that "95% of the [world's] people WANT to be led by the 5%", and claimed this can be proven because "the 95% DO NOT WANT TO KNOW what really goes on in government." Byrd believed that in order for this world to survive, mankind must take a "giant step in evolution through creating a superior race." To create this "superior race," Byrd believed in the Nazi and KKK principles of "annihilation of underprivileged races and cultures" through genocide, to alter genetics and breed "the more gifted -- the blondes of this world."

As Byrd's captive audience (literally), I absorbed information that the other so-called masterminds behind the New World Order would never have revealed for security reasons. But Byrd regarded me as "his" object, a game-piece that he could strategically move through life as though he were playing a chess game. He perceived me as totally under his control with no possibility of my ever being rescued, surviving, and recovering my mind and memory. Byrd likely would have talked to a post, and I filled the role as his silent sounding board.

My CIA Operative mind control handler Alex Houston was often scheduled to perform at the Swiss Villa Amphitheatre in Lampe, Missouri, which is yet another installation where I was programmed. Swiss Villa was a cover for a CIA Near Death Trauma Center of which there are several across the country. It is a remote, high security resort, enclosed with military barbed wire fences, that swings its guarded gate open to the local public for country music concerts. The small Amphitheatre covers the covert activities occurring inside, which includes U.S. Government CIA cocaine and heroin distribution operations and mind control projects.

Swiss Villa, like the Mount Shasta, California compound, was also used as a training and operations camp for the Shadow Government's paramilitary projects referred to by Senator Inouye (D. HI). I learned that this not-so-secret military buildup, sanctioned by corrupt members of our government, consisted of special forces trained robotic soldiers, numerous black unmarked helicopters, and the highest technological advancements in TOP SECRET weaponry and "Star Wars" electromagnetic mind control equipment. These paramilitary compounds were intended for global policing of the New World Order through the Multi-Jurisdictional Police Force.

"A Most Dangerous Game" was often played at Swiss Villa and involved CIA agents, politicians, and others who would attend the resort just for the sport of hunting humans. Kelly and I both were hunted at Swiss Villa. The tortures and rape after being caught were extensive and sufficiently traumatized our minds for ensuing programming, as well as for creating memory compartmentalization for the high level operations we witnessed behind the villa's patrolled fences. It was at Swiss Villa that I was taught "THE "Most Dangerous Game" was one where a slave tried to escape and reveal what he or she had learned. If the hunters could not catch and stop the slave, then the black helicopters patrolling the area would. And if all else failed, the "Eye in the Sky" would locate him or her, and a torturous death was supposedly imminent.

According to my abusers, my deprogrammer and primary advocate Mark Phillips and I have embarked on "THE Most Dangerous Game" through efforts such as releasing this book and turning a spotlight on the Shadow Government to reveal its members' identities and their crimes against humanity. Mark Phillips and I are determined to beat them at their own "game" by arming the "95%" with the truth that perpetrators "don't want them to know!"

---

[1] Dick Thornburgh is listed in Houston's CIA memo book, which is now in my (and others') possession.

[2] Please note that, while still Sheriff of Youngstown, Ohio, Traficant was investigated and subsequently indicted for federal racketeering, drug distribution, and Mafia connections. However, he was acquitted through careful CIA jury manipulation and he went on to become the U.S. Representative he is to this date.

[3] Once gaining "eyes to see and ears to hear," this "you can run, but you can't hide" theme is so widely used it is visible from Hallmark greeting cards to Interstate overpasses to the lock-in song by the rock group Police "I'll Be Watching You."

[4] A good friend of mine who remains a victim to date was "married" to Kristopherson on the night she wed her mind control handler -- much the way I had "married" Byrd when I wed Houston. The crucifix used in her Larry Flynt "wedding night" porn photos was mirrored rather than crystal.

[5] Kristopherson nearly strangled me to death with his penis, which had further sexually excited him, late in the summer of 1987 during another incident related to Byrd.

CHAPTER 8

CIA'S WAR ON DRUGS OPERATION: ELIMINATING COMPETITION

I no longer had any mind of my own. I was absolutely void of free will and was now totally robotic. So was Kelly. We wore our Charm School smile at all times, and did exactly what we were told to do. The only characteristic noticeably out of place was Kelly's age-inappropriate programmed vocabulary and mannerisms. Outsiders attributed this to her traveling within the country music industry. My public image was a programmed personality that always smiled, looked and talked like the proverbial "air-head" blonde that kept outsiders away by socializing only within my controlled environment. This lifestyle appeared quite normal for my role as Houston's much younger "wife" in the country music industry.

When we were not traveling, I began each day at 4:00 A.M. with a minimum of 2 hours aerobic exercise. Afterward, I tended farm animals and did other chores, then cooked Houston a large country breakfast which neither Kelly or I were permitted to share. Houston would then order me to work to exhaustion on his 100-acre farm while he watched. These chores included hauling, stacking, and feeding out hundreds of bales of hay to our livestock each year; maintaining miles of electric fencing; cutting acres of grass with a push mower an average of twice weekly; busting concrete with a sledge hammer and mixing and pouring new cement; digging by hand and maintaining a two acre vegetable garden for canning; cutting, hauling, and stacking firewood for Houston, his neighbors, and friends; shoveling pick-up truck loads of creek gravel to fill in enormous potholes in the gravel road leading to 11 rural residences including Jack Greene's; and anything else Houston could think of that would wear me down. Houston's exhaustive, slave-driving work orders made my father's seem benevolent in comparison. The "best" of days were rough.

I ate "like a bird [Byrd]," following Byrd's orders of 300 calories per day -- with no sugar or caffeine. My metabolism was low. I was trained to compute calories like a machine, eating more like a rabbit than a "bird." I had to count every calorie, from a simple taste of what I had to cook for Houston to semen. Houston ensured that Kelly and I never got more than two consecutive hours of sleep per night. He accomplished this through automatic mental "alarm clocks" that woke us up at two- hour intervals -- Kelly with asthma, and me with panic. These tactics contributed to Kelly's and my total inability to resist mind control.

Traveling in the country music industry was no easier than existing on Houston's farm in Tennessee. It certainly lacked the glamour that outsiders usually associate with entertainment industries. CIA covert drug operations had permeated the industry. Entertainers were used to buy, sell, and distribute cocaine brought into this country by the U.S. government for the purpose of funding the Pentagon's and CIA's Black Budgets. Nashville's local government, from my perspective, was totally corrupted by these criminal covert operations. Cover-up, murder, drugs, and white slavery prevailed. Entertainers usually made it big only when they participated in CIA operations and/or were slaves themselves. I know of numerous entertainers in need of rescue and deprogramming from their mind controlled existence, because it was discovered that voices could be harmonically tuned through mind control to captivate audiences. To quote my father, "Spies, like singers and actors, are made, not born." These entertainers have endured much of the same programming as I to permit them to carry out government operations in the course of their travels. Norwegian Caribbean Lines (NCL) cruise ships depart regularly from Miami, Florida and travel throughout the Caribbean and Mexico. NCL provides pleasure cruises to the public complete with "entertainment" like that of Alex Houston while carrying out CIA operations. Sue Carper, former director of entertainment procurement for all NCL cruise ships, would ensure that government covert activities staging were properly orchestrated. She rotated entertainers like Houston from ship to ship in order to avoid the scrutiny of clean U.S. Customs and Immigrations inspectors. I routinely took cruises with Houston, muling cocaine and/or heroin out of Haiti, the Bahamas, Mexico, the Virgin Islands, and Puerto Rico to fund covert operations. While I was robotically carrying out transactions as ordered, I was also prostituted to South and Central American drug lords and politicians, as well as filmed pornographically. Houston made sure I was in the right place at the right time and switched me into the proper mode for each activity I was forced to carry out. In the early 1980's, this included passing messages to and from Senator Byrd, Baby Doc Duvalier, my Cuban contact, Puerto Rican drug lord José Busto, and others.

In keeping with NCL's Caribbean operations, Byrd adjusted his use of programming themes to include the mirror-reversal, interdimensional, Air-Water mind control theme used on me by NASA and the Jesuits. I often saw dolphins playing in the ocean while being transported from port to port via the cruise ships, but the popular "whales and dolphins" mind control theme was avoided in favor of a theme more suitable to my experience; that of the Sea- Bird -- Robert C. (Sea) Byrd. He told me, "Atlantis[1] has long been the epicenter of alien activity. The path is so well worn that there are holes in the fabric of time and space whereby airplanes and ships, even people, timelessly seemingly disappear, transformed into another dimension alien to this world. Likewise, we (aliens) came in, entering through the mirror reflection of the hole in the fabric of space, the deep blue sea. Some of us entered earth's plane as whales and dolphins. And when we emerged from the sea, some of us came flying out. Or is that in? At any rate, we are here. Watch for the flying fish when you are out to see/sea. When you see one, you will know it is kin to me. A flying fish by any other name is a C. Byrd. A sea bird. Robert C. Byrd."

The drug business was booming for the CIA, and the only "War on Drugs" I witnessed was that launched by the CIA against its competition. As quickly as I brought the NCL suitcases of drugs into the Port of Miami, they were usually transferred to Houston's factory custom built Holiday Rambler motor home. Concealed compartments were built into the walls for hiding the illegal drugs. If I drove the drug-filled motor home on to Nashville rather than deposit the drugs enroute at Warner-Robbins Air Force Base in Macon, Georgia, the bulk was stored in the Hendersonville Mormon "food storage" Bishop's Warehouse. Some cocaine was delivered to a music distributor in Nashville, Tennessee, where it was carefully packaged in participating entertainers' cassettes, for delivery along their carefully scheduled travel routes. Houston always kept a large amount of the cocaine for his own use and distribution. Oftentimes he ordered that I deliver the drugs to specific entertainers at the Grand Ole Opry and/or at the local shopping mall when we were not traveling. Most often, however, the larger loads of drugs remained concealed in the motor home for distribution to CIA drug drops while we traveled the country music industry. These CIA drug drops included an abandoned amusement park near Youngstown, Ohio; Diamond Caverns[2] campground in Park City, Kentucky; and Swiss Villa Amphitheatre in Lampe, Missouri. I was aware that tons of drugs were being handled via our military, but the hundreds of pounds I muled were targeted for exclusive private distribution.

An example of a typical Caribbean drug operation centered around the NCL port of call, Key West, Florida. Houston took Kelly and me to a nearby tennis court under the guise of playing tennis. In reality, I was to meet with CIA Operative Jimmy Buffett, who devoted more time to the proliferation of CIA criminal covert activity than he did to his music career cover. Buffett was playing tennis. Referring to him as though he were to be my tennis instructor, Houston said, "There's your instructor. As soon as he gathers the balls, he should be over here to meet you."

Noticing us, Buffett strode over and shook hands with Houston. "Hi, Jimmy," Houston said as though they were old buddies.

"Hi, Alex and Elemer," Buffett responded, sarcastically using Houston's stage name.

"Oh," Houston said. Never one to know an insult when he heard it, he continued, "What do your friends call you?"

"What does it matter to you?" Buffett asked. "Uncle calls me Jim. I take it you're not the contact."

Houston pointed to me. "She is."

"That's more like it," Buffett smiled. "A little Byrd told me I'd be meeting with a Diamond in the Rough."[3]

"I prefer a Diamond in the Buff," he said. "I've got a studio across the street."

As we walked toward his studio, I was oblivious to the meaning behind his conversation with Houston and commented, "I understand you're an instructor. I wish I had brought my racquet."

"I'm not that kind of an instructor," Buffett explained. "I'm a point man for Uncle. And you've got an appointment with me. I have some instructions to give you." As we entered his studio, he said, "Welcome to paradise," and gestured me in. We went into the small living quarters, which may have appeared even smaller due to the electronic equipment, acoustic guitars, and furniture that filled the room. A black mirrored coffee table, atypical of cocaine users I'd known, was the clearest spot in the room. A gold razor blade, cocaine residue, an ashtray full of marijuana roaches, and a fanned deck of card with the queen of hearts on top lay on the table. Tropical plants further cluttered the room. Standing between a perched, stuffed parrot and a banana tree, Buffett was saying, "Key West is a key place to be. It's the key to the Caribbean -- Cuba, Panama -- anyplace that means anything to Uncle these days. I hold the keys. I'm keeper of the keys and I hold a few of yours." Looking at his parrot, he continued, "The bird/Byrd says you respond to pair-o- dice, look deep into the parrot eyes."

I did as instructed, and Buffett popped out the bird's ruby red eyes, which actually were dice, into his hand. "Roll your eyes high while I roll my pair-o- dice," he ordered as he rolled the dice across the table. Stopping at the deck of cards, he picked up the jack of diamonds. "I am a jack of all trades," he cryptically continued. "And I trade in whatever Uncle orders. An order has been placed. You must follow orders and go to that place. Go to the White House Inn at the pier. Carry your laundry bag (full of cash) with you, and see the man in black. (My Cuban contact almost always wore a conspicuous black trench coat.) There is a laundromat on the dock itself.

They do all my laundering for me, and will be expecting you. Watch for the sea-man with the duffel bag. When you see the military green duffel bag, approach the desk. When he says, "I need this laundered, but I do not have the time," you say, "Welcome to Paradise. I will make sure it is cleaned and delivered on time." Then give him your duffel bag of 'laundry' and say, "This has been properly laundered for you." Take the duffel bag. It will be light as a feather. Return to the Inn and enjoy the buffet."

Changing modes, Buffett unzipped his shorts as he asked, "Do you like a buffet? I have a Buffett buffet for you now. And it is Paradise!"

I carried out the drug transaction as ordered, the whole ordeal lasting a matter of minutes. A buffet was spread in the courtyard of the White House Inn at 4:00 PM just as Buffett said it would be. But due to the food and water deprivation necessary to maintaining my mind controlled trance, Houston forbid me from carrying out this last part of Buffett's instructions.

Alex Houston Enterprises was another side business that Houston used to cover for his CIA criminal covert activities. It included the relabelling of G.E. capacitors for the "energy savings" companies, Queen Electric and Phase Liner, he shared with his former wife and first CIA mind controlled slave. She was a Catholic processed Puerto Rican blonde beauty. These G.E. capacitor banks were sold internationally as energy saving devices, when in fact they provided one more means of transporting drugs from the U.S. around the world.

It was Houston's G.E. capacitor scam that provided me insight into the elaborate Long Island docks drug network run by U.S. Congressman Gary Ackerman (D. NY).[4] I first met Ackerman in 1981 when Houston was booked into the Woodberry Music Festival with known CIA mind control victim Loretta Lynn.[5] Loretta's road manager, Neo-Nazi pedophile Ken Riley, who was also Alex Houston's best friend, often assisted Houston in handling me. Riley in turn handed my Charm School programmed keys, codes, and triggers to Congressman Ackerman, who skillfully accessed my *Alice in Wonderland* mirror theme programming. After snorting a couple of lines of coke, he stepped into the center of a three way mirror where he positioned me and proceeded to sexually gratify himself in my throat. Ken Riley, and other involved members of Loretta's band, all laughed as Ackerman stumbled around the room while pulling his pants up from around his ankles and complaining that he "couldn't stand for sex like that." The term "Ackerman Syndrome" was coined after that in reference to sex that drained a man of his energy, and circulated among "those who know" for years.

[1] NCL cruise ships routinely pass through the so called "Bermuda Triangle," and Byrd did not miss this opportunity to tap into old programming base installed by Senator J. Bennett Johnston.

[2] When Mark and I turned in detailed information on this drug drop to law enforcement, our lives were endangered to the point that a foreign Intelligence officer intervened and subsequently saved our lives through a timely tip off.

[3] "Diamond in the Rough" was a term used to describe an MPD/DID slave actively engaged in programming via torture conditioning.

[4] Congressman Ackerman's Caribbean cocaine and Asian heroin operations have not hindered his position on the Congressional Post Office and Civil Service Committees, nor the Asian and Pacific Affairs Committee. It is important to note that, as a matter of Congressional record, Ackerman openly opposed compulsory drug tests for all federal employees.

[5] Senator Byrd proudly claimed Loretta as his mind controlled slave and told me, "I literally made Loretta what she is today, and she is maid to order." Loretta's son and secondary mind control handler, Ernest Ray, told me, "I know what the Byrd did to my mother. I can get away with murder All I gotta do is call him and I'm free as a bird/Byrd."

CHAPTER 9

RONALD REAGAN'S AMERICAN DREAM:
A PANDORA'S BOX OF NIGHTMARES

My mind controlled existence became more complicated after Senator Byrd introduced me to then President Ronald Reagan in the fall of 1982[1] at a White House political party. Byrd told me, "When you meet the Chief, imagine him with his pants down. He's most comfortable knowing you are imagining him with his pants down. He doesn't want formality." Former president Ford had conditioned me to dread the Office of President, and I mechanically went through the motions of meeting Reagan.

Reagan admittedly had seen the *How To Divide a Personality* and *How to Create a Sex Slave* videos made in Huntsville, Alabama. He acted very pleased with me as though I had participated in them willingly. Within the first few minutes of meeting Reagan, he was giving me acting tips to utilize in government operations and pornography!! "When you become your part, your performance increases, which in turn increases your ability to do your part -- for your country. 'Ask not what your country can do for you, Ask what you can do for your country' -- your part," he instructed. Somehow, Reagan's reminder of Ford's and VanderJagt's conditioning to Kennedy's quote seemed more patriotically significant that "simply" sexually entertaining politicians by waving a flag in my bottom. After gazing deep into his self professed "kaleidoscope eyes," each metaphorical phrase he spoke became life and breath to me.

Reagan explained to me that the illegal CIA covert activities I was forced to participate in were "justified" as they funded covert activities in Afghanistan and Nicaragua. He explained, "America's Freedom Train is spanning the globe and sex is but a sidetrack to the ultimate course of freedom. Our job of procuring and transporting arms is the most difficult part of all. But it can and must be done. How can a man with no arms fight? These operations are necessary as American people raise too much hell about violence already, and it is better they're not informed of our supporting wars they cannot understand the significance of."

I realize now that Reagan twisted reality to fit his personal perceptions rather than to adhere to Byrd's philosophy of providing "excuses" for what he deemed "the order of things." In typical Reagan fashion, he did not perceive mind control as slavery, but as "an opportunity for those who otherwise would have nothing in life." He claimed that multigenerational incestuously abused children like myself, or "previously impoverished baseball players from third world countries and slums, are provided an opportunity to 'be all they can be' through making a 'contra-bution' to society, our nation, and the world, by utilizing their talents to maximum potential." With this attitude, Reagan displayed pride in the sick role he played as *The Wizard of Oz*, directing Project Monarch slaves like myself.

That night, Senator Byrd acted in the capacity of a pimp and prostituted me to Reagan. Referring to me as though I were a machine, Reagan asked Byrd, "Does she run on chemicals?" meaning specific CIA drugs.

Byrd answered, "She takes it in spurts." I noticed that Reagan's eyes lit up with perversion and understanding of Byrd's statement, which meant that I "shared" whatever drugs were in his system through his urine.

Reagan later told me he preferred sex slaves equipped for this task since he, as President, should not have to get up in the night to urinate.

"Well," Reagan said, holding up his glass, "All I've had to fuel her with is alcohol. That's not much of a jolt from a 'whiz of a Wiz[ard]." Byrd chuckled at Reagan's Oz cryptic joke and removed his gold cocaine vial from the inner pocket of his suit. He and Reagan discretely turned their backs to the party while Byrd "spoon fed" Reagan the drug up his nose.

Before I left with Reagan, Byrd informed me that "Uncle Ronnie doesn't sleep with his mommy [Nancy]," and that he preferred snuggling into his LL Bean light blue flannel sheets in his nightshirt and ridiculous nightcap because "they're warmer, softer, more comfortable, and don't snore."

Later, in his bedroom, Reagan accessed my sexual programming, and I became "my part" as a prostitute to "Uncle Ronnie." Reagan did not move during sex. After all, that was "my duty." And my duty was to please him, whatever it took, and it took more time than anything. Reagan never hurt me (he always made sure someone else did that) and used this as a "bond" to the little child ("Kitten") personality he always accessed for sex. Reagan's most apparent personality kink was his love for bestiality pornography.[2] According to my handlers, his passion for pornography escalated its manufacture and distribution during his administration. He wholeheartedly approved and encouraged the porn industry for funding covert activity.

Many commercial and instructional (private) pornography films I and others participated in, referred to as "Uncle Ronnie's Bedtime Stories," were manufactured solely for his pleasure -- oftentimes according to his instruction, using Freedom Train slaves. After my initial meeting with Reagan, I was used in numerous films that were produced predominantly at Youngstown Charm School and/or by his "Chief Pornographer"[3] Michael Danté, specifically to satisfy his perversions. These included a wide range of cryptic themes, but were mostly bestiality. Reagan often watched the videos while I was prostituted to him, requiring me to re-enact the porn however possible.

I first met Reagan's Chief Pornographer Michael Danté, AKA Michael Viti, at an elite Nashville hotel where he was attending "charity" Golf Tournament festivities. Like CIA Operative Charlie Pride's Pro-Am Golf Tournament in Albuquerque, New Mexico, this "charity" tournament provided a cover for the cocaine and white slavery operations that dominated the event. Houston and I often attended such "charity" events, as did Danté, but it was only after having met Reagan that Danté's and my paths crossed as arranged.

Dante' took me to his hotel room after our initial introduction. He snorted a few lines of coke, looked me over as though I were merchandise, and accessed my sex programming. He then arrogantly asked me if I knew who he was. He told me he lived in Beverly Hills, California and made movies. I thought he was referring to his box office flop *Winterhawk* until he said, "Uncle Ronnie sent me. He wants me to make movies with you as your 'contra-bution.' We're gonna have a good time, then he's gonna have a good time, and everybody's happy. You'll like that, won't you Baby? Get dressed. We're going back downstairs and make arrangements."

Danté telephoned me often, professing "our love" through command reinforcements and making arrangements to meet me in specific places for producing Uncle Ronnie's Bedtime Stories and commercial porn. These locations included, among others, Tennessee, Florida, the Caribbean, and

California. He often talked of owning me in the future, painting a picture of what life would be like living with him. His attitude toward women was atypical of slave owners and handlers, and he often quoted scripture to justify his dominance. "No arguments," "speak only when spoken to," "take a good beating now and then just to keep you in line," "see to all my comforts and housework," and "be on call 24 hours a day when I need a good whore." He gave me a slave bracelet -- a trademark of his porn -- and said, "A woman needs a chain. It's a public reminder of total commitment and devotion. A reminder of the chain-of-command. A woman is tied to her man. No man should be tied to a woman."

Danté's Connecticut Italian roots are in the Mafia, and it was a well-established fact that organized crime and government had a close working relationship where criminal covert activities were concerned. I met many of Danté's associates, and we already shared a few common contacts who were conduits between the Mafia and CIA. These included Congressman Guy VanderJagt, former President Gerald Ford, then Governor of Pennsylvania Dick Thornburgh, Congressman Jim Traficant, Congressman Gary Ackerman, and Ronald Reagan.'

Danté related to me, "When Reagan was Governor [of California], we went to Dodger [baseball] games together and sat in the Press Box. I got to know him real well and we got along. So, he and Tommy [LaSorda, Dodger manager and their mutual friend] and I would continue partying after the game. I brought him a few girls (slaves) and we did business. Really, Tommy LaSorda brought us together -- you'll like him. I'll take you to meet him. We'll go to games together all the time, every chance we get. You'll love that, won't you Baby? You like a Press Box, Baby? Dick says you do."

I wasn't surprised that Dick Thornburgh had talked about his previous, perverse sexual activity with me at a baseball game back east any more than I was surprised to learn that Danté knew Thornburgh through their mutual political and baseball ties.

Dick Thornburgh was Governor of Pennsylvania during my tenure as a Presidential Model mind-controlled slave. He used his influence to bring Houston into Pennsylvania state and county fairs year after year for the purposes of cocaine and pornography distribution, as well as for prostitution of me to him on a regular basis. Thornburgh was a heavy cocaine user, and was deeply involved in CIA covert activities -- particularly Project Monarch. He was a firm believer in mind control, not only for sex training and government operations, but for sports. An avid baseball fan, Thornburgh had much to share with Reagan, Danté, and LaSorda.

I had been giving Handwriting Analysis lectures on NCL's Norway cruise ship (my cover for covert operations) in 1987, and Thornburgh and his friend Chicago Cubs Baseball Scout Jim Zerilla were in attendance. Afterward, Zerilla offered me a job with the Baseball Commission analyzing handwriting of their "million dollar babies" baseball players before they were signed up. Thornburgh explained that the job may not fit into my schedule. Nevertheless, we met on several occasions during the course of the cruise, always for sex, but business was discussed as well.

My programmed mind contained a "baseball computer" that was created for Reagan, and used by many including Thornburgh, LaSorda, Danté, and Zerilla. It was packed with the kinds of statistics in which they were interested; the codes, keys, triggers and hand signals of certain mind controlled baseball players. Zerilla and Thornburgh were cruising en route to the Dominican Republic to the CIA baseball mind control farm to scout

127

out new slaves. They talked excitedly about the prospect of winning large sums of money through gambling on rigged games. I had been aware for years that many pro players, particularly LaSorda's Dodgers, were mind-controlled and triggered to win or lose according to their owners' bets and favors. The Dodgers, Reagan's "favorite American pastime" ball team continuously won the World Series during his Administration. The Mafia was in on the bet rigging, and information was passed to certain ones through Thornburgh and others as gleaned from my "baseball computer" programming.[4]

To this day I am not certain who instigated the plastic surgery to which I was forcibly subjected, but soon after meeting Reagan and Danté I was scheduled for breast implants. Perhaps it was done for pornography. Perhaps it was Reagan's preference. I tend to believe it was a combination of the two and ordered since my breasts were no longer lactating. In the first commercial porn film Reagan had directed Danté to produce in St. Thomas, U.S. Virgin Islands my breasts were still tender and swollen from silicone implant surgery.

My appearance was not the only "make over" I endured after meeting Reagan. Aquino and I were called to Washington, D.C. to revise my base core programming to override Senator Byrd's control for security reasons. Since Reagan had been shot, he took extra precautions to ensure his safety which included directing Aquino as to how he wanted me programmed. Much to Aquino's dismay and embarrassment, Reagan admired the occult role that this Army Lt. Colonel played for mind-control traumatization purposes, as it fit in with the public promotion of religion Reagan had launched. Reagan claimed to believe that the masses were easiest to manipulate through their religion, as were mind-controlled slaves like myself.

While Reagan had Aquino in D.C., he demanded that he wear his black ritual robes to a White House party to reinforce the controlling superstitions of a few South/Central American diplomats. Aquino appeared foolish in the eyes of his peers. They knew Aquino's image was only a guise for Psychological Warfare, but his appearance at the White House in costume made Aquino look like he believed his own facade. Aquino got even with Reagan. Minutes before I was prostituted to Reagan that evening, Aquino ordered me into a closed side room where he very quickly had intercourse with me. When he finished ejaculating, he slapped me on the behind and disrespectfully said, "Take that to the Chief."

Earlier that day, Reagan instructed Aquino how to program me in keeping with "spin" programming depicted in the "How to" videos. "Program it," Reagan said, referring to me as though I were an object, "under number one. I like the number one. Its the first, the best, and it promotes confidence -- like 'I've won'." I observed Aquino giving him the intellectually disgusted look he reserved for anyone with the fortitude to make a suggestion to him, but tempered his reaction by giving some thought to the request. Since the "How to" videos showed the 6th revolution to "ignite the heat of hell" for sex, no one would suspect I had sex programming under the first revolution. It would take some modification of my initial programming, but Aquino was sold on the idea. By programming me according to Reagan's instruction, Aquino would be able to provide added protection for Reagan whereby any program I was under at the time would immediately become replaced by Reagan's number one as quickly as I saw him. This effective safety measure infuriated Byrd the first time he saw me instantaneously switch out of his control in Reagan's presence.

Additionally, Reagan discussed how Aquino could use me on various military and government installations to provide "Hands-On Mind-Control Demonstrations" of the "latest advancements in training" by displaying the diversity of my "Presidential Model" programming. Reagan said the Hands-On Demonstrations could "educate our boys in the military to the wonders of the mind control phenomena." "Hands-On" meant my sex programming would be used to "peak their interests and lock (bond) them in." After all, "entertaining the troops is a long time American tradition." Aquino did the programming, and Reagan began making arrangements for the demonstrations -- which brought me back around to Dick Cheney. Cheney would be acting in the capacity of my "Commander" for the Hands-On Mind-Control Demonstrations and other covert operations from then on.

[1] Since I had no concept of time under mind control, the '80s seemed like one long day to me, whereby discerning exact dates is extremely difficult. Furthermore, I was programmed to believe that every encounter with certain individuals was "the first time." I do know that I had been conditioned and programmed in preparation for Reagan since 1978 at NASA's Cape Canavaral in Titusville, Florida.

[2] Reagan preferred illicit pornography videos such as bestiality, while his favorite pornographic magazine was Larry Flynt's Hustler.

[3] Although Hollywood's Dante' rivaled Larry Flynt for the title of "Chief Pornographer" producing video versions of Hustler's stills, Flynt was unequivocally the official White House Pornographer. Dante's covert filming of political perversion for blackmail purposes failed to gain him the international notoriety Flynt maintained through his New World Order colleagues such as Presidents Reagan, Bush, and Ford; CIA Director Bill Casey; U.N. Ambassador Madeleine Albright; Senators Byrd and Spector; Congressmen Trafficant and VanderJagt; Governors Thornburgh, Blanchard, and Alexander; and various World Leaders such as Prime Minister of Canada Mulroney, President of Mexico de la Madrid, and Saudi Arabian King Fahd... to name a few.

[4] Having been out of circulation since my rescue did not preclude my ability to "predict" winners according to political favors: from George Bush, Jr's Texas Rangers to the Toronto Blue Jays' victory during the Canadian political heat of NAFTA.

CHAPTER 10

"COMMANDER" DICK CHENEY & REAGAN'S
"HANDS ON MIND CONTROL DEMONSTRATIONS"

Please note: In order to maintain the integrity of documenting my experiences using precise and photographic detail, I have recorded events and quotes as they occurred in reality. Please excuse any offensive and foul language, but this is the way Cheney presented himself.

I was attending another White House cocktail party where, as usual, I was taken aside for a meeting and escorted to a large office. There, Reagan and Cheney were having their "before cocktail party" cognacs, and Reagan's cheeks were already flushed. He was in a hurry and quickly explained the purpose of the meeting.

"You're the kind of girl who could hold a man in line. [He was cryptically referring to the lines of military personnel I was forced to have sex with.] That's why I've selected you to tour a few Air Force Bases with the Colonel [Aquino] and demonstrate for our boys in the service what a Presidential Model is trained for, a kind of "hands on" demonstration. But you'll have to audition for the role." Reagan drained his glass and gestured toward Cheney as he strode for the door, adding, "Do what he says. He's your commander."

It had been eight years since I had been hunted and brutalized by Cheney in Wyoming, and apparently, he wanted to see how my programming had progressed before agreeing to use me in Reagan's "Hands-On Mind-Control Demonstrations." He grabbed me roughly by the hair and slung me onto a black leather chair, tipping my head backwards over the high studded arm. "Audition here," he snarled. Since I last saw him, I had undergone Wizard of Oz Tin Man programming, which he accessed to accommodate his large, thick penis. He placed his hands on my jaw while he said, "Soon we'll have you purring like a well oiled machine. All of your moving parts are pivotal and gliding with ease. Melt into my hands. I'll hold your jaw to keep it from slipping while you slip through a window in time." He then jerked my jaw out of joint, and roughly gratified himself in my throat.[1]

As he lit his cigarette, I slowly regained focus enough to realize I was in pain. The back of my head hurt from being thrust into the studs on the chair, and I slowly lifted my head. My owner, Senator Byrd, had just walked in and realized Cheney had already completed the "audition." Referring to compartmentalizing my memory via stun gun high voltage, Byrd asked, "Did you fry her?"

Cheney, 'cocksure' of himself as always, answered, "She can't have fucked all of Washington" (indicating that no one would believe me anyway, even if I did reach this point and talk). Cheney put out his cigarette and said as he went out the door, "She'll work. Tell Ronnie she'll work."

When Byrd saw that my lips were bleeding, he called Cheney a "son of a bitch" under his breath, as this damage would prevent my fulfilling other assignments that were planned for me. Byrd touched his finger to my swollen lips and tasted the blood (and Cheney) several times. Then he slapped me hard across the face, which re-aligned my jaw but caused more blood to flow down my chin. He took a box of tissues from the desk and threw it at me, the corner hitting me in the forehead. "Wipe yourself up. You're just getting started. I'll see to it you get what

130

you've got coming to you."

Fortunately for me, Byrd had cause to return to the formal cocktail party and did not have time to brutalize me further. My face was battered, mouth torn, and my throat felt torn and stretched. I had difficulty swallowing for some time, and could not speak. I certainly was in no condition to return to the cocktail party, and was escorted out by agents/guards.

Before I could leave Washington, Byrd made good on his threat and arranged for me to meet with Cheney in a blue bedroom in a part of the White House so remote that "no one could hear my screams and moans." But Cheney implemented Oz theme "Silence" conditioning anyway as he proceeded to brutally sexually assault me.

"Byrd tells me you need a good whipping. But I'm not certain which instrument you prefer, so I brought them all." Cheney had a riding crop, a whip, and a cat-o-nine-tails laid out on the bed. He beat me quick and hard as though he were releasing his tensions rather than savoring my pain like Byrd did. I regained consciousness when Cheney slid a pillow under my neck, steered me by the hair, and bent my head back. Survival instinct kicked in when he positioned himself above my head. I hoped to satisfy him before he became deadly brutal again. But he quickly pulled out his liquid cocaine sprayer, sprayed my throat, then proceeded to get rough. At one point he yanked my head aside and asked, "Was that a tooth?" and grinned. It was imperative that I kept my teeth off him because, according to Aquino's programming instruction, I was subject to death if a tooth was ever felt by anyone. Cheney knew this was my programming and manipulated me with it often. I resumed "satisfying him as though my life depended upon it, because, of course, it did." This is another Aquino programming line Cheney knew and used. When he was gratified, he flopped over and slept. I had been instructed to leave immediately because Cheney absolutely did not want me near him when he slept (some insiders say he is paranoid), and I began dressing. I was escorted out.

In preparation for "running bases" for Reagan's Hands-On Mind-Control Demonstrations, I underwent a great deal of programming by both Aquino and Cheney. Cheney laid the ground rules while Aquino carried out the programming detail and performed the demonstration with me on various military and NASA installations.

Reagan wanted the demonstrations to include all programming depicted in the "How to" films, additional programming instilled since the videos were made, delivery of drugs when applicable, and sex according to Aquino's instruction with whomever/however many were present at the lecture. Cheney's personal "touch" to the demonstrations was to have me programmed to vaginally internally electric prod myself with a high voltage cylindrical cattle prod -- truly an example of total mind control.

I was routinely escorted arm-in-arm "Oz style" by two agents to Cheney's downstairs office in the Pentagon. Sometimes Byrd took me in. Other times Cheney walked me through the building, particularly if we were going to his "Bunkhouse" personal quarters. Cheney's office was equipped with black leather furniture, a huge messy brown desk, massive book shelves, and an hour glass that he always used in keeping with Oz programming, to assure me that my life was on the line under his command. As a programmed MPD, I had no concept of time. The hour glass was a visible way for me to see "my time running out" and actually grasp the concept.

The first time I reported in, Cheney shuffled through the clutter on his desk, picked up a paper and began reading:

"Number one. I am NOT your friend, and I don't want to see you unless I order you to report in. Number two. Follow the Colonel's [Aquino] orders, as it is the chain of command. What he orders you to do, is a command from me. Follow it to the letter, as though your life depends upon it, because [he looked up and grinned wickedly] of course, it does." His cold eyes bore into mine as he walked around to the front of his desk. "Any questions?"

I knew he "was NOT my friend," but he already "saw me" sexually on other occasions. I was perplexed and hesitated. Even though I remained silent, Cheney sensed my hesitation and became enraged. He got up in my face, poked my breast bone with his finger and roared, "Don't even THINK to question anything I say! There is no question as to what I do, what I think, or what I say, because I am absolutely above questions -- especially YOURS!! Your orders are clear. Now get out of here! I have work to do!"

Throughout the next three years, U.S. Army Lt. Colonel Aquino used me in the Hands-On Demonstrations on numerous Army, Navy, Air Force, and NASA installations across the U.S. according to Reagan's plan and Cheney's orders. The Top Brass privy to the demonstrations ranged from three at a time to roughly twenty. In closing, Aquino always "persuaded" them to line up while I was forced to perform sexually on command with each one. The larger groups were physically painful, while the smaller groups often involved unapproved variance from the routine, such as revealing Reagan's bestiality perversions. The wide array of "switching" my personalities that Aquino incorporated into the demonstrations, and the vast amount of high voltage and torture to which I was subjected, left me exhausted and physically devastated for days after each one of Reagan's Hands-On Mind-Control Demonstrations.

---

[1] My jaw is permanently damaged from Cheney. I have chronic TMJ.

132

CHAPTER 11

"POPPA" PHILIP HABIB

My (CIA operative) handler Alex Houston was scheduled to perform with country music entertainer Loretta Lynn at the Playboy Club in Atlantic City, New Jersey in the spring of 1985, and he admittedly did not want me there for the performance. He explained that after his show, he intended to "dress up like a carrot as lunch for the Bunnies" and I would only be in his way. But I had White House business to attend with a different kind of "rabbit." Reagan had arranged for me to meet with his personal attache', Philip Habib (now deceased), who always played the cryptic role of the *Alice in Wonderland* White Rabbit to mind controlled slaves. Houston had no choice but to take me along once the orders came down.

CIA operative Ken Riley, the Neo-Nazi pedophile who functioned in the capacity of Loretta Lynn's road manager and Project Monarch mind control handler, was Alex Houston's closest friend. Riley often made arrangements through Loretta's and Houston's shared talent agent, Reggie MacLaughlin, for all of us to travel together -- particularly when it involved government covert operations such as this Playboy Club gig did. Loretta's singing career and political ties into CIA covert operations have always been synonymous. Riley escorted her in and out of the White House on numerous occasions during the Reagan Administration. By natural attrition, this put Riley in a secondary role as a "backup" handler for me as he often returned from D.C. with orders for and/or concerning me. Houston and Riley shared much: CIA covert operations, country music interests, Neo-Nazi and U.S. Government mind control, Project Monarch methodologies, slave running[1], pornography, cocaine, and pedophile activities. Kelly and Riley's young daughter were often filmed pornographically together, and endured the sexual assaults of Houston and Riley[2] together on numerous occasions.

This trip to Atlantic City provided me an opportunity to talk with Loretta while her husband, Mooney, Riley and Houston met for business. Loretta and I had so much in common that our time together had been restricted from the time we met in Minneapolis, Minnesota in 1981 and discussed our victimizations.[3] While alone in Loretta's dressing room at the Playboy Club, we discussed a wide range of topics from motherhood to the White House. We talked about Reagan in terms of his role as *The Wizard of Oz*, but mostly we recited the general praises we were trained to say. We talked about Reagan's "favorite" music by Air Supply, which he had supplied to us both via Riley. Air Supply's cryptic NASA/Project Monarch theme recordings became "life and breath" to us both according to Reagan's intention, which locked in our programmed devotion for him. We discussed the recent Inauguration party Loretta had attended at the White House. (I was aware she had entertained there as Houston relayed information to Riley pertaining to his recent trip to Panama to meet with Panamanian Dictator and CIA operative Manuel Noriega in order that Riley deliver the information to Reagan during the Inauguration party.)

Loretta and I switched personalities spontaneously as we inadvertently triggered each other with the shared cryptic language to which we were accustomed. We discussed forbidden subjects including Noriega and Byrd until Riley and Houston caught us and separated us as though we were a couple of naughty kids. I learned more than I was supposed to about Loretta while in Atlantic City, but was never permitted another opportunity to speak with her so freely.

This trip to Atlantic City was multi-purpose, which was not unusual for government operations in which I was forced to participate. I had a major cocaine transaction involving Noriega to attend at the airport; a message to deliver to Philip Habib pertaining to the Contras, and another programmed in by Habib in answer to Reagan; country music "entertainment" aspects; and prostitution to Habib according to Reagan's instruction.[4]

As the sun was setting over Atlantic City, Houston activated the Project Monarch Oz programming that was used for high level covert operations, and had me dress accordingly. I wore real and faux diamonds to signify my "Presidential Model" business role, rubies to signify my Oz programmed prostitution personality, and emeralds to signify my Oz programmed drug business. This physically indicated to my contact(s) which mode of operation I was under at the time. Rarely did I wear all three indicators at once, but they certainly applied in this operation with Habib. Houston led me down the waterfront boardwalk toward the hotel casino where I was to meet Habib, walking like the Oz Scarecrow and singing, "Follow the Yellow Brick Road."

Houston led me up the elaborate escalators of the hotel to a high stakes gambling area where Habib was playing cards. The guard at the door did not let Houston through, and I was sent to Habib's table on my own. When I approached, Habib leaned back in his chair to hear while I quietly recited in Oz cryptic, "I've come such a long, long way to see you. Uncle Ronnie sent you something."

"What would that be?" he asked loudly as he leered at me and chuckled. I could not respond because I was under heavy program. He handed me his room key and pulled me close as he hypnotically whispered, "Use the key. Put it in the lock. Turn. Open the door, and step through a window in time." The other gamblers at Habib's table were getting impatient, and I quickly exited the gambling room.

When I arrived in Habib's room, two of his bodyguards accessed my programming. "Chiefly speaking," I began reciting Reagan's message. Arrangements were made for the two guards to pick up a fair sized shipment of cocaine the next morning that was arriving on a small military "brass" airplane. Houston and I would then board the plane and fly to D.C. where I would complete my part of this operation.

When Habib arrived, he ushered me into the bedroom part of the suite and began disrobing, down to his boxer shorts and gartered socks. Referring to a recent Danté porn film I was used in, he said, "I liked your ruffled tennis panties..." then threw me a pink teddy and ruffled panties resembling the tennis outfit commanding, "Put it on." I complied. He threw me a stuffed toy cat on the pillows and explained, "That kitten is going to keep this Kitten [pointing to me] from screaming. We're going to play Tweedle Dee and Tweedle Dum." (S&M games) Habib physically resembled the violent *Alice in Wonderland* characters, especially in his boxer shorts. The hysterical controlled laughter that rose in my throat would only have intensified his abuse and was (fortunately) choked back by terror as he began attaching heavy rope ties to the four posters of the bed. On command, I crawled onto the bed and lay on my stomach while he tied me so tightly I was stretched. He shoved the stuffed cat under my mouth, then entered me roughly from behind and said, "Come to Poppa."

The intense pain as he brutally sodomized me was outweighed by a high voltage stun gun as he jolted me repeatedly to create the perverse jerking movements and rectal muscle constrictions he desired. I soon passed out from the blinding high voltage of his stun gun. It was nearly 3:00 a.m. when I stumbled out the door with the stuffed cat in my hands, nauseated, disoriented, and in extreme pain. The cool ocean breeze helped revive me as Houston marched me back to the Playboy Club.

Houston knew I had been programmed with a message for Reagan that I would deliver the next morning in D.C. As usual, he began to access it immediately. His quick timing somehow permitted him to penetrate the electricity and programmed codes (designed to keep the information repressed) and accessed the information. Houston kept a written record of any messages he was able to access (along with photos and ledgers) for his personal profit and future blackmailing purposes, should he need to protect himself. In this case, I surmise from Houston's Panama activities, conversations I overheard between him and Riley, and my recollection of the messages he accessed, that his purpose in extracting this information was for his personal profit in backdoor dealings with Noriega. I understood it was these kinds of dealings that eventually contributed to Noriega's downfall with the CIA.

Morning arrived before I was allowed to sleep, and I felt exhausted and "spacey" as I waited by the curb for Habib's body guards to pick Houston and me up and take us to the airport. A small military airplane was parked in a restricted fenced in area as we arrived at the airport. The two bodyguards conducted their business and quickly loaded the trunk with the bundles of cocaine as planned. Houston and I boarded the airplane and flew to Washington, D.C., where I delivered Habib's message to Reagan. The bank transaction numbers later checked out to be a Cayman Island account number.

Philip Habib was directly involved in various DIA/CIA Operations I was forced to participate in throughout the Reagan/Bush Administration. Although Dick Cheney maintained his role as my Commander for these Operations, Habib directed my actions where International "Diplomatic Relations" were concerned. Cheney orchestrated events from behind his desk, whereas Habib was active in the field as Reagan's attache'.

The following Operations, documented in their entirety from my experience perspective only, most likely involve other aspects to which I am not privy. In typical DIA/CIA manner, scant "need to know" information resulted in the "left hand not knowing what the right hand was doing." Nevertheless, the overall criminal purpose of Operation Carrier Pigeon and Operation Shell Game, documented herein, does not change.

---

[1] Riley, over time, owned several slaves.

[2] Riley, like my father, Wayne Cox, and others, remains apparently immune from prosecution for his crimes against children and humanity, as it is considered a matter of "National Security" under the 1984 Reagan Amendment to the National Security Act.

[3] I still have the handwritten note from Loretta that prompted our forbidden conversation, and I hope that someday Loretta will gain the piece/peace of mind that comes with rehabilitation.

[4] In the course of deprogramming, I found retrieval of this information much quicker than it would have been had Houston not accessed it previously, against government policy, and for his own personal gain

CHAPTER 12

OPERATION CARRIER PIGEON

The term "Pigeon" is one with which I have been familiar since the early 1980's when I first began delivering messages between my "owner" Senator Byrd and Puerto Rican drug lord and CIA operative, José Busto. Houston had simply explained to me then, as we fed the flock of pigeons roosting at the Old San Juan Cathedral, that Pigeons were used as messengers. The DIA's U.S. Army Lt. Colonel Michael Aquino often activated my Pigeon programming during the Hands-On Mind-Control Demonstrations.

Dick Cheney further defined the term "Pigeon" when I learned of Operation Carrier Pigeon in the mid '80s. He said, "You have been selected from the flock [of programmed slaves] for the Carrier Pigeon Operation for the purpose of carrying messages from point A to point B as ordered. Pigeons, once they fly the coop, find no freedom in flight, but carry out their task of delivering their message from point A to point B by the shortest possible route -- a direct route. I will direct your route and you will deliver messages as ordered."

But no one defined my role as a Pigeon more eloquently that President Reagan during the course of Operation Carrier Pigeon.

The cryptic "pigeon language" utilized by all participants in the operation was intermixed with Wizard of Oz, Alice in Wonderland, and "Genie in the Bottle" cryptic programming themes. While Pigeon meant messenger, "Carrier Pigeon" referred to the U.S. Air Force aircraft that actually transported the arms and drugs. "Pigeon Droppings" included the sometimes multi-national dispersal of the arms and drugs after they reached their destination. "Pigeon Holing" meant covering up the criminal activity. These definitions, as I understood them then and understand them now, may well include deeper, more diverse meanings than I have perceived.

Habib's favorite programming theme was Alice in Wonderland, Through the Looking Glass due to its international recognition and relation to the ultra- effective NASA mirror, time, and infinity space programs for instantly dissociating programmed participants. He habitually spoke in Alice in Wonderland cryptic language, and even used it for sex as was evidenced by his Tweedle Dee and Tweedle Dum brutal games of perversion. Due to Habib's orchestration of Operation Carrier Pigeon, this CIA covert operation was littered with Wonderland mirror themes from beginning to end.

My CIA handler Alex Houston had just returned from a brief solo trip "to Florida" with an elaborately wrapped box. "It's from a friend of yours," he told me as he handed me the box. "Let's go into the bedroom so you can unwrap it and see it through the 'Looking Glass'." Cryptically triggered, I mechanically walked to the bedroom as ordered.

I removed the silver metallic bow and wrappings from the box and found an expensive, elegant dress made of an unusual shimmery silver fabric. A sheet of plain white stationary written in Philip Habib's recognizable shaded blue script lay on top of the dress. It read:
The heat you radiated when we last met
melted my mirror.
I had it made into a dress just for you,
cut to accentuate your figure
so that when you melt into it,

You lose yourself into
the pool of liquid mirror.
Step into the Looking Glass
Sink deep within its pool
and straddle dimensions in time.
I'll see you there...
along with my friends.

It was signed: "Passionately, Phil Habib," with his name written upside down under a line as though it were a mirror reflection.

Houston knew there would be a note, and ordered "Let me see your note," snatching it from my hands. He gestured toward the dress. "Go ahead and try it on while I read this note. Now let's see, what does it say? 'Come to Poppa'?" I took the dress from the box. It did not feel like anything I'd ever felt before. It was cold like satin, but thin like silk. I started crying quietly, afraid that Habib would somehow show up if I had it on.

"Put it on and I'll zip you in," Houston said as he took another note from his wallet and read it as I undressed:

There's a pair of magic shoes to wear with your dress,
Something in-lightening,
to transport you faster than the ol' ruby slippers (Oz)
The shoes, like the dress, are made just for you,
and when you wear them you'll be fit for a King.
I'll send them for you at the appropriate time.

Houston tucked the note back in his wallet. "See. You're not going anywhere now. You'll meet him at the White House when you have shoes to wear with it. Just slip it on."

I did. Houston accessed Habib's Wonderland brutal sex programming for his own gratification. Afterwards I hung the dress in Kelly's closet with my other trigger-significant clothes; out of sight, out of mind. Until the shoes arrived...

Habib "sent the shoes for me" soon afterward. They were shiny black with what appeared to be silver lightening bolts down the high heels and sides. In place of dinner that night, Houston gave me a "Wonderland Wafer" (MDHMA- XTC CIA designer drug "Ecstasy"). The wafer, like all those supplied by Habib, bore his trademark that read "Eat me." I began to prepare for the night out as instructed. Houston zipped me into the dress, and turned me to face the mirror. As I slipped into the shoes, Houston took another note from Habib out of his pocket and read:

Something in-lightening to tranceport you faster
than the ol' ruby slippers.
Click your heels together (I obeyed) and be there in a snap.
Electrifying -- with the rumble of thunder.
Bolting through time
So you won't be late for a very important date.

Houston hit me with his stun gun and I passed out. He then drove me to the Nashville airport where I boarded a small plane to Washington, D.C.

I found myself at the White House with Byrd, attending another small cocktail party of about 20-30 people. After we spoke with Reagan, Byrd pointed me in the direction of Philip Habib and sent me over to him. My eyes were locked on Habib's as he hypnotically said:

Melt into your melted mirror
for an electrifying ride.
Look deep into the black
of my melting mirror eyes.

137

See you reflecting me, reflecting you,
reflecting me - you - me - you - me
until we melt together and sink deep
into the other side. Habib took me to a quieter spot in an adjoining room and held up another Wonderland Wafer as he said in Alice in Wonderland cryptic, "Welcome to Wonderland, Kitten. This is a very important date. I haven't time to explain." He gave me the wafer and continued, "Eat it, and I'll take you through the door."

Habib took me by the hand and led me to the doorway of another room. It was a dining room of sorts where an informal array of guests was gathered. As soon as Habib appeared in the doorway, King Fahd of Saudi Arabia quickly excused himself from the table and approached. He was wearing a multicolored robe and headwear with a black-brown rope band. I was instantly repulsed by his "wicked" lecherous gaze. I stepped back into the other room in fear. Habib introduced him. "This is one of 'my friends' I mentioned in my letter."

I robotically responded, "Its a pleasure to meet you" and extended my hand as taught in Charm School. Fahd bent over to kiss my hand. As he did, his evil black eyes bore into mine as he softly said, "Your beauty warms my embers. See them glowing deep within the darkness of my eyes -- igniting into flame - black flame." He laughed wickedly at the effect of his use of NASA hypnotic conditioning.

Habib slapped him on the shoulder as though they knew each other well and there were no formalities between them and asked, "Am I right? Is that fit for a King?"

The three of us went into another room that appeared to be a guest bedroom that Habib was occupying. He closed the door and told me, "Diplomatic relations are very important. You know the old saying 'when in Rome do as Romans do'. Well, he's a King. Get on your knees. His wish is your command. Satisfy his deepest wishes. It's your turn for a magic carpet ride, so turn your Genie free."

Fahd was sitting in a chair by a coffee table. As I knelt on the carpet in front off him, his piercing black eyes seemed to stab into my brain like swords. I could not turn away. He stroked my neck with his index finger, activating oral sex programming. "I have heard about you and am in-tent on having you." Somehow he found the slit in his robes and parted it as he continued, "Come into my tent. A feast has been spread for you." He spread his legs and exposed his penis -- one of the nastiest I had ever seen -- like a black nightcrawler worm that smelled and tasted strongly of spice. Habib watched as I carried out my orders, much to the pleasure of Fahd.

Then Habib went to the chest of drawers and began pulling out his electric prod and bondage equipment as he explained, "Now let me introduce you to my other 'friend'. I need to bottle up a message with your Genie and send it out to sea. You know what to do. Begin undressing now."

I did as I was told and lay on my stomach on the bed while Habib sodomized me. He used his electric prod equipment and programmed me with a message to deliver to General Manuel Noriega while on an upcoming NCL cruise.

I was at sea on board an NCL cruise ship bound for their private island in the Bahamas, Stirrup Cay, which was to be my rendezvous point with Noriega. "Bottled up" in my mind through the recent 'Genie in the Bottle' programming, was a cryptic message from King Fahd to Noriega. It was a moonless night whereby the Caribbean waters appeared as black as the night. I could not distinguish the sky from the sea in accordance with NASA hypnotic conditioning. I gazed, totally entranced, from the rear of the cruise ship. Houston used the opportunity to hypnotically enhance Habib's previous programming, while traumatizing me with the threat of being thrown overboard. The thought of "treading water in the inky blackness while the lights of the ship fade further -- and further - away -- until all is black and I sink -- to the depths of the sea" did not seem so horrible in light of the fact that I was to be the bearer of bad news to Noriega in the morning.

Upon arrival to NCL's Stirrup Cay, Houston and I began our usual walking trek to the farthest end of the island where the CIA operations radio station and equipment were located. In a hidden cove on the island's back side was a smaller island of sufficient size to conceal Noriega's personal yacht, anchored behind it. As Houston and I made our way along the cove's beach, we came upon an old wooden boat half buried in the sand and a man sitting beside it. Because I was in a different personality, I did not recognize the man as my contact who ran the Stirrup Cay control tower for drug trafficking and covert activity. I asked him how he got there. He began his charade, which, due to the depths of my trance, I believed in its literal text, while Houston heard quite a different story:

"I shipwrecked." John (the name I called him) pointed to the boat half buried in the sand, "That's all that is left of my boat."

I asked, "Why haven't you been rescued?"

He cryptically replied, "I sent a message in a bottle and I expect a response real soon. Good thing I had these coconuts [he was carving one] and all that 'sugar' in the hull to sustain me."

Houston laughed, immediately realizing that 'sugar' meant cocaine and said, surprised, "In the hull?" as he bent down to look inside the wreck. I looked, too. There was more white cocaine and (dark) cocaine paste than I could mule (carry) in one walking haul, even with both of my tote bags full. But I could not comprehend reality in the midst of this charade, and therefore commented that he was fortunate that both the "white and brown sugar" had made it through the wreck.

Houston said, "So, they cast you away, huh?"

My contact laughed and sniffed, "Yeah, cast me away with all that 'sugar' -- that's nothing to sniff at." He looked up as Houston informed him a speedboat was approaching. I looked out across the cove beyond the little island and finally noticed Noriega's yacht. A "black mirror" finish speed boat, which matched the upper smoke glass windows of Noriega's yacht, was approaching. John told me, "Probably has something to do with that message I sent. Help me wave him in." I did. He handed me a coconut and, using it as a scramble and excuse for me to join him on Noriega's yacht, persuaded me to board the speed boat with him. Houston stayed behind to guard the cocaine that had obviously already been delivered from Noriega's yacht.

When we pulled up to the rear of the yacht, I was helped on board by Noriega's armed guards. I noticed there did not seem to be any big parties going on as was customary, and Noriega seemed unusually abrupt and businesslike. He was not drunk this time. Upon command from John, I delivered Fahd's message:

"I am under command to deliver a message from King Fahd. The Caribbean is becoming volatile. Trouble in Jamaica. Trouble in Cuba. Even trouble in Panama. Dominican Republic must be launching point for missiles and artillery that are being channeled through Cuba. Concluding arms deal, Carrier Pigeon must be detained until all transactions are cleared. Banco de Panama to receive Contra Aid after all steps leading to me have been swept away by the shifting sands [of time], and all pigeon droppings pigeon holed. Our business is concluded. Let us part on friendly terms."

My personal perceptions of history as it happened in reality remains somewhat distorted, as I had no access to "news" outside of my mind controlled environment. In order to keep my memory retrieval free of contamination, I completed the deprogramming process before "educating" myself through books and news. I have since learned that what was reported as news was often distorted propaganda, and many events were never reported at all. Therefore, I do not know of the "troubles in Jamaica and Cuba" to which King Fahd referred. I was aware, however, that due to outside scrutiny, Houston had recently met with Jamaican officials in Kingston pertaining to ceasing the long standing criminal covert operations. As for Cuba, I only knew that I was no longer meeting with my Cuban contact. In Panama, I knew Noriega himself was the object of controversy. The "arms deal" was the final stage of Operation Carrier Pigeon where the planes were to wait in Saudi Arabia until all bank transactions were cleared and the load was ready for disbursement. Saudi Arabian King Fahd would then fund the Contras via Noriega for Reagan after all evidences had been properly covered up -- just as he had done in Afghanistan. After the shipment, there would be no further deals through Noriega involving Fahd, because Noriega could no longer be trusted. Besides, Fahd had increased diplomatic relations with Mexico for covert operations, and Iran-Contra was just beginning to heat up.

Noriega did not seem to be upset by the news of losing Saudi Arabian business, although he was somber and took some time to respond. His translator was working over some complex computer equipment after I delivered the message. I left Noriega's yacht with John and a brief message for Dick Cheney at the Pentagon.

Back on Stirrup Cay, Houston was anxiously waiting to begin transporting the cocaine back to the party area of the island. There, NCL workers were cleaning up from the cruise ship's beach party cookout, which was NCL's excuse to stop the ship. After I muled the first heavy load of cocaine in my tote sacks, Houston approached one worker familiar with the drug operation and informed him we had a heavier load than usual and needed to make another trip. The worker directed us to a huge empty food container used for transporting cook out supplies from the ship, and gave us the key. We locked the first load in the container, and I took my empty tote sacks, plus another straw bag back for another haul. With the second load, Houston even carried some cocaine himself. We had to run quite a distance through the island woods in an attempt to make it back to the ship's shuttle before scheduled departure time. When we arrived, the beach was nearly deserted, as all the passengers had been taken back to the ship. All that remained was the food container and the NCL worker who was hurrying us onto the shuttle and on board the ship, which was waiting for us.

When the cruise ship docked at the Port of Miami, Puerto Rican drug lord and CIA operative José Busto was acting as a U.S. Immigrations officer (commissioned by the Drug Enforcement Agency through the CIA), which he often did for NCL. Busto helped us clear ship undetected with the large load of cocaine. The drugs were packed into suitcases, then loaded into Houston's specially made motor home which was parked in NCL's guarded, restricted parking lot. Most of the cocaine was dropped off as usual at Warner Robbins Air Force Base in Macon, Georgia, to be distributed to destinations unknown to me. The money generated by the sale of cocaine was supposedly used to fund a major arms shipment into Saudi Arabia. These weapons were reportedly distributed among several neighboring countries. The profits were then relayed into Reagan's Contra Cause.

A large quantity of cocaine was retained by Houston for his own use and delivery for personal profit through his country music industry contacts. Some of the cocaine would be delivered by me to Saudi Arabian Ambassador, Prince Bandar Bin Sultan, Fahd's own "Homing Pigeon."

I carried a message from Warner Robbins Air Force Base in addition to the message from Noriega agreeing to Fahd's terms back to Dick Cheney at the Pentagon. Cheney then prepared me for the final phase of the operation. This was a meeting with Prince Bandar (who Cheney, Houston, and others referred to as Sultan) in Nashville, Tennessee where he often visited corrupt friends. There, I would relay a message of agreement to Fahd's terms between Noriega and the U.S., as well as confirm all Air Force flights (Carrier Pigeons) and bank transactions. In turn, Fahd's "Homing Pigeon" would relay the messages to Fahd so that the seemingly long running drugs for arms deals would draw to a successful conclusion.

Dick Cheney cautioned me, "Sultan will be in Nashville having dinner with friends at the Stockyard." (The Stockyard was a popular country music dinner club known for its CIA criminal covert activity involvement.) Cheney glanced at the list on his desk and continued, "Among others, those friends would be [Mayor] Fulton[1] and [Sheriff] Thomas.[2] They are considered a threat to the operation. They're not discrete. Thomas in particular is not to be trusted -- he's an ass and too crooked. So, Sultan must leave the table before the message is delivered. Any questions? Good."

I certainly had no questions this time. I did not need him to caution me about Nashville's Mayor Richard Fulton whom Houston had prostituted me to, and Sheriff Fate Thomas. I had known the pair for years, had been cautioned about them before, and had no respect for them at all. Together Thomas and Fulton had indiscreetly perpetuated the total corruption that had permeated Nashville's $2.8 billion country music industry, which ran the city of Nashville. They ran the city's business from a bar -- the Stockyard -- while they drank and openly used cocaine. If I had had the capacity to wonder, I would have wondered what a "Homing Pigeon" so critical to the conclusion of this international criminal covert operation was doing with such low level sleaze. As it was, I could only sense relief at not having to deal with them, too.

Prince Bandar Bin Sultan's reputation for sex and drugs was widely known in Nashville. But much of my information pertaining to his activities came from one of my closest Project Monarch friends. She is an entertainer's daughter who was prostituted regularly to Sultan when he was in town, which was often.

When Cheney was through with me, Byrd escorted me to the White House to see Reagan, who also cautioned me about the Prince. Reagan was aware of Habib's having activated me sexually with King Fahd, and made it clear that my scheduled rendezvous with Prince Bandar would not include the usual sex.

Reagan joked in Byrd's presence, "Birds [Byrds] may well be eaten by a Kitten [Reagan's pet name for me], but not Homing Pigeons. Homing Pigeons taste foul." Byrd laughed. Reagan continued, "Homing Pigeons have one purpose. Passing messages. Throughout history world leaders have passed messages to and from each other by way of pigeons. Messages that have set the course of events that have altered the course of history. Homing Pigeons are loyal and dedicated to their task, flying over seas, yet never pausing long enough to even quench their thirst -- giving no thought to their own needs. When a pigeon is released, he takes a direct course to his destination. Dedicated to delivering the very messages on which history was founded. Why, even Noah relied on a pigeon to traverse the seas to bring back a message of hope. It is your duty to attach an added message to the Homing Pigeon -- one of peace, from our homeland to his: One from the President of the United States to King Fahd of Saudi Arabia, ... [Omitted due to international ramification.]"

Byrd was visibly inspired by the speech. I was literally saved by the bell from another boring, long winded recitation that Reagan had just inspired in Byrd when Cheney telephoned me back to his office. It was still morning and Cheney had appeared very busy, hurried, and irritable when I had seen him just a short time earlier. My heart was heavy in expectant anticipation of the physical and sexual brutality Cheney's moods normally incited. Yet I was relieved to escape the torturous "picture painting" competition that experience had taught me Byrd and Reagan were about to embark on. My heart lightened when my escort left me at Cheney's office and I noticed his foul mood had changed dramatically.

"I understand you ordered me to report in, Sir." Cheney looked up from his desk where he was shuffling through papers and tying up loose ends before leaving his office.

"Sit down," he ordered. "I just got word that the Genie in the Bottle 'Cast- away' Operation is complete and I intend to pop a cork or two of my own in celebration of its successful conclusion. I have time on my hands and want you to join me. The bunkhouse is being prepared..." Cheney apparently thought of something, went to the door and told the guy who had escorted me, "Make sure there's some Wonderland Wafers in the bunkhouse." He walked to his desk, picked up the phone and said, "I'm outta here" into it and slammed it down. I followed Cheney out the door, and we turned to the right rather than the left outside his office and walked to his personal quarters referred to as the bunkhouse. It was decorated in Cheney's western style in browns and tans, with leather furniture. There was no food (maybe some nuts stashed somewhere), but plenty of bottles of alcohol.

I was swollen and bleeding vaginally, the bottom of my shirt was soaked in blood, and my belly hurt deep inside when my escort finally came for me early the next morning. Staying around Cheney while he slept was as deadly a mistake as removing his clothes or questioning him -- it was forbidden. This time he broke his own rule, and did not even punish me for it when morning arrived. He had spent so many hours drinking alcohol and using his enormous penis as an assault weapon that he passed out shortly before my escort arrived. As I walked into the hall, I doubled over from pain. My escort turned to Cheney and remarked, "Christ, Cheney."

Cheney lifted his head and proudly slurred, "Now you know why they call it 'Dick'."

Back in Tennessee, my CIA paid gynecologist, who knew I was under mind control, covered for my abusers as usual and wrote me a prescription for swelling and pain. I was still in pain and ill from my exposure to Dick Cheney and his high voltage torture and brutal sex when Houston drove me to Nashville's Stockyard Nightclub for my rendezvous with Prince Bandar Bin Sultan.

A waitress led me to the Saudi Arabian Ambassador's table where he was drinking with Mayor Fulton, Sheriff Thomas, and Metro Police Chief Joe Casey.[3] I approached him and said, "If you please, Sir [Oz], I am under command to deliver a message to you from the Pentagon. There is to be no horse play [sex games]. We must get down to business." There was laughter from everyone at the table. I continued, "My message is brief and I only need a moment of your time away from your dinner."

The Prince's face grew more serious and we left the table. He touched the waitress' arm and she pointed to a door across the hall that led to an empty room. We stood just inside the room, and I quickly delivered my Pigeon cryptic message:

"The Carrier Pigeon (Air Force airplane) will take flight ... and will keep its promise (the agreed load) while all transactions (both bank and distribution) are procured through the designated diplomatic channels (Habib.) Your bonus, one crystal, three cuts await you. The President of the United States gives his word to King Fahd: ..."

He told me his driver would meet me out front of the Stockyard and instructed me to put the cocaine in the back. I left the building to rejoin Houston at the car in order that the cocaine could be delivered. A white stretch limousine was pulled up in front of the Stockyard; Chief Casey's assigned Metro Police Officers guarded the area, and the cocaine was transferred into the back seat of the Prince's limo. Houston and I immediately left the area. My part in Operation Carrier Pigeon was concluded.

---

[1] Richard Fulton and his bank were under Federal investigation as of 1991.

[2] Fate Thomas is currently serving time in a Federal penitentiary for bribery and extortion.

[3] Recently under Federal investigation for corruption

CHAPTER 13

OPERATION SHELL GAME

Sometime prior to the death of CIA Chief William Casey, I was in Washington, D.C. for a briefing on Operation Shell Game. Iran-Contra was politically explosive at this time, and U.S. Senator Allen Simpson (R.Wyoming) had a plan to set Panamanian General Manuel Noriega up to take the fall for cocaine aspects of the investigation. Noriega had become yet another source of embarrassment to the Reagan-Bush Administration. The need to convince him to be discrete about his involvement in U.S. criminal covert activities had reached alarming proportions. Noriega had been an intricate part of arming the Nicaraguan Contras for Reagan, as well as an international hub in the cocaine operations that funded the black budgets for ultra secret projects such as Project Monarch. My CIA operative handler Alex Houston's shadowy back door drug dealings with Panama further exemplified the kind of "honor among thieves" rules that Noriega routinely and openly violated. My role, my "Contra-bution," was but a small part of the over all picture. Nevertheless, Operation Shell Game was one of the more significant and informative covert operations in which I had been forced to participate.

My role began one cold, rainy day when Houston dropped me off at the Washington Monument where I was met by two agents, who triggered me to go with them by flashing their IDs. They escorted me to the large White House office where I had first met Cheney to "audition" for the Hands On Mind Control Demonstrations some years before. As usual, Cheney and Reagan were drinking, this time to excess for so early in the day. Reagan's cheeks were flushed and his voice slurred as he greeted me, "Well, hello, Kitten. Dick and I were just discussing the plight of the Contras since this Ollie North thing broke out." Cheney's alcoholic foul mood was immediately apparent. He was agitated as usual at Reagan's informality in my presence. Apparently I had come in during a serious discussion about Iran-Contra as Reagan's mood was more somber than I had ever seen it. He took a drink and looked out the window. "Americans believe in their country -- baseball, hot dogs, and Ollie North." Cheney snorted a laugh at what seemed to be an ongoing joke between them about "hot dogs and Ollie North." Reagan continued, "And I believe in the Contra cause and all that we have accomplished. And I'm damn proud of it! Its not 'Law and Order'. No, its Order and then Law. Order must come first because without it, law would be ineffective. Sometimes we must rise above and beyond the law to establish that order [he glanced seriously at Cheney] -- or a new [world] order. As President, that is my responsibility. Establish order through democracy by spreading democracy throughout the world. With order, there is peace. Right now in Nicaragua the people are crying out for democracy, for peace, and I cannot turn a deaf ear to them. Not even in view of Ollie North's troubles. True Americans know he is a hero. That's why we must rise above the law to establish order by fulfilling the wishes, the hopes, the dreams of those brave men fighting for freedom by doing our part in spreading democracy." Reagan was gesturing into the air, apparently lost in the poetry of his own ranting.

Cheney lost patience and jumped from his chair to sneer at me and poke his finger in my chest while he said, "Order is all that matters, and you're going to follow mine."

Reagan turned back to us. "I'm glad you brought that up, Dick. Kitten, you have a role in establishing this order. With the same patriotic passion that burned in your bosom for the freedom fighters of Afghanistan, you will carry out your orders for the Contras. Dick will define your role and provide you with all you need and all you need to know from the ol' Wizard's bag in the basement [Oz programming in Cheney's Pentagon office]. So, you run along now and do as he commands."

Senator Allen Simpson was in Cheney's office when we arrived. Cheney flipped over the hour glass to let me know my life was on the line according to Oz programming. Cheney gestured to Simpson and began, "Operation Shell Game is Simpson's brain child, so he's master of the game and he's going to teach you the rules. The objective of the game is to see 'who's left holding the goods'." Pointing to Simpson, he commanded, "Listen to 'im."

Simpson stood up and began cryptically talking. "You are going on a 'Princes Cruise' [Noriega's Yacht]. The Baby's Ear Shell is your pass key. I will provide you with yours at the appropriate time." He took the "shell" out of his wallet. It was approximately 1 1/2 inches long and was translucent pink, shaped and detailed exactly like a baby's ear. Simpson noticed the relief cross my face as I realized it was not a real baby's ear. He smiled. "These are but empty shells of the life they once possessed. Like you are -- empty and void of life. A shell. In one ear and out the other. I have your ear now LISTEN. If they hold the pass key, you listen. When you hold the pass key, you speak. In one ear and out the other -- never again to be retrieved."

He returned the shell to his wallet and continued, "Listen. Follow orders. The Colonel [Aquino] will be there and you will follow his orders and provide a demonstration Hands On style for the General [Noriega]. It will be different, yet the same, so follow the Colonel's orders closely."

Cheney roughly grabbed my hair and pulled my head back, got right in my face and said, "Or, I'll get her, my pretty, your little girl. Follow orders as though her life depends upon it because it does. Or the next baby's ear will be taken from Kelly. So listen. When you see the baby's ear, you will listen." He spun my head in the direction of the hour glass as he released my hair. He was sneering and Simpson looked as though he thought Cheney overdid it. I was relieved it would not be my job to "soothe Cheney's savage beast" sexually that day.

Cheney took me back to the White House office where we had started. He and Reagan shared another drink. Reagan patted my hair back in place where Cheney had pulled it, which made me feel safe somehow since I could not comprehend that he was behind my ordeal with Cheney. Reagan switched my personality to where I no longer regarded him as "Chief," but instead as "Uncle Ronnie." He did this by reaching into his Jelly Belly jar and giving me one. Certain colors and flavors triggered certain programmed responses. Uncle Ronnie must have had other "Kittens" conditioned to the military green watermelon ones because he kept an excess amount of these in his numerous jars.

Cheney said, "How in the hell you drink cognac and eat those god damn jelly beans is beyond me."

Reagan responded, "Well, Dick, you don't have to have a Jelly Belly if you don't want to. I was just giving one to Kitten, here."

"Damn right I don't have to have a Jelly Belly, but you're going to have a jelly belly if you keep that shit up." Cheney finished his drink.

Reagan chuckled, "Now, you know I watch my figure . . ."

145

"Figure this," Cheney interrupted. "What are you going to do with the Contras?" Cheney slammed down his drink and headed for the door.

"Exactly what I've been doing." Reagan turned to me, "C/mon, Kitten. Let's take a walk. I need my evening constitutional."

Reagan was in no mood for sex, and it was a relief to be away from Cheney. He took me outside for a walk in his "Secret Garden," where he said he goes to "think and solve the world's problems." We walked down a cement path he referred to as a "Yellow Brick Road." After sitting quietly on a cement bench for a while, he said, "If you follow the Yellow Brick Road, it leads right to the Wizard's lair -- the Oval Office. How would you like to see where Uncle Ronnie really solves the world's problems?" I felt like a little girl with her daddy going to see where he works with no real concept of the experience. The guard at the Oval Office door ensured I was returned to my escorts when Reagan was through "sneaking me in" to his office. I was then taken back to Washington Monument where Houston was waiting in the car as though I had never been gone at all.

Operation Shell Game brought me back in touch with former President Gerald Ford early one misty fall morning. Ford's continued relationships with my abusers had given me cause to remain in touch with him throughout the years, particularly since he and my father were still jointly active in the Michigan organized crime drugs and pornography operation that had launched me into Project Monarch so many years before.

Ford was about to embark on a game of golf with my father on the otherwise "Closed for the Season" golf course next to my father's expensive house in affluent Grand Haven, Michigan. My brother, Mike, was with my father and me as we rendezvoused at the Club House with Ford and the Secret Service personnel assigned to him. Ford told my father he would "catch up with him and Mike at the third hole" and to "leave us to our business." I was maintained in "Silence" until Ford and I were out of range of the Secret Service men, and I recited a message from Reagan instilled prior to the Shell Game.

"If you please, Sir," I began in Oz cryptic, "I have a message for you from Uncle Ronnie. Its a 'humming telegram' [oral sex game] to see if you agree that our National Anthem should be changed to America the Beautiful." (Reagan was actually serious about changing our National Anthem.)

Ford responded, "We may have to see about that later. First, we've got some other 'holes' to attend before the sun gets up any higher."

As he teed up his golf ball I asked, "Do you still golf a lot now that you're no longer President?"

He said very seriously, "I golfed a lot when I was President. But now, I just keep up with events from the golf course. I've earned the privilege of monitoring the progress of America's Freedom Train at my leisure." He turned to face me, "Do you play golf yet?"

"Very well, Sir, when permitted." (Houston always ensured he won.) Ford was openly amused by my answer and handed me his club. "Give it your best shot." I outshot him the first stroke and his amusement vanished. I gave him back his golf club as ordered.

At the end of the second hole, Ford said, "I'd like to have a word with you." He took me over to some trees off the fairway and turned to me with his arms crossed over his bulging chest, raised himself up taller, and bore his shark-like eyes into mine. "Lend me your ear." I had the Baby's Ear Shell with me as ordered, took it out of my back pocket and handed it to Ford. He began talking as though I were a machine and he was dictating a message. "Take this message to Dick Cheney, Pentagon. The Mob has agreed to transfer the $2.3 million [porn profits] to the Bank of Credit and Commerce International. Let's pool our money now and we'll be swimming in it. This operation has been an enterprising success. Let's keep it that way. Cease agreement with Panama. All Mexican channels are implemented [cocaine and heroin]. Hail to the Chief." He took a step away and added, "And you [he poked my chest like Cheney] take care of my friend, Dick. Here..." he handed me the Baby's Ear. For meanness he added "over and out," and did the sign of the (satanic) horns at my eyes which deepened my trance significantly since I had been conditioned so heavily to this by Byrd.

After he hit the golf ball, he asked, "How's my friend Allen Simpson these days?"

"Very well, Sir." I noticed he bristled as he missed another shot. His temper was rising. When he wanted to add more to his message, he took out his frustration on me.

"Gimme that fucking shell." He wiggled his fingers at me. That wasn't the pass phrase and I did not trigger. He grew louder and more agitated, "Where's that Baby's Ear." I still could not respond. "Lend me your god damn ear!!" he roared at me. Close enough.

"Yes, Sir," I responded meekly as I dropped it in his hand.

He proceeded. "Tell Simpson to take care of my friend Dick Thornburgh. Get back to me on it." He returned the ear. We could see my father waiting at the next hole and Ford said he might "bean him one" with his next stroke. He swung, but missed my father.

When we met up with my father at the third hole. Ford set up his ball first, of course, and waving his club at me said, "Get out of here before I get teed off." My father pointed the way with a thumb over his shoulder and let out a shrill whistle. My brother, Mike, walked me through the bushes and back to my father's house.

My sister Kelli Jo was waiting tearfully for my return. She was MPDed and horrified of Ford. She and my little sister Kimmy and I had all been forced to sexually gratify Ford just prior to a special ordered porn film titled *Three Little Kittens* whereby his semen was filmed "anonymously." I was aware that Ford had initiated both of my sisters the way he had me in Cedar Springs, and they, too, dreaded his brutal and degrading sexuality. I hurried past my sister to make sure my daughter, Kelly, was OK. Cheney's threat to her life was ringing loud in my ear.

I did not see the Baby's Ear shell again until Kelly and I arrived in Bradenton Beach, Florida. I drove the motor home into Florida with Houston and Kelly along, and dropped Houston off at the Tampa airport, since he did not have a role in Operation Shell Game. He "had business at Boys Town in Omaha, Nebraska" where the wayward boys were being traumatized and sexually abused in accordance with the Catholic involvement in Project Monarch. Survivor Paul Bonacci of the infamous Franklin Cover-up case has named Alex Houston as one of his abusers there in Boys Town. Houston often went to Boys Town or other similar "vacation resorts" while I was on covert government business. Kelly and I drove on to Bradenton, where we checked into a participating campground on the bay across from MacDill Air Force base. It, too, was "Closed for the Season".

The recreation room of the campground was actually a harmonics programming operation, and the offices were filled with elaborate computers consistent with high-level CIA operations. The day Kelly and I met with Senator Simpson, I had been instructed by campground workers

147

to drive to nearby Santa Maria island where we were to collect unusual shells. Kelly and I were on the "wild side" of the island hunting sand dollars because they had "birds" in them. As we walked through the shallow water, Kelly scared up a Stingray, which sent us screaming for the shore. Simpson was on the beach laughing, looking out of place in his Cagney hat and grey suit with legs rolled up and polished shoes in hand. He seemed familiar with the beach. When we reached the shore, he struck up a conversation about shells. It wasn't until he told us about the Baby's Ear Shell and opened his wallet to retrieve it that I triggered and knew who he was. As he took it out, he also flashed his ID signaling us to go with him. Considering Kelly, he had slipped a shell into the sand for her to find that looked like an eye in a spiral. He used this as a hypnotic induction to control her, comparing it to Bush's Eye in the Sky.

Simpson showed me the shell in his hand and began, "You. You alone will take the shuttle boat to your Princes cruise. It willful leave the dock from your own backyard (Oz) at 7:30 P.M. Dress appropriately [Houston had ensured the proper attire had been packed]. You will be escorted to the conference room and on into the top deck. You will see as you approach the ship [Noriega's yacht] the top deck is surrounded in black mirrors. Look deep into the mirrors, that is where you will be. And where I will be when next we meet." We walked a little further up the beach to where the motor home was parked and, referring to the Baby's Ear, Simpson said, "They're very rare indeed. This one is the right ear. You must go to the other side of the island, out Long Boat Key, to find its match. The Colonel (Aquino) has the baby's left ear and will meet you at the Pier at 4 P.M. Stop at the little market on the corner and call. Then its just down the street a little ways."

I followed instructions robotically. Kelly and I watched from the pier as four big, armed (with machine guns) emotionless (programmed?) guards scanned the area as Aquino emerged from a car. Kelly said, "Mom, lets go." I remembered Cheney's threat and assured her I would protect her, though I could not comprehend from what.

When Aquino approached with two Dobermans on leashes, I told him Simpson had sent me there looking for the left baby's ear. He opened his hand to reveal "all that was left -- the baby's ear -- the dogs had devoured and consumed the rest of the baby." It was bloody, ragged, and bluish rather than pink. Whether or not this was an actual baby's ear, the impact was the same. I put Kelly further behind me away from the dogs. I stood traumatized and entranced, ready for command. Aquino instructed me in full detail on the night's activities, and that I was to leave Kelly with campground personnel until my return.

That evening I was taken to Noriega's yacht in the bay via a small motorboat. I triggered and tranced further as I approached the familiar "black mirrored" yacht according to plan. I was helped onto the back of the yacht by Panamanian "palace" guards who kept me there at gunpoint until I was cleared and my Baby's Ear pass key accepted. I was escorted past the Air Force Base officials, their wives, drug people, and the vast amounts of cocaine laid out for them. I recognized several of the guests, including Oliver North and Puerto Rican drug lord Jose' Busto. I was led up the stairs to the conference room where Aquino, Noriega, and Simpson were waiting. Simpson! I realized I must "be on the other side of the black mirror" and I gazed out into the darkness.

Simpson spoke softly, "You're on the other side of the black mirror now [NASA programming], peering though the blackness out to sea. Sea of black. Riding on a sea of black, drifting, drifting from the winds. Deep into the blackness. Drifting through the sands of time. Black sands, yielding shells -- such as this Baby's Ear." He pressed it into my hand signaling it was time for me to speak. I addressed Noriega.

"If you please, Sir, I have a message from the President of the United States of America: The successes we have enjoyed in our shared endeavors are now history in the making, whose course cannot be altered -- regardless of the imminent lifting of the veil by well intentioned do-gooders. As this veil is lifted, it may shed light on you. So you must have your house in order, as does Ollie North, and cease any and all detectable activity. I will do my best to keep you under shield and out of view if you comply with these orders and cease all detectable activity at once."

Noriega reacted as anticipated, obviously insulted by the message. In the ensuing moment of chaos, Aquino hypnotically waved his hands in front of Noriega and dramatically spread out his satanic black cape (worn for impact on Noriega's superstitions) which appeared to fill the room. Noriega all but bowed to him as Aquino's control over him was complete.

Aquino's manner was side-show-style rather than the usual somber tones used on Military bases for the Hands On demonstrations. "General, for your entertainment and in respect and appreciation of your successful enterprising 'Contra-bution', the Chief has sent his Presidential Model to demonstrate the latest technology in mind control advancements. With the flip of a switch, this Pigeon becomes a Kitten [I began undressing]. Quite a different animal."

Because of Noriega's superstitious beliefs, the whole idea of switching personalities apparently frightened him. I know Noriega believed whole heartedly in mind control, but could not grasp the concept of multiple personalities (which I now believe he perceived as demonic possession). Therefore, he did not adhere to the idea of one slave being trained for both business and pleasure. Aquino, whom Noriega already perceived as a "devil" working for Reagan, was manipulating his beliefs masterfully. The impact of this demonstration and Operation would prove to be Psychological Warfare of the highest order.

Aquino ordered me to lie on the bed and invited Noriega to look closer at what the "Wizard" -- "his Chief"(Reagan) -- could create. Noriega stepped closer to see what Aquino was pointing out to him between my breasts. A large, carved baphomet appeared. Aquino had hypnotically regressed me to the time of its making which caused it to seemingly "suddenly appear" right before Noriega's eyes. Noriega jumped back, ignorantly terrified of this scientific phenomenon. I believe Noriega stayed in the room for the rest of the demon-stration simply because he was frozen in fear. Aquino hit me with a cat-o-nine- tails and I shrieked in pain. Noriega jumped. Aquino hit me with it again, this time activating me to respond sexually as though pain were pleasure -- a mind control concept that Noriega more readily grasped. Then Aquino pointed out that the baphomet had disappeared. While Noriega looked, Aquino used Byrd's hypnotic induction as he cut me between the breasts with a knife saying, "In like a knife sharp and clean, I'll carve out what I want." My trance had been deepened to the extent that my circulatory system was slowed. Therefore I did not bleed until Aquino hypnotically changed my trance level. He then told Noriega that the baphomet carving had "retreated to the depths of my body and soul, possessing me and inciting the heat of hell." He commanded me to show my "face", the vaginal mutilation carving of the baphomet face. As I did, Aquino offered Noriega my sex. As predicted, Noriega's eyes bulged in terror and revulsion. While Aquino told him his "rejection of me had killed me," I ceased breathing and moving as conditioned. Noriega was dumfounded as Aquino laughed wickedly and threatened, "Even death will not permit her -- or you -- escape from the Wizard's power." He explained that I was the "Wizard's own" and "under his spell" and could therefore "re-energize myself and come back to life." He put a vaginal prod in my hand and ordered me to masturbate myself with it, pushing the button to electrically jolt myself internally upon command. Noriega's eyes were enormous. He paled to a sickly grey, his mouth fell open and he ran out the door while Aquino assured him that he had "no where to run, no where to hide from Reagan's powers."

Noriega predictably interpreted the demonstration as a threat from the depths of HELL, which should have been enough to heed Reagan's commands to break the drug trafficking ties immediately. (Apparently this is not the case as is evidenced by Noriega's continued Florida incarceration.) Aquino and Simpson doubled over with laughter as they congratulated themselves on a job well done. Simpson finally ordered me to dress and escorted me to the back of the yacht to ensure the guards put me on the shuttle boat rather than kill me because of Noriega's horror.

As I approached the dock of the campground, the boat driver told me I would find Kelly asleep in the 'recreation' room. I ran to her, and, fearful of Cheney's threat, made sure her ears were still intact. I was immensely relieved to find them still there and to know she was "OK" (I could not think to wonder what she had endured in my absence.) I illogically felt like a "good mom" for "doing my part right so Kelly could live." Never before had I experienced such a sense of danger to us both and my relief was proportionate. I lovingly held her in my arms the rest of the night.

CHAPTER 14

CLINTON COKE LINES

I met up with Bill Clinton again in 1982 at a county fair in Berryville, Arkansas. Alex Houston was "entertaining" there due to the close proximity of the CIA Near Death Trauma Center (a.k.a. slave conditioning and programming camp) and drug distribution point at Swiss Villa in Lampe, Missouri. I had just endured intense physical and psychological trauma and programming. Clinton was campaigning for Governor and was backstage with Hillary and Chelsea while waiting to make a speech. Clinton stood in the afternoon sun with his arms crossed, talking to Houston about him and "his people" (CIA Operatives) being booked into specific areas for the duel purpose of entertaining and carrying out specific covert drug operations.

From my perspective, those who were actively laying the groundwork for implementing the New World Order through mind conditioning of the masses made no distinction between Democratic and Republican parties. Their aspirations were international in proportion, not American.[1] Members were often drawn from, among other elitist groups, the Council on Foreign Relations. Like George Bush, Bill Clinton was an active member of the CFR, as well as a Yale Skull and Bones graduate. Based on numerous conversations I overheard, Clinton was being groomed and prepared to fill the role of President under the guise of Democrat in the event that the American people became discouraged with Republican leaders. This was further evidenced by the extent of Clinton's New World Order knowledge and professed loyalties.

Clinton understood that I had just been through "hell" in Lampe, and took it all in stride as he focused on his speech. He not only was well aware of the mind control tortures and criminal covert activities proliferating in Arkansas and the neighboring state of Missouri, but he condoned them! Just as there are no partisan preferences in this world dominance effort, neither are there any strong individual state considerations or boundaries, either. I knew from experience that Clinton's Arkansas criminal covert operations meshed with the Lampe, Missouri center where he routinely tended business and claimed to "vacation," staying in the compound's resort villas.

In 1983, Houston took me to Lampe for routine trauma and programming while he was scheduled to "entertain" at the amphitheater. Also scheduled to perform were Bill Clinton's and George Bush's friends Lee Greenwood and CIA Operative, slave runner, and country music singer Tommy Overstreet. Greenwood and Overstreet were active in both the Lampe, Missouri and Lake/Mount Shasta, California CIA compounds. Clinton was flown in from Berryville, Arkansas by helicopter for the shows as well as for a business meeting.

Before Clinton arrived, Greenwood and Houston were in the backstage dressing rooms snorting line after line of cocaine. Houston, always eager to make an extra penny to pinch, attempted to prostitute me to Greenwood. "She's the real performer," Houston said. "She performs all kinds of sex acts upon command. For a small price, she's yours."

Greenwood laughed, and referring to my Huntsville, Alabama NASA programming said, "I've spent more time in Huntsville than she has, and I know full well who and what she is -- a 'space cadet' programmed for sex. She's a modified version of Marilyn Monroe."

Tommy Overstreet had walked in and heard what Greenwood said, "How much time have you spent in Shasta?"

"Shasta?" Greenwood looked arrogantly at Overstreet and smiled knowingly as he said, "You don't 'spend time' in Shasta, you maintain the concept if you can. I haven't lost any time there, either, if that's your next question. I go there quite a bit. Enough really to override Houston's suggestion with ease and take what I want, when I want, and how I want it."

Greenwood began expertly accessing my sex programming and told the others in the room, "you all can come and go as you please, but I've been made an offer that I am going to use." He ordered me to undress and bend over the desk where he roughly sodomized me as he said, "You're going to think its daddy all over again."

When Greenwood was through with me, I was ordered out into the amphitheatre concert area. During intermission, I met up with Swiss Villa manager Hal Meadows, Tommy Overstreet, and Governor Clinton in the hall. Clinton was wearing a cap that read "Diesel Trainer" which I was told to equate literally as "these-will-train-her." Puzzled, I looked at his cap and asked, "Are you a conductor?"

Clinton smiled and said, "Of electricity." Overstreet laughed as he continued, "Actually it means I check cabooses. How's yours?" I squirmed. Apparently Greenwood had bragged about sodomizing me. They laughed even harder as Clinton said, "Still running, I'm sure."

Houston stepped out of the dressing room to greet Clinton. "Hi, bud." Houston extended his hand. "I hear you made Governor."

"I hear you deliver a hell of a one liner," Clinton replied, cryptically referring to cocaine and NOT Houston's so-called comedy routine. "I'm always aspiring to achieve new heights."

"Well, come on in," Houston invited. "I have enough [cocaine] to put us all into orbit." I walked into the dressing room with them as Houston was saying to Clinton, "I suppose there are no limits for you since you're across the [state] line."

"What line?" Clinton feigned surprise and ignorance. He looked at Hal Meadows as he continued, "You mean I've left that state of mine? In the state of mind I'm in, there are no boundaries anyway." He walked over to the table and snorted a line of cocaine. "I come here to get away from it all. This kind of business is pleasure."

"So where's that young wife of yours?" Houston asked, referring to Hillary.

"She's with friends." Clinton sniffed the coke further up his nose. "She's minding her own business. I'm just here to unwind, see the show, maybe do a little hunting [referring to A Most Dangerous Game]. I've got a bird [helicopter] ready to fly me back when I'm through. Hey, speaking of 'Byrd' [he gestured my way] I hear she's moved up to the big house [White House]." Referring to his friend and mentor Senator Byrd he asked, "So what's his position now?"

"The same." Houston answered. "Probably like this..." Houston pantomimed a lewd sodomy pose while everyone laughed. "He still runs the show."

Clinton kept his eyes fixed on Houston's "caboose" and said, "Why don't you show her [referring to me] the way out and show me that again?" If I could have

thought at that moment, I would have realized Bill Clinton was/is bisexual. I had no personal sexual experience with Clinton beyond witnessing him engaged in homosexual activity during an orgy at Swiss Villa.

Immediately following the Swiss Villa incident, Houston was scheduled as usual to perform at the county fair in Berryville, Arkansas. There, Houston and I had been visiting with long time Clinton friend and supporter H.B. Gibson when we parted company to attend a private meeting at the mansion of Clinton's bisexual friend and supporter Bill Hall. Hall had reportedly made his fortune in the pre-fabricated log home business, and the Clintons were staying in a guest villa patterned after those at Swiss Villa. Hillary had taken toddler Chelsea to the villa while Clinton and his aide/body guard attended the meeting. Tommy Overstreet was also in attendance as this directly coincided with the recent Lampe meeting. We all sat in Hall's sunken living room on two couches facing each other with a black mirror coffee table between us. Hall had cut numerous lines of cocaine on the table, and everyone present -- including Bill Clinton -- was inhaling it through $50 bills rolled into straws. The conversation ranged from CIA, drugs, and politics to the Swiss Villa Amphitheatre and country music. At that time, a major effort was underway to move Nashville, Tennessee's country music industry to the Lampe area (it has since literally moved to nearby Branson), in closer proximity to the CIA cocaine operations that leached the industry.

Tommy Overstreet was attempting to convince Hall, who was obviously no stranger to the drug (cocaine) business, to join the high level CIA cocaine operation that was funding covert activity. They discussed the possibility of Hall transporting cocaine from Berryville, Arkansas to Nashville, Tennessee to be in on the ground level of what would soon be one of the largest and most prolific CIA cocaine operations -- the Branson, Missouri country music industry. By enlisting now, the contacts and customers that Hall would procure could "politically and financially bolster him for life." Additionally, Overstreet discussed the viability of using Hall's own company trucks to transport the drug throughout Atlanta, Georgia; Louisville, Kentucky; and Jacksonville, Florida as well as Nashville, Tennessee and Lampe, Missouri. These key CIA cocaine routes coincided with Hall's established truck routes, according to the insiders present at the meeting. Hall was being offered the "opportunity of a lifetime" as his role would also include laundering money through his business to fund the black budget covert operations. Hall appeared nervous and skeptical, and Clinton and Overstreet attempted to maintain a "light" atmosphere by joking that Hall could change the name of his trucking line to **"CLINTON COKE LINES"**.

Hall was not convinced and began to raise questions as to the longevity of the operation and how he was going to protect himself. Although Hall was very adept at the cocaine business, he voiced concern that he found it easier to trust those who were not with the CIA operations than he did U.S. government protected participants. Clinton reassured him that it was "Reagan's operation," but Hall was concerned that some faction of the government would "shut it down like a sting operation" without warning and leave him literally holding the bag. Houston laughed and explained that "no one was going to cut it [the drug business] off." He assured them it was far too lucrative and that there would "always be a market" for drugs -- a market controlled by those criminals implementing their New World Order.

Clinton added to what Houston said, talking in local colloquialisms. "Bottom line is, we've got control of the [drug] industry, therefore we've got control of them [suppliers and buyers]. You control the guy underneath ya' and Uncle [Sam] has ya' covered. What have ya' got to lose? No risk. No one's gonna hang ya' out to dry. And whatever spills off the truck as it passes through [he laughed and snorted another line of coke] you get to clean up."

Hall smiled at his friend, which was apparently interpreted as consent. Clinton motioned for his aide to get his ledger. Overstreet began pulling out his paperwork, and Hall neatly cleared the table of the remaining coke lines.

Clinton gestured to me and told Houston, "Get her out of here."

Houston didn't move and laughed. "She's a Presidential Model. She's kept secrets bigger than yours."

Clinton responded, "I don't care. Get her the fuck out of here."

Hall's wife led me away and locked me in a back bedroom. After an indeterminate period of time, I heard her telephone Hillary at the guest villa. She then drove me up the mountain through the dark to meet with Hillary. Although I had previously met Hillary we had very little to say to each other -- particularly since I was still dazed and tranced from the tortures I had endured at the CIA Near Death Trauma Center in Lampe. Hillary knew I was a mind controlled slave, and, like Bill Clinton, just took it in stride as a "normal" part of life in politics.

Hillary was fully clothed and stretched out on the bed sleeping when Hall's wife and I arrived. "Hillary, I brought you something you'll really enjoy. Kind of an unexpected surprise. Bill ordered her out of the meeting and I took her to my bedroom and made an interesting discovery. She is literally a two faced [referring to my vaginal mutilation carving] bitch."

"Hmm?" Hillary opened her eyes and sleepily roused herself. "Show me."

Hall's wife ordered me to take my clothes off while Hillary watched. "Is she clean?" Hillary asked, meaning disease free.

"Of course, she's Byrd's," she responded, continuing the conversation as though I were not there. "Plus, I heard Houston say something about her being a Presidential Model, whatever the hell that's supposed to mean."

"It means she's clean," Hillary said matter-of-factly as she stood up.

I was not capable of giving thought to such things back then, but I am aware in retrospect that all Presidential Model slaves I knew seemed to have an immunity to social diseases. It was a well known fact in the circles I was sexually passed around in that government level mind controlled sex slaves were "clean" to the degree that none of my abusers took precautions such as wearing condoms.

Hall's wife patted the bed and instructed me to display the mutilation. Hillary exclaimed, "God!" and immediately began performing oral sex on me. Apparently aroused by the carving in my vagina,[2] Hillary stood up and quickly peeled out of her matronly nylon panties and pantyhose. Uninhibited despite a long day in the hot sun, she gasped, "Eat me, oh, god, eat me now." I had no choice but to comply with her orders, and Bill Hall's wife made no move to join me in my distasteful task. Hillary had resumed examining my hideous mutilation and performing oral sex on me when Bill Clinton walked in. Hillary lifted her head to ask, "How'd it go?"

Clinton appeared totally unaffected by what he walked into, tossed his jacket on a chair and said, "It's official. I'm exhausted. I'm going to bed."

I put my clothes on as ordered, and Hall's wife drove me back down to the mansion where Houston was waiting for me. The meeting apparently had been a success. I heard discussions throughout the remaining years between Houston, his agent Reggie MacLaughlin, and Loretta Lynn's handler Ken Riley pertaining to Hall's successful branch of the CIA cocaine operation emanating from Arkansas. No discussions were as poignant and revealing as those between Alex Houston and CIA operative country music entertainer Boxcar Willie.

BoxCar Willie burst onto the country music scene after an ad campaign of high tech hypnotically persuasive produced television commercials that strategically made him an overnight sensation and "star." The country music industry's Freedom Train needed a conductor to lead the industry and fans to Branson, Missouri, and BoxCar Willie was placed in the driver's seat. Like the Pied Piper of Hamlin, BoxCar Willie succeeded in his role of trance-ferring the industry in close proximity to the Lampe CIA cocaine operations.

BoxCar Willie was one of the primary ground level contacts that Bill Hall made after Clinton convinced him to cash in on the cocaine benefits of the country music industry transfer. Houston and BoxCar Willie discussed Hall's lucrative dealings throughout the years in my presence while traveling the country together, billed on the same shows, including performances at the Swiss Villa Amphitheatre. I had much contact with Boxcar Willie personally since my government sponsored cocaine runs often coincided and intermeshed with his. But I never knew BoxCar Willie as well as my daughter Kelly knew him. Kelly has named Boxcar Willie as one of her primary sexual abusers in three different mental institutions, and has voiced frustration at the lack of justice. "Why am I the one locked up while my abusers remain free?" she constantly pleads. I assure her I am doing all I can to blow the whistle on BoxCar Willie for her, and expose his role in transferring the country music industry to close proximity of the Lampe, Missouri CIA cocaine operation as outlined by Bill Clinton.

---

[1] Loyalty to the sovereignty of our country is non existent under New World Orders. "President" Clinton poses no more leadership or loyalty to our country than Ronald Reagan did since both follow(ed) New World Order directives from former U.N. Ambassador and CIA Director George Bush.

[2] Hillary Clinton is the only female to become sexually aroused at the sight of my mutilated vagina.

155

CHAPTER 15

NO MORE BEATING AROUND THE BUSH

It was a sunny fall day in 1983 when U.S. Congressman Guy VanderJagt met with my CIA operative mind control handler Alex Houston, my then 3 1/2 year old daughter, Kelly, and me on the steps of the U.S. Senate in Washington, D.C. Kelly appeared familiar with VanderJagt, although I had never previously remembered seeing her in his company. Even so, I could not think to realize he was, in fact, sexually abusing her just as he had me when I was a child. VanderJagt knelt on one knee in front of her to talk with her, assuring her that "today was a special day" because she would "see Uncle George [Bush] while mommy sees Uncle Ronnie [Reagan]." He stood up and took her by the hand, saying in *Alice in Wonderland* cryptic language, "Let's go on an Adventure together" and led her quietly and robotically away.

I met up with Kelly again that afternoon at the White House, both of us literally "on our toes" and standing at attention in Reagan's office. In retrospect, I wonder at the measures of control inflicted on my 3 ½-year old child to cause her to perform so robotically and behave "so well" as she silently stood with the plastic smile and unblinking eyes, in the presence of President Reagan, Vice President Bush, and (later Defense Secretary) Dick Cheney. Reagan appeared to gaze at Kelly, with her long blonde hair cascading down the back of her blue pinafore dress, completing her Alice in Wonderland appearance. Reagan seemed to pose no direct threat to her sexually as he said, "She is adorable, a model child."

Reagan then gestured towards Bush and said, "This is my Vice President George Bush. People don't usually know what the role of the Vice President is because he's always behind the scenes making sure everything that the President wants done happens the way its supposed to." He looked at me and said matter-of-factly, "I catch the public's attention (he made a gesture in the air that was eye catching) while the Vice President carries out orders."

Bush's close friend Dick Cheney said, "And "gives them.""

"Right," Reagan said. "An order from him is like an order from me."

Bush was wearing canvas boat shoes and a cardigan sweater as he knelt on one knee in front of Kelly in order to talk to her on her level. Bush used the children's television program *Mr. Rogers' Neighborhood* to scramble/confuse young victims' (like Kelly's) memory of contact with him and his sexual abuse. His physical resemblance to TV's Fred Rogers was deliberately exaggerated by his choice of clothes and mannerisms and is further compounded by his developed vocal impersonation. Using his best Mr. Rogers voice he said, "Come here, Little One. I want to ask you something. Do you watch *Mr. Rogers' Neighborhood?*"

"Yes, Sir," Kelly responded.

Bush told Kelly, "Well, I'm kind of like Mr. Rogers when he makes his puppets move and talk -- like your daddy (Houston, ventriloquist) does with Elemer [his dummy]. Only I'm like Mr. Rogers because I have lots of puppets-- only mine are people. I even have a King [Fahd] just like Mr. Rogers.[1] I pull the strings (he pantomimed marionette hand movements) and I talk through them. They say my words and we create all kinds of exciting Adventures. Right now I'm building a new Neighborhood (the

156

New World Order). The stage is set, and I have hold of everyone's strings. I need you to help me -- together we can pull your mother's strings. She's in my Neighborhood. That means you're in my Neighborhood, too."

It seems obvious to me now that Bush was referring to those actively engaged in implementing the New World Order through chaos and mass mind control (a.k.a. media conditioning) as "The Neighborhood." Of course, I was unable to consider disputing Bush's statement, and Kelly was certainly not of a mind to see beyond Bush's twist on her favorite television program. Kelly's big blue eyes grew even wider as she responded, "I am?" Bush stood up and took her hand. "C'mon. Let me show you my Neighborhood." He led her out the door.

Kelly became violently physically ill after her induction into George Bush's "Neighborhood" and from every sexual encounter she had with him thereafter. She ran 104-6 degree temperatures, vomited and endured immobilizing headaches for an average of three days (as is consistent with high voltage trauma). These were the only tell-tale evidences aside from the scarring burns left on her skin. Houston forbid me to call a doctor, and Kelly forbid me to comfort her, pitifully complaining that her head "hurt too bad to even move." And she did not move for hours on end. Kelly often complained of severe kidney pain, and her rectum usually bled for a day or two after Bush sexually abused her. My own mind control victimization rendered me unable to help or protect her. Seeing my child in such horrible condition drove my own wedge of insanity in deeper, perpetuating my total inability to affect her needs until our rescue by Mark Phillips in 1988.

Kelly's bleeding rectum was but one of many physical indicators of George Bush's pedophile perversions. I have overheard him speak blatantly of his sexual abuse of her on many occasions. He used this and threats to her life to "pull my strings" and control me. The psychological ramifications of being raped by a pedophile President are mind shattering enough, but reportedly Bush further reinforced his traumas to Kelly's mind with sophisticated NASA electronic and drug mind control devices. Bush also instilled the "Who ya gonna call?" and "I'll be watching you" binds on Kelly, further reinforcing her sense of helplessness. The systematic tortures and traumas I endured as a child now seem trite in comparison to the brutal physical and psychological devastation that George Bush inflicted on my daughter.

As soon as the door closed behind Bush and Kelly, Dick Cheney reached over to Reagan's desk from his seat and flipped over the hour glass. (Oz) "Her [Kelly's] time is running out. You'd better pay attention and follow orders as though her life depends on it, because from now on [heh heh] it always does! If you make one mistake - one -- then I'll get her, my pretty."

Reagan said, "George is like a director. He makes sure the stage is set to implement the New World Order as I envision it. Then he makes sure everyone has a script and knows their part. He tells them how to speak and when to speak. How to dress and [patting my head] how to wear their hair. He gets everything and everyone in place and hollers, 'Action!'" Reagan shouted through his hand as though it were a megaphone and rambled on, "All the world's a stage. I'm the Wizard. But he is directing the show so you better pay attention and learn your part well from him."

Cheney interrupted, "George and I will be working closely on a few projects together, and when you see him, you'll see me. When you're given orders from him, you're given orders from me."

157

"She knows the chain of command, Dick," Reagan injected, referring to his perception of who was in charge, and in what order. President, Vice President, Habib, Cheney, Byrd, etc. may have been the chain of command in Reagan's mind, but Cheney's definition was necessary to my understanding. From my perspective, the chain of command was clearly Bush, Cheney, Habib, Reagan, Aquino and lastly, on a par with my handler Houston, Byrd, all of which was subject to change at any given moment. Cheney just rolled his eyes at Reagan's comment and never slowed down as he continued, "Right now a stage is being set and you will be directed by the Vice President on just how he wants you to do your part in setting the stage for Mexico's role in the New World Order."

Reagan jumped in again, "With the world in order, there will be world peace. By strategically placing an American Patriot dedicated to the cause of spreading democracy in all parts of the world, we can influence the thinking of every nation's leader and paint for them a picture of freedom and American values that they'll never forget. They'll spread it to the people and the whole planet will be of one mind -- one purpose -- one cause. Freedom. You'll be talking with some of these friends and leaders from time to time on my behalf."

Bush slipped back into the meeting, without Kelly. Cheney continued, "Taking orders from me and your new director -- the Vice President. Lesson number one. You know what Miami Vice is. Undercover drug agents taking control of the drug industry. A Vice President is just that -- an undercover drug agent taking control of the drug industry -- for the President."

Bush spoke up. "Mexico is a problem. They've got lots of drugs, but not the brains nor the means to sell it outside their own country. So how can we take control of their [growing] drug industry when we can't even get our hands on it? It's your duty as an American citizen to open the routes and initiate freedom from poverty throughout their nation by offering them cash as a means of enticing their drug industry right into our grasp by bringing it right up to our doorsteps."

"Operation Greenbacks for Wetbacks," Cheney said, laughing. Bush laughed with him.

Bush regained his composure to conclude, "Your assignment begins in Miami with NCL (Norwegian Caribbean Lines) and ends when you return from Mexico with word of success."

Cheney caught my eye with a hand gesture that directed my gaze from Bush to the hour glass, which was running out fast. By then I was deeply tranced and lost touch with my surroundings all together while my trance was timelessly deepened for further programming. I left the White House with a message for the Vice President of Mexico, Carlos Salinas de Gortari, from the Vice President of the U.S., and with one very sick child.

---

[1] Mr Roger projects through puppets on his show, and one of his key characters from the Land of Make-Believe is King Friday the 13th.

CHAPTER 16

OPERATION GREENBACKS FOR WETBACKS

My CIA mind control handler Alex Houston and I boarded the Norwegian Caribbean Lines ship bound for Cozumel, Mexico, with a large, black, soft side suitcase packed full of cash and a proposal of "prosperity" from the U.S. This proposal, programmed in me by Vice President Bush, was supposedly initial diplomatic groundwork for the North American Free Trade Agreement (NAFTA).

It was my understanding then that the North American Free Trade Agreement was considered a significant step in implementing the New World Order through mind manipulation of the masses. According to Byrd, propaganda disguising the true purpose of NAFTA included the concept of "free trade" which the U.S. and Mexican governments had long since shared. "Free trade" of child and adult mind controlled slaves, cocaine, heroin and businesses has been not-so-secretly proliferating for years. My own father joined the "run for the border" via U.S. State Department and Mexican subsidized business incentives and opened yet another branch of his U.S. Department of Defense-given-business in Mexico. This was part of the "free trade" agreement that I know personally has been operating smoothly from at least 1984. In an effort to maintain the illusion that the agreement would not create a negative economic imbalance between Mexico and the U.S., tourist areas of Mexico were deliberately built up, enhanced and Americanized with U.S. dollars. These funds were provided through CIA covert Black Budget operations of drug and slave trading, as well as directly through the Senate Appropriations Committee of which Senator Robert C. Byrd is chairman as of this writing.

I certainly do not purport to understand international business, nor have I attempted to "educate" myself through what I know to be propaganda slanted and filtered periodicals. How money interfaces in world markets has been well documented. For example, who supports whom in which financial endeavors is apparently far too complex for even BCCI attorneys and investigators to sort through. My personal perspective on Mexican, U.S., and Saudi Arabian buildup of Mexico's economy is limited to my own experiences. My understanding is further affected by deliberate misinformation from the criminal perspectives of those who were in control of my mind's knowledge base and actions. From time to time, Senator Byrd used me as a robotic sounding board. He told me what he wanted me to hear, and this was structured more toward stroking his own enormous, warped ego than it was to educate me in world finance.

Senator Byrd claimed "the money game is simply a game of control," and lives by his adopted Golden Rule of "He who holds the gold makes the rules." He told me in so many words that "by appropriating funds to all (viable) projects ushering in the free trade agreement, and allocating lesser amounts to U.S. social systems such as our 'criminal' justice system, I control our country and our place in world markets. All the world is a stage, and I own the theater!...you can bank on it!"

Senator Byrd's twisted reality echoed in my mind when America was bought (stolen) and sold by Presidents Bush and Clinton in the recent passage of NAFTA. "I would never run for President -- Oh, I'd win if I did," Byrd bragged. "But why should I run for an office that is beneath me? I can make a President look good, or I can make him look bad by strategically appropriating funds." Byrd and others I knew boasted that he was one of those (corrupt power brokers) responsible for Bill Clinton's being "chosen" and elected to the office of Presidency. And the last minute bids and dealings with those Congressmen holding NAFTA's deciding votes proved "strategic appropriations" indeed made Clinton "look good" in his NAFTA "victory."

At the La Celiba Hotel in Cozumel, Houston maintained my food and water depravation for mind control purposes, even during our dinner meeting in the hotel's restaurant later that evening. Although the restaurant was "officially" closed due to the late hour, a mariachi band, one waiter, four stationed armed guards, my Mexican dignitary contact, his two assistants, and handler Houston and I were present. During the meeting, arrangements were made to meet with Mexico's then Vice President Salinas the next afternoon at a nearby military installation. I would also deliver a message as usual from Senator Byrd at the nearby Consulate's office pertaining to U.S. financial support for creating propaganda to insure the illusion of economic equality in Mexican tourist areas. These funds were simply to further the ongoing shared goal of easing into New World Order domination through carefully contrived smoke and mirror tactics.

The next afternoon, Houston escorted me to the high security fenced government installation for my meeting with Salinas. According to Bush, Salinas was regarded by the Reagan-Bush Administration as superior in power to Miguel de la Madrid who was officially President of Mexico at that time. The upcoming Mexican "election," which was no more an election than Reagan's second term, was to place Salinas in the office of President to coincide with Bush's destined Presidency. To insure that this "strategically placed American Patriot" would be voted into position, Reagan informed me that the U.S. would "guard the integrity" of "elections" by covertly "overseeing" them, among other strategies. Salinas was to be President at all costs.

Although President De la Madrid was considered by Bush to be the stepping stone to the ultimate reign of Salinas/Bush's (already established) diplomatic relations, he was regarded with all due respect in a manner conducive to "no margins for error." His full cooperation was tantamount to establishing Bush's and Salinas' goals via free flowing drug markets and Mexico's cooperation in subversively funding and supplying Reagan's Nicaraguan Contras. De la Madrid worked in close association with Salinas so that a smooth transition of power would maintain U.S.-Mexican relations and efforts already in place.

"A message to Salinas is a message to the President," Cheney had explained. Not only would the message be relayed to de la Madrid, but for the most part Salinas was the one responsible for working with George Bush since they would both come into power during the most critical point in the promotion of NAFTA -- passing it by the American people and into law. President Reagan, Mexican President de la Madrid, Vice President Bush, and Mexican Vice President Salinas were all "of one mind -- one effort" toward economic expansion and growth for our southern "neighbors in the New World Order" through what I experienced was based on "free trade" of drugs, children, and pornography. Vice President Bush told me that this (criminal) activity was regarded as Mexico's "only means of rapid economic advancement and freedom from poverty since the people were slaves to their own inability to advance in world markets."

When I arrived at the military installation with the aforementioned suitcase of cash in hand, I was taken to Salinas' "office" through a series of electronic gates guarded by officers in white uniforms. Salinas sat at his desk, which was small and functional (i.e. military issue), set on a highly polished wooden floor in a vast room virtually void of decor and personal effects. This created an air of military practicality. I set the suitcase in front of Salinas and began relaying the message I had been programmed to deliver.

"I have a message from the Vice President of the United State of America to our neighbors in Mexico. America is willing to share its wealth through a trade agreement with Mexico. We'll trade our cash for control over Mexico's cocaine and heroin production. By controlling your drug industry, we can open the border between our countries to allow a free flow of cocaine and heroin into the U.S., bought and paid for in American dollars to build Mexico. Eventually this could dissolve the border between our countries altogether as Mexico's economy grows to match ours. If we begin today, this dream could be realized by the turn of the century -- sharing the same continent, sharing the same wealth. Why? The drug industry already dictates what the Mexican government can or cannot do. By giving the U.S. control of your drug industry, Mexico regains control over her government. Re-established power backed by U.S. dollars will bring Mexico on an economic par with America. We can begin by spreading the word through the (drug) cartels that the U.S. is covertly willing to open the borders to free drug trade by making agents available to show you the passage and routes through which the drugs are to be delivered. Only U.S. agents can bring Mexican heroin and (South American) cocaine across the border, and likewise they will bring the cash in. Explain to those select few who control the drug empires that the cruise line (NCL) agreement is going into mass expansion, tearing down the border between our countries enough to allow for as many drugs to come in as Mexico can deal out. When do we begin? Immediately. The cash is at hand. [I gestured toward the suitcase which Salinas unzipped to find full of cash.] Deliver whatever amount of brown heroin you have at hand as a means of confirmation to the agreement. Keep the change as a token of the change and good fortune that has befallen Mexico from its neighboring nation."

As I finished Bush's message, Salinas immediately took a note pad from the desk and scrawled a quick note. He passed it to a guard who was stationed at the door. He stood up, smiled, and leaned over his desk as he extended his hand in a warm handshake. I was escorted out. Houston found me on the front steps of the installation and together we were escorted through the barbed wire fences and back onto the streets of Cancun.

I waited in a small clearing nearby for an indeterminate length of time, playing with a large iguana. Finally, a taxi cab driver pulled up and honked his horn three times, signaling me to pick up a fist sized ball of Mexican brown heroin. The heroin was crudely wrapped in brown paper, tied with twine, and measured approximately the size of a baseball. As quickly as the cab driver left, Houston, who was standing some distance away with two uniformed men, signaled me to join him. We were then driven to the airport where we boarded a U.S. Air Force aircraft to Washington, D.C.

Immediately upon arrival at Andrews Air Force Base just outside of Washington, D.C., I was taken to Senator Byrd who then escorted me to Dick Cheney's Pentagon office for a meeting with Vice President Bush. I was ill and vomiting from the high voltage administered in Mexico to compartmentalize my memory. I was allowed to use Byrd's magnetic pass key card to unlock the maze of doors that led to the Ladies Room. I was still wearing my inappropriate-for-D.C. cruise clothes and carrying the heroin in my tote bag when I met with Bush to confirm Mexico's agreement to his proposal. Bush took the heroin for himself, obviously pleased with the quality of the product. Cheney laughed and told Bush he needed to "confiscate the Contra-band."

Bush replied, "Over my dead body" as he laughed at Cheney's Contra joke.

"If you don't share some of it, that could be the case," Cheney said. "Pitch it here."

Bush struck a pitch pose, wound up, made a fake out pitch, and joked in baseball banter, "Its a 'high fly' ball. You're going to have to steal." He tossed the heroin in the air, caught it, and strode for the door. Cheney got out of his chair, pointed to the door, and ordered me "Out."

Houston and I were flown in to Montego Bay, Jamaica and transported to Ocho Rios to board our next NCL cruise ship.

CHAPTER 17

ABOUT FACES

Soon after Kelly was inducted into George Bush's "Neighborhood" through horrific sexual abuse, Bush enforced his controls on me. Our mind control handler, Alex Houston, had taken Kelly and me to Washington, D.C. for separately scheduled meetings with Bush. Kelly had already been escorted by agents to her rendezvous with him that morning, during which time I had been ordered to one of U.S. Senator Robert C. Byrd's offices located in the nearby F.B.I. Hoover Building. There, Byrd reinforced his holds on me by claiming control of the Justice Department and "proving" once again that I had "no where to run and no where to hide." My horror reaction was compounded when Byrd looked at his pocket watch and notified me in *Alice in Wonderland* cryptic language, "You're late, you're late for a very important date," referring to my meeting with Bush.

I sprinted from the Hoover Building, encountering Houston who waited just outside. Houston hurried me to the Smithsonian where I waited for my escorts as instructed at the "Face Changing" exhibit. This computerized exhibit illustrates how an individual's face can take on a radically different appearance by slightly altering any single feature.

The exhibit fascinated me as a programmed MPD since multiples often experience the unnerving phenomena of routinely not recognizing themselves in a mirror due to switching personalities. A multiple's face often changes slightly with each switch, which "validates" the religious communities' perceptions of so-called "demonic possession" in occultism. Logic quickly dispels this belief when it is realized that everyone's expression changes according to emotion, by skin color and tones, blood pressure, and by tightening or relaxing specific micro muscles. An MPD's face changes are more exaggerated when these natural conditions are combined with the results of sophisticated programming. "Charm School" teaches subconscious control over these natural phenomena as a ready-made disguise on government slaves such as myself, as well as to enhance sex slaves' "beauty" to their maximum potential. I was incapable of thinking or logically understanding my fascination with the display, as I stood totally enthralled, waiting for my escorts as ordered.

As the escorts approached, I was relieved to see Kelly with them. Though she was visibly tranced and traumatized, the fact that she was alive was all I was capable of grasping. When she saw the "Face Changing" exhibit, she excitedly exclaimed, "Uncle George just read me a book about this!" Before I could hear anymore, I was led away, leaving Kelly with our handler, Houston.

I was then quickly taken to Bush's Residence Office, which here-to-fore was unfamiliar to me. Although it had slate blue plush carpets and fine furnishings like the White House office, lattice work and smaller rooms provided a different air. I sat in a hard back wooden chair as ordered, while Bush carefully positioned himself in front of me on a little wooden footstool. This allowed me clear visibility of the large book that he held in his lap. All illustrations faced me, while all text except the last page was printed in the holder's direction. This book was a unique, high tech piece of art specifically designed to enforce Bush's favorite method of programming, "You Are What You Read." The juvenile face depicted on the front of this hardcover book gave it the appearance of a children's storybook. It was entitled *About Faces*.

Bush explained the dynamics of "changing faces" and "becoming what I read." Although I had been conditioned to this idea all of my life through Disney stories, *The Wizard of Oz, Alice in Wonderland*, etc., I was not prepared for Bush's version of "You Are What You Read" programming explanations. The illustrations themselves were elaborate, consisting of mirrors and hypnotic depictions. He seemingly made the book come alive in my mind as he read page after poetic page of hypnotic, metaphorical language, all the while creating powerful illusions. His impersonations of the characters further enhanced the desired effect of fantasy becoming reality. This extraordinary effort to scramble reality would have worked - perfectly -- had it not been for another victim and myself discussing it only a few days later The purpose of Bush's book was clearly explained within the first few pages, which included the following passage:

I am the Vice President when circumstance demands,
And I am your Commander, you'll follow my commands.
The first command's important - It is one you will heed,
When I send you a book, you are what you read.

Throughout my tenure as a Presidential Model mind controlled slave, I was provided specific books according to Bush's program. These books, delivered through pre-established channels such as Ken Riley, Alex Houston, and even Ronald Reagan, came complete with specific commands on how they were to be interpreted and used. Some books were used to instruct me on operations; some were an attempt to scramble my memory with fantasy; others were used to load my mind with pertinent data such as bank account passbook numbers, and so on.

I was provided a paperback book entitled *Afghanistan*, from which I absorbed history, current political events, and the strength of the Afghani Freedom Fighters. I have since learned that the book I read was never publicly released in the text it was provided me. According to instruction, the book was delivered back to Bush as quickly as I finished memorizing it. I wonder in retrospect if any part of it contained fact beyond how I was supposed to perceive it.

I read stories of espionage, including Robert Ludlum's *Bourne Identity*, and William Diehl's *Chameleon*. Mostly I was provided steamy sex novels for further training as well as scrambles. Kelly was conditioned to fairy tales, Steven Speilburg's *ET*, NASA NSA operative George Lucas' *Star Wars*, and the nightmarish *Never Ending Story*. Steinbeck's classic *Of Mice and Men* caused Kelly constantly to quote the dependent character of Lenny for years saying, "Tell me what to do, George." She still does this each and every time I am allowed to visit with her in the mental institution. The attending therapist overseeing the visit has yet to pick up on this programming cue, and I am forbidden by Juvenile Court order not to discuss Kelly's past or therapy.

Bush's most effective example of "You Are What You Read" in his book *About Faces* occurred during his reading of the page depicting lizard-like "aliens" from a "far off deep space place." Claiming to me to be an alien himself, Bush apparently activated a hologram of the lizard-like "alien" which provided the illusion of Bush transforming like a chameleon before my eyes. In retrospect, I understand that Bush had been painstakingly careful in positioning our seats in order that the hologram's effectiveness be maximized. U.S. Army Lt. Col. Aquino's occultism provided trauma sufficient to maintain my Project Monarch mind controlled existence despite his inability to affect my core spirituality. Therefore, I was not routinely subjected to the other favorite "trauma of choice" -- alien themes -- like many slaves (including Kelly) I knew had been. The effect of Bush's illusion hologram on such victims is binding and strong. Even Aquino envied the mind shattering effects of Bush's alien theme visual traumas to the extent that he wrote and published his own comic book sequel to Lucas' *Star Wars*. While occultism is easily dispelled with reason and fact, Bush's alien theme continues to be reinforced through NASA's involvement in mind control atrocities. Additionally, California's 24 year incumbent Senator Alan Cranston of the Select Committee on Intelligence has perpetuated this trauma base for decades, as have others. Despite my having escaped routine "alien" theme traumas, Bush's "You Are What You Read" hologram proved devastatingly sufficient for him to gain total control of my robotic mind from that moment on until my rescue in 1988.

By the time Bush reached the last page of his *About Faces* book, I was so traumatized I instantly "became what I read" when I read the last verse aloud as ordered:

I am a True Patriot living an American Dream,
I will become my role when you pull my string.
I will become my part, so I can 'be all I can be'
'Cause just like the Vice President, I am what I read.

CHAPTER 18

IN THE MEAN TIME

My life seemed to lead me at an accelerated pace after being subjected to Reagan and Bush. My handler Alex Houston egotistically claimed it was his and Elemer's (his alter-ego dummy) popularity that kept us traveling so extensively within the country music circuit. When we weren't traveling the Caribbean and Mexico via NCL ships, or driving his cocaine loaded motor home to strategically booked shows across the U.S., we were routinely moving in and out of Washington, D.C. All along the way, my daughter and I were either prostituted, used in commercial pornography, or filmed in Michael Danté's "Chief" bestiality pornography as ordered by Uncle Ronnie Reagan.

Occasionally our travels would take us to Michigan, where Houston made certain we stayed with my family. Trips to my father's house were devastating but informative. My mother had developed deep psychological scars above and beyond her own MPD condition and became an insomniac. My father by this time was routinely traveling to London, Germany, and Mexico, and taking the family to Florida's Disney World and Washington, D.C. My older brother, Bill, still worked for and with my father, traveled with him annually to "hunt" in Cheney's Greybull, Wyoming lodge, and maintained his wife and three children under trauma base mind control according to my father's instructions. My brother, Mike, ran a video store to front some of my father's and Uncle Bob Tanis' lucrative porn video business. My sister, Kelli Jo, became a belly dancing contortionist excelling in "gymnastics" since she became "as flexible as Gumby" according to her prostitution programming. She worked her way through school in children's day care centers, admittedly spotting, for my father, abused children for potential "chosen ones" candidates. In 1990 she graduated to open a licensed day care, "Little Learners" in Grand Haven, Michigan for my father. My brother Tom (Beaver) is a Compu-Kids (CIA Project) programmed computer genius. My brother Tim broke his leg (in the same place my mother had broken his leg years before) due to following my father's sports programming above and beyond human capability. And my youngest sister, Kimmy, became hysterically obsessed with "Mr. Rogers," expressed immense fear of her huge "electric" doll house that lit up at night to look like the White House, and was under a doctor's care for anorexia by age seven. I look forward to the day I can help them all, and justice is served on my father.

Since I was using parts of my brain I would not have used under normal circumstances, I developed the ability to read backwards as naturally as I could read forwards. Houston tapped into this typically occult based phenomenon as a means of "scrambling" road signs to promote amnesia of where we were traveling. He further compounded his effort by conditioning me to read phonetically and literally, and alternated his "scrambling" methods. "Zoo"s became "ooz" and "ooz" translated to "oz". Arkansas read "Our Kansas", and Missouri became (and was!) "Misery." East became West, and highway 66 became 99. When I traveled, I "literally" did not consciously know if I was coming or going. If an outsider happened to ask me about where I'd traveled, I mechanically replied, "The towns all run together and look alike after awhile." Commands delivered in the same language twisting manner were natural for me to follow. "Role with it" was easier for me to become according to Reagan's acting definition than it was to go with the flow by "rolling with it." Phrases like Wyoming Senator Alan Simpson's "In a switch of an "I" (personality)/ "eye"(hypnotic blink)/ "i"(the letter), complaint becomes compliant. The parts of my brain I was forced to function with were not conducive to "normal" thinking.

Nor could I have appeared "normal" to outsiders had they cared to see beyond my superficial programmed cover personality. I did have occasion to mix with "outsiders" at the local library where I took Kelly for her books on days when we were not traveling. By age 6, she tested at the 7th grade reading level. I also emerged from my closed environment to tend to Kelly's schooling. She maintained straight As, but her poor attendance record threatened to violate state requirements. Once when the librarian asked where Kelly would be traveling to waive library book due dates, or the teacher inquired as to Kelly's absences, I gave the usual response of, "the towns all run together and look alike after awhile." If they pressed for specifics, I ran through a series of religious phrases such as "praise the Lord", to compensate for my lack of answers. People tended to overlook and accept "religious fanaticism" personality peculiarities, which combined with my "role" traveling the country music industry, kept outsiders at a distance for years.

My "religious fanatic" cover personality was cultivated at the Brentwood, Tennessee Lord's Chapel "nondenominational" (Pentecostal) church, through the CIA Operative preacher "Reverend" Billy Roy Moore (who has since fled to Arkansas due to a local murder scandal).

Moore transported cocaine from the Caribbean for the CIA, at least during the Reagan Administration, under the guise of so-called "missions,"[1] ie. Christian ministries. It most likely was not the intent of the Christians dedicated to their Caribbean ministries to be used by the CIA and Moore to inadvertently mule drugs into our country. Even CIA agents operating under "need to know" partial information were denied the full scope of what they were actually participating in. Many seemingly willing participants were manipulated, provided "justification," and deliberately misled to believe they were serving their country, rather than destroying it from the inside out.

"Pastor" Moore combined his knowledge of Kelly's and my programming keys, codes, and triggers with his use of metaphorical language to maintain and/or direct our mode of operation. Moore's "following" consisted primarily of government mind controlled slaves and handlers, including the Mandrells, Jack Greene and his slave, the Oak Ridge Boys, and others. He instructed us on how to vote, which political issues to support, and to follow other "religious" political leaders such as his and Manuel Noriega's friend evangelist Jimmy Swaggart. "Religious counseling" from Moore equated to maintaining mind control programming through "God's Orders." And "God's Orders" often came by telephone.

Houston constantly prostituted Kelly to anyone "in the loop" who was willing to pay. When she wasn't being prostituted, she was being filmed pornographically. By 1984, Michael Danté routinely filmed Kelly in pornography, since kiddie porn was as lucrative as bestiality. He filmed Kelly and me in Las Vegas, Nevada and various other locations throughout the Caribbean, California, Florida, Tennessee, and in my home state of Michigan.

This created professional conflict with long time kiddie pornographers formerly associated with Houston. Houston's close friend in Waycross, Georgia, pedophile Jimmy Walker, managed the Okefenokee Swamp Park and had participated in black budget funding operations for years on both the cocaine and pornography levels. His counterpart, Dick Flood, refused to participate in any more pornography after Danté came on the scene. Even the Huntsville, Alabama NASA/DIA/CIA appointed "law enforcement" officers could rarely succeed in their bidding for Kelly's video taped performances unless directly ordered by Senator Byrd. Danté considered himself her future owner as well as mine, and maintained control of our porn "business" ventures through serious U.S. Government and international Mafia methodisms/connections.

Jimmy Walker, the same photographer who had taken pornographic "wedding night" pictures for Larry Flynt, recently had other photographs of me published in *Hustler*. When Danté found out, he was furious. Larry Flynt and Danté both worked for the CIA, had Vatican and Mafia connections, and deliberately appealed to Reagan's perversions using Project Monarch mind controlled slaves. What Flynt could not "legally" publish, Danté ran through the underground. Flynt and Danté lived on opposite coasts, which, despite their similarities, still was not far enough apart to sooth their differences. Waving his hands in dramatic Italian gestures, Danté furiously spouted a string of obscenities over Flynt's publishing photos of what he deemed "his property." Accusing Flynt of going to extremes to gain favor/protection from the government, Danté shouted, "He's a bigger whore than the girls he promotes!"

Michael Danté's pornographic filming abilities served several purposes. Aside from producing porn according to Reagan's own (well known) perversions and instructions, Danté was present during many key international government "gatherings." Oftentimes when I and others were prostituted to various government (New World Order) leaders, Danté had hidden cameras filming perverse sexual acts apparently for future black mail leverage. These videos were scandalous in proportion and were usually ordered by Reagan. Danté turned the videos over to Reagan, and covertly kept copies to protect himself. Danté converted a small room of his Beverly Hills mansion into a security vault, where he kept his personal copies of the international blackmail porn tapes there.

Among these internationally scandalous tapes are numerous videos covertly produced at the supposedly secure political sex playground in northern California, Bohemian Grove. According to Houston, Danté's high tech undetectable cameras used fiber optics, and fish eye lens were in each of the elite club's numerous sexual perversion theme rooms. My knowledge of these cameras was due to the strategically compromising positions of the political perpetrators I was prostituted to in the various kinky theme rooms.

I was programmed and equipped to function in all rooms at Bohemian Grove in order to compromise specific government targets according to their personal perversions. "Anything, anytime, anywhere with anyone" was my mode of operation at the Grove. I do not purport to understand the full function of this political cesspool playground as my perception was limited to my own realm of experience. My perception is that Bohemian Grove serves those ushering in the New World Order through mind control, and consists primarily of the highest Mafia and U.S. Government officials. I do not use the term "highest" loosely, as copious quantities of drugs were consumed there. Project Monarch mind control slaves were routinely abused there to fulfill the primary purpose of the club: purveying perversion.

Bohemian Grove is reportedly intended to be used recreationally, providing a supposedly secure environment for politically affluent individuals to "party" without restraint. The only business conducted there pertained to implementing the New World Order, through the proliferation of mind control atrocities, giving the place an air of "Masonic Secrecy." The only room where business discussions were permitted was the small, dark lounge affectionately and appropriately referred to as the Underground.[2]

Sex slaves were not routinely permitted in the Underground for security reasons, leaving the lounge's small stage as the only source of "entertainment." This entertainment ranged from would-be talents such as Lee Atwater, Bill Clinton, and George Bush to CIA Operative entertainers such as BoxCar Willie and Lee Greenwood. On one occasion I was instructed to meet with former President Gerald Ford in the Underground where Lee Atwater was picking and singing. As I walked through the smoke filled room to Ford's table, Atwater interrupted his song to cryptically acknowledge my unwelcome presence by singing choruses of "Over the Rainbow" and Byrd's song for me "Country Roads" while emphasizing the lines of "Almost heaven, West Virginia."

My purpose at the Grove was sexual in nature, and therefore my perceptions were limited to a sex slave's viewpoint. As an effective means of control to ensure undetected proliferation of their perverse indulgences, slaves such as myself were subjected to ritualistic trauma. I knew each breath I took could be my last, as the threat of death lurked in every shadow. Slaves of advancing age or with failing programming were sacrificially murdered "at random" in the wooded grounds of Bohemian Grove, and I felt it was "simply a matter of time until it would be me." Rituals were held at a giant concrete owl monument on the banks of, ironically enough, the Russian (rushin') River. These occultish sex rituals stemmed from the scientific belief that mind controlled slaves required severe trauma to ensure compartmentalization of the memory, and not from any spiritual motivation.

My own threat of death was instilled when I witnessed the sacrificial death of a young, dark haired victim at which time I was instructed to perform sexually "as though my life depended upon it." I was told, "...the next sacrifice victim could be you. Anytime when you least expect it, the owl will consume you. Prepare yourself, and stay prepared." Being "prepared" equated to being totally suggestible, i.e. "on my toes" awaiting their command.

After returning to Tennessee, Houston attempted to distort my Bohemian Grove experience by instructing me to "prepare myself for imminent death." He ordered me into a bathtub of cold water, placed ice cubes in my vagina, then transferred me to his bed. There he tied a coroner's type tag on my toe, and hypnotically deepened my trance to the point where my heart and breathing were nearly stopped. Then he gratified himself on my cold, still body through faux necrophilia -- reportedly one of his favorite perversions. Houston had "perfected" his perversion to the extent that he handed the keys to my death-state programming to Lt. Col. Michael Aquino for use in Reagan's Hands On Mind Control Demonstrations. My death-state also further equipped me in my role of "anything, anytime, anywhere with anyone" to be accessed at Bohemian Grove.

The club offered a "Necrophilia" theme room to its members. I was so heavily drugged and programmed when used in the "necrophilia" room, that the threat of actually "slipping through death's door" and being sacrificed "before I knew it" did not affect me. My whole existence was balanced precariously on the edge of death as a matter of routine anyway. My robotic state did not permit me the "luxury" of self-preservation, and I could only do exactly what I was told to do. My necrophilia room experience was only for the purpose of providing Danté a compromising film of a targeted member anyway.

Other perversion theme rooms at the Bohemian Club included what I heard Ford refer to as the "Dark Room." When he not so cleverly said, "Let's go to the Dark Room and see what develops," I understood from experience that he was interested in indulging in his perverse obsession for pornography. In the Dark Room, members had sex with the same mind controlled slave they were viewing in porn on a big screen television.

There was a triangular glass display centered in a main throughway where I was locked in with various trained animals, including snakes. Members walking by watched illicit sex acts of bestiality, women with women, mothers with daughters, kids with kids, or any other unlimited perverse visual display.

I was once brutally assaulted by Dick Cheney in the Leather Room, which was designed like a dark, black leather-lined train berth. As I crawled through the leather flaps covering the narrow entrance, I heard Cheney play on the word "berth/birth" as the soft blackness engulfed me. With the small opening covered, the blinding darkness enhanced the sense of touch and provided an option of anonymity. Cheney jokingly claimed that I "blew his cover" when I recognized his all-too-familiar voice and abnormally large penis size.

There was a room of shackles and tortures, black lights and strobes, an opium den, ritualistic sex altars, a chapel, group orgy rooms including poster beds, water beds, and "kitten" houses. I was used as a "rag doll" in the "toy store," and as a urinal in the "golden arches" room.

From the owl's roost to the necrophilia room, no memory of sexual abuse is as horrifying as the conversations overheard in the Underground pertaining to implementing the New World Order. I learned that perpetrators believed that controlling the masses through propaganda mind manipulation did not guarantee there would be a world left to dominate due to environmental and overpopulation problems. The solution being debated was not pollution/population control, but mass genocide of "selected undesirables."

---

[1] Moore often operated under the cloak of World Vision.

[2] The wooden sign was carved to read: U.N.DERGROUND

CHAPTER 19

E.T. PHONE ROME

Anyone attending the Bohemian Grove on a regular basis was referred to by those in the know as a "Grover." One such Grover was Ronald Reagan's then-Secretary of Education, Bill Bennett. Bill Bennett, who later became "Drug Czar" during the Bush Administration, wrote the so-called *Book of Virtues* and was/is? vying for the office of President. Bennett is apparently very close to his brother and fellow Grover, Bob Bennett. Although Bob Bennett holds the position of Legal Counsel to President Clinton, it is apparent that the brothers recognize no party lines.

It was clear to me that there were no partisan differences amongst those ushering in the New World Order, any more than there was loyalty to our *Constitution*. The close relationship I witnessed between the Bennett brothers, like the marriage between Clinton's and Bush's 1992 campaign managers James Carville and Mary Matlin, should raise questions as to their agenda.

When Bill and Bob Bennett together sexually assaulted my daughter Kelly and me at the Bohemian Grove in 1986, I had already known Bill Bennett as a mind control programmer for some time. Bennett anchored his Jesuit/Vatican based programming of me in my Catholic conditioning initially instilled via the Rite to Remain Silent. Through further manipulation of my "inner- dimensional" perceptions, Bennett believed he had forever compartmentalized his personal secrets of perverse sex with his brother Bob and my then six-year- old daughter. Bennett also had manipulated my mind in accordance with Vatican "Orders" via Byrd's Jesuit College programming center in West Virginia. He used his role as Jesuit programmer for the purposes of carrying out his efforts as Education Secretary to implement Education 2000.[1]

In order to program my mind for my role in bringing Education 2000 into the "Volunteer State" of Tennessee's school system, Bennett used sophisticated mind manipulation to set the stage -- the same kind of mind manipulation propaganda executed on national and international scale. Bennett's penchant for manipulating minds is apparently rooted in his knowledge of Catholic/Jesuit mind control techniques.

When I met Bennett at a White House cocktail party in 1984, I was wearing the rosy cross necklace that Guy VanderJagt and Father Don had presented to me during my first communion, to signify the mode of program I was operating under at the time. Byrd had ordered that I wear it for the occasion.

Byrd was already talking with Bennett when a White House butler led me in to see Byrd.[2] Byrd was saying, "I was just talking about you with my friend, Secretary of Education[3] William Bennett."

"Bill," Bennett corrected, sweeping his lecherous gaze over me as though I were merchandise. "How do you do?"

"As I am told, thank you," I said as I extended my hand as trained.

Bennett clumsily fingered the rosy cross necklace, blowing his alcoholic breath in my face as he said, "Your necklace is as beautiful as you are, and no doubt, as significant in purpose. Where did this come from and what does it mean to you?"

"From my first communion," I responded. "Guy (Byrd interrupted to clarify 'VanderJagt') gave it to me to consummate my holy communion."

Byrd corrected me, "<u>Commemorate</u> your holy communion."

"She doesn't need a translator, Bobby," Bennett laughed. "I'm hearing her loud and clear."

Byrd left me with Bennett, who went into a long winded recitation on an interpretation of the *Bible* deliberately intended to further distort my Catholic instilled perceptions. "Christ was an alien in this land," he was saying in accordance with his learned Jesuit mind manipulation techniques. "Once he landed in earth's plane, it was plain to see he was a leader in interdimensional travel. <u>We</u> (Jesuits/aliens) followed his lead since he was the first to slip into earth's dimension. In Christ's transformation from porpoise[4] to purpose, he lost his will to earth's demands. He lost his porpoise, so to speak." Totally "trance- fixed," I listened as Bennett rattled on and on. "When Christ emerged from the deep to inhale of earth's atmosphere, time began ticking. It was not recognized or acknowledged until Christ's passing, however. We began marking time with his death. BC - AD -- or is that AC-DC?" Referring to high voltage used to compartmentalize memory, he continued, "No, AC in DC stops time. At any rate, we followed his lead. He referred to you as sheep. He knew you needed to be led. He led us. He led you. He led us to you. We're here to lead you. The transformation is perfected now, updated with the latest in alien technologies whereby we no longer have to follow Christ's course to the grave. We can transcend dimensions free of the confines of earth's gravitational pull. The time is now, and we are here to lead you. We know your mind. That's how we make you mind. Make you mine. Make you a mind. Make you mine. Journey with me now..."

Bennett manipulated my perceptions until, at last, he informed me, "You and I will be working closely together on a global education project." Sweeping his hand around the crowded room, he continued, "This atmosphere is not conducive to the kind of work we need to be doing. Something else just came up that demands immediate attention. Let's complete tonight's business with pleasure, beat it out of this dimension, suspend your suspended animation, and get with the program."

In one of many White House bedrooms available for such purposes, Bennett led me into bed. "I told you we were going to beat it out of this dimension, and that's exactly what I intend to do. A little Byrd told me you like a whip. Since I am not the Senate kind, I'll just represent the majority by giving you what you need most."

Bennett apparently found perverse pleasure in whipping me. With my wrists bruised and my body stinging with pain, Bennett lit up a cigarette and cryptically asked, "Was that your first cum-union with an alien?"

He threw me my clothes, and ordered, "Make yourself presentable. Make sure your wrists are covered. I'm not waiting around for you, I'll see you in the morning."

Bennett left. After awhile I was escorted back to Byrd, with whom I spent a brutal, short night. On the way to his room, Byrd told me, "You've got work to do come morning with Mr. Bennett. Working for him is like working for me. We are working in conjunction with the state Governors in an effort to implement the global 2000 education formula for the future. I am excited at the prospect of meddling in the future through what I accomplish today. Since I hold this country's purse strings, it is up to me to delegate as much funding as is necessary to implement the educational program. I've withheld funding and withheld funding to the point where the individual states must rely on federal funding to get them out of hot water financially. I am ready to do just that so long as they follow my guidelines. Mr. Bennett is working out the details of this plan, and will be sharing much of that with you. I need you to do what you do best by enlisting the full cooperation of state government at the upcoming Governor's Convention. I have never demanded Conventional sex of you before, but this time is different. Persuade these Governors at their weakest moment -- bring them to their knees while you are on yours, and convince them that global education is the gateway to the future if there is to be any future at all."

Early the next morning, deep underground in the NASA's Goddard Space Flight Center mind control lab near D.C., Bill Bennett began preparing me for the program. NASA uses various "CIA designer drugs" to chemically alter the brain and create exactly the mind set required at the time. Huntsville, Alabama's NASA drug of choice, "Train-quility," created a feeling of absolute, peaceful compliance and a sensation of walking on air. The drug administered this time was sufficiently similar to Tranquility to create total compliance. The beating I had endured the night before had rendered me helpless, anyway, and I could barely crawl up onto the cold, metal lab table as the drug took effect.

In the darkness surrounding me, I could hear Bill Bennett talking, "This is my brother, Bob. He and I work as one unit. We are alien to this dimension -- two beings from another plane."

The high tech light display swirling around me convinced me I was transforming dimensions with them. A laser of light hit the black wall in front of me, which seemed to explode into a panoramic view of a White House cocktail party -- as though I had transformed dimensions and stood amongst them. Not recognizing anyone, I frantically asked, "Who are these people?"

"They're not people, and this isn't a spaceship," Bennett said. As he spoke, the holographic scene changed ever so slightly until the people appeared to be lizard-like aliens. "Welcome to the second level of the underground. This level is a mere/(mirror) reflection of the first, an alien dimension. We are from a transdimensional plane that spans and encompasses all dimensions."

"Infinite dimensions," Bob injected. "Infinite dimensions spanned simultaneously."

Bill said, "No limitations."

Bob softly sang, "Let freedom ring."

"There truly is no where to run and no where to hide from us. We're who is looking from behind the Eye in the Sky," Bill continued.

"We're watching you," Bob said. He sang a line from the popular rock song "I'll Be Watching You."

"I have taken you through my dimension as a means of establishing stronger holds on your mind than the earth's plane permits," Bill Bennett was saying. "Being alien, I simply make my thoughts your thoughts by projecting them into your mind. My thoughts are your thoughts."[5]

The brief message Bennett programmed me with pertaining to Education 2000 was to be directed to state Governors at the upcoming convention while delivering a packet of information:

"The children. We must consider the children. Think for a moment beyond tomorrow. Our children are the future. Their future lies in education. We can control the future today by regulating education. Our thoughts and plans for the future -- put in their text. A text they can understand. Children's text books. The highest levels of government, the most brilliant minds on the face of this earth would like input into the future

173

by way of the children. You, as Governor, are in a position to provide that link. Global Education 2000 is ready for implementation. Look into it. Look into it and see the future."

[1] Education 2000 was designed to increase our children's learning capacity while destroying their ability to critically think for themselves. You can learn more about Education 2000, also referred to as America 2000 and Global 2000, through reading: Educating for the New World Order by B.K. Eakman, published by Halcyon House ISBN # 0-89420-278-2-3441000, and A Critique of America 2000: An Educational Strategy by Kathi Simonds, published by Citizens for Excellence in Education.

[2] Anytime I was taken to "see Byrd," I was deliberately reminded of his name, (Robert) C. Byrd and "its alien mirror reversal," Sea-Byrd as a triple bind lock in.

[3] Bill Bennett, who was still acting as Chairman of the National Endowment of the Humanities in 1984, was designated (tapped) to become U.S. Secretary of Education through his allegiances to George Bush and the New World Order. In 1985, Reagan (Bush) officially appointed Bennett as Secretary of Education. Apparently Byrd considered my "Need to Know" Bennett as Secretary of Education pertinent to my role in the Global Education project.

[4] Jesuit/NASA based whale and dolphin programming suggests that water is a mirror to other dimensions and is the means by which aliens have mixed with our population.

[5] If this were so, why did he have to audibly tell me?

CHAPTER 20

NEW WORLD ORDER OF THE ROSE

Still feeling drugged from the programming session instilled in me by Bill Bennett at the nearby Goddard Space Flight Center, I attended a White House cocktail party later that night as instructed. Dressed "to Order," I wore a slinky black dress that gathered at one hip decorated in rubies, with a red rose barrette in my hair. "The Chief called for her," my Secret Service escort told the butler as he left me at the door. The lights were dim and the air was formal as the butler led me through the unusually large crowd of people. He released my elbow, aiming me in the direction of then President Ronald Reagan.

As I walked through the crowd toward Reagan, I saw familiar faces associated with the "Order of the Rose.[1]" Across the room, Bill and Bob Bennett were laughing with Dick Cheney. Then-Governor of Pennsylvania Dick Thornburgh was engaged in conversation with Senator Arlen Spector. Within the farthest reaches of my expanded peripheral vision, I saw George Bush talking with his U.N. confidant Madeleine Albright[2]. Knowing I could see him as though I had eyes in the back of my head, Bush subtly signaled me to join them.

"You know Madeleine Albright," Bush began. Expertly using terminology from previously instilled Catholic Jesuit beliefs, he continued, "She's the reverend mother of all sisters (slaves). She's so close to God that an order from her is an order from Him." Albright snickered, apparently impressed with Bush's "witty" manipulation of program verbiage. "She rose in the U.N. through me to implement the New World peace process."

Albright said to me, "I hear you're a world (whirled?) piece." "Who told you that?" Bush demanded.

"Larry Flynt, for her stint in Jamaica[3]" she quickly explained.

Bush threw up his hand in apparent disgust at the idea of sex relating to someone with two digits in their age. "Spare me," he said.

"That's my job," Albright said matter-of-factly with a smile of pride. She shooed me away while condescendingly saying, "I'll see you tomorrow at the OAS (Organization of American States) office. Now, you run along and go play." Noting that her nonspecific orders left me unable to determine which way to turn, literally, she aimed me back in the direction of Reagan.

Reagan was dressed in a dark navy blue suit and red silk tie. His red rosebud[4] boutonniere instantly triggered me into a Jesuit "Order of the Rose" sex slave mode. "Well, hello, Kitten," Reagan said, blowing his cognac breath in my face as he bent over to kiss my hand.

"Uncle Ronnie..." I said, sexually responding as conditioned.

Reagan turned to the man beside him and said, "Brian, this is one more of those benefits of the New World Order I was telling you about. Kitten, this is Brian Mulroney, Prime Minister of Canada."

The connotations of my childhood experience with the former Prime "Minister" of Canada, Pierre Trudeau, suggested that Mulroney was Jesuit -- as did the mode I was operating in. He, too, was wearing a red rose boutonniere signifying his involvement and commitment to the Order of the Rose.

"It's a pleasure to meet you, Sir," I said as I extended my hand.

"The pleasure is mine," Mulroney said as he kissed my hand. "Please, call me Brian."

"Yes, Sir, Brian," I responded, my brain still whirling with the NASA designer drugs.

Chuckling but insistent, Mulroney reiterated, "I am not a Sir."

Reagan jumped in, "He is a <u>Prime</u> Minister, which means he is more important than your average Minister, and certainly more important than any Sir. Brian is my friend."

"Oh, Brian," I said, finally understanding.

"O'Brien is her father's name," Reagan told Mulroney. "She is of Irish descent and hails from Michigan."

Brian turned to me, "I've been in your neck of the woods here recently -- in one of my favorite get-aways -- on Mackinac Island."

"Mackinac Island was her launch point into the project," Reagan explained in terms used by those familiar with mind control operations. Mulroney apparently was aware of my mind controlled state and leered at me as though I were merchandise. Reagan noticed his interest and proceeded to function in the capacity of a pimp. "I highly recommend you take her along with the rest. She is an excellent game piece for you to use in any position. And there's security. Her head is in the ethers and come tomorrow, she wouldn't know you from the man in the moon. I'll give you the keys later."

Expertly using Order of the Rose signals and triggers, Mulroney said, "Just give me the key to her heart, and she's mine."

"You are wise in the ways of the world," Reagan commented.

"I have to be on top of things. Its a New World Order," Mulroney said matter-of-factly.

As a guard led me away, I heard Reagan tell Mulroney, "You will be on top of the world soon."

I was searched by uniformed Canadian body guards and pointed in the direction of one of the White House's many bedroom suites. When I opened the door, I saw three blonde sex slaves undressing and preparing the bed -- one of whom was my close friend and Senator Arlen Spector's slave.

I excitedly called my friend's name. "What are you doing here?" I asked as we hugged each other.

"Small world," she said, as she always did when we were thrust together in various places for prostitution and/or pornography. This universal term was often used among those familiar with the Small, Small World Disney- developed mind control program.

I hugged my friend again. "Wow, it is a small world. I'm so glad you're here." I had no comprehension of our predicament and could not see beyond the moment.

"Hell girls! It is a small world!" Mulroney entered and strode across the room, tossing his coat on a chair and loosening his tie. "Watch it get smaller and smaller as we rocket further and further away." He slipped out of his shoes, suspenders, and pants while he continued his hypnotic metaphors. "Soaring through the sea of black space. As the world gets smaller and smaller and smaller, then sinks into the black sea of space." Removing his boxer shorts, he announced, "I brought you here for a purpose..." and proceeded to access our sex programming.

In retrospect I know it was no coincidence that my friend and me were brought together to satisfy Brian Mulroney's perversion for mind controlled slaves. Identically mirror programmed, we operated in unison.

The delicate red rose tattoo on my friend's left wrist signified her enslavement to the (New World) Order of the Rose to which Mulroney belonged. My friend and her young daughter reportedly were often transported across the U.S.-Canadian border at Niagara Falls for prostitution to Mulroney. The sexual abuse of her precious child was used as a trauma base to maintain control of her mind just as Kelly's abuse traumatized me. Mulroney had previously accessed sex programming at Niagara Falls in my friend and me -- along with our daughters -- to satisfy his sanctioned perversions as though it were "business as usual." Had I been capable of connecting events, I would have felt enormous relief that our daughters were not forced to participate in his sexual assault this time.

"Mission" complete, I slipped on my dress and prepared to leave. Mulroney pointed to me and cryptically said, "I'll be seeing you around. Maybe I'll see you in Mackinac. May be somewhere in time." In three lines, Mulroney expertly tied the immediate moment to childhood cues and current Mexican NAFTA operations, as well as prepared me for my next encounter with him on Mackinac Island.

[1] "The Order of the Rose" was an emblem of those ushering in the New World Order. "Orders from the Rose" were orders from George Bush.

[2] Reagan first introduced me to U.N. Ambassador Madeleine Albright as "my mentor" in Jesuit operations in the Caribbean. "Madeleine Albright is a Saint," Reagan told me, forming my perception of her. "The Mother Teresa of the Caribbean."

[3] While I was in Jamaica under Albright's (via Bush's) instruction, Larry Flynt photographers took advantage of my being there to use the picturesque Dunns River Falls as a backdrop for pornographic photos to be used in Hustler.

[4] Reagan's red rose triggered a sexual mode usually used to compromise/blackmail dignitaries and lock them into loyalty to the Order of the Rose.

CHAPTER 21

GLOBAL EDUCATION 2000

My programmed role toward implementing Education 2000 according to the plans of those ushering in the New World Order brought me back in contact with former Governor of Tennessee, Lamar Alexander, and eventually Canadian Prime Minister Brian Mulroney.

I had met Lamar Alexander in 1978, at a satanic ritual I was subjected to in an affluent neighborhood of Nashville, Tennessee. Lamar Alexander presided over this sex oriented occult ritual with full understanding of my Project Monarch mind control victimization and the impact his actions were having on my mind. It was my experience then, and intermittently throughout the years, that Lamar Alexander's sexual perversion was to bring his victim to the point of death through oral suffocation.

During the course of publicly exposing Tennessee's need for education reform as instructed, I was in contact with Commissioners, Superintendents, Mayors, and Lamar Alexander. Lamar Alexander, who followed Bennett as Bush's Secretary of Education, worked in close association with Bill Bennett to manipulate the minds of the masses to accept Education 2000 as the ONLY means of education reform. When Ned McWherter was moved into the office of Governor to rubber stamp federal projects, Lamar Alexander maintained influence over state politics. At the same time, he maintained influence over national politics through his role as chairman of the National Governor's Association in 1986.

As the 1984 Governor's Convention drew near, I met with Lamar Alexander at the Stockyard nightclub where he was drinking with his long time associate and partner-in-crime, Nashville's Mayor Richard Fulton. In the basement bar of this old, converted stock yard was a modified antique "Shoe Shine" booth, where the term took on new meaning. A key to a private shoeshine booth could be obtained by those in the know through Stockyard owner, Buddy Killen. This closet sized booth was lined in mirrors and had a small bench where Lamar Alexander sat after our business was concluded. I knelt at his feet as ordered to perform oral sex. Programmed sex slaves such as myself were trained to go long periods of time without drawing a breath, and users such as Alexander stretched this time to the maximum.[1]

On this occasion, Alexander apparently exceeded the maximum. I do not recall completion of my programmed task. It was afterhours when my mind control handler, Alex Houston, dragged my limp body from the booth, roused me, and ordered me out of the building. Buddy Killen opened a back door that once was a cattle run, and Houston half-dragged me out the back exit unseen.

The night of the Convention, Alex Houston's youngest daughter, Bonnie,[2] was to join me. Bonnie and I were close to the same age, and together we dressed for the occasion. As a prostitute, Bonnie was familiar with Lamar Alexander and his perversions but nevertheless was excited at the prospect of seeing "old friends" at the Convention via Louise Mandrell,[3] who would be entertaining there. The comradery between Alex Houston and Irby Mandrell that developed during Bob Hope's U.S.O. tours in the 1960's lasted for decades due to their shared involvement in running mind controlled slaves for Byrd. Bonnie shared in this friendship with the Mandrells and was looking forward to seeing her "friends" in the band.

I, too, was looking forward to talking with Louise Mandrell, but for a very different reason. Barbara had just endured her near-fatal car crash, and I was deeply concerned for her welfare. Throughout the 1980's while traveling under the guise of the Country Music Industry, Alex Houston toured with Barbara and/or Louise Mandrell on a regular basis. Occasionally Barbara and I saw each other in "church," the Hendersonville Lord's Chapel. This church was an offshoot of Billy Roy Moore's Lord's Chapel, and was pastored by his mind controlled slave, Mike Nelson, who became close friends with Barbara.[4] Alex Houston and I were present when Mike Nelson broke program, and attempted to flee for his life with Barbara Mandrell. The pastor was subdued with a stun gun and immediately relieved of his position, while Barbara frantically sought answers to the questions the two of them had managed to raise.

Alex Houston was touring with Louise Mandrell in 1984 when Louise had a "premonition" of Barbara's eminent demise -- much the same way Loretta Lynn "psychically predicted" her son's murder. Like the murders of Loretta's son and Country Music entertainer Keith Whitley, I was aware of Barbara's planned accident before it occurred due to Alex Houston's direct involvement. These traumas were also used as a means of locking in my mind controlled belief that I had "no where to run and no where to hide." Worst of all, I could not think to speak of what I knew due to my own absolute mind control. While Barbara physically survived her ordeal, her voice was silenced as planned.

When Bonnie and I arrived at Opryland Hotel, we hurried to the ballroom where Louise Mandrell would be performing. My concern for Barbara detracted me from my appointment with Lamar Alexander until one of Louise's dancers who knew of my role put me "back on track."

"What are you doing here?" he demanded. "You're supposed to be at Rhett Butler's restaurant NOW."

I hurried to the restaurant where Lamar Alexander was having dinner with Senator Byrd and several governors. Byrd was participating in the function for reasons unknown to me, but I was aware that he had fiddled at the Opry. Byrd stopped eating just long enough to acknowledge my presence, "Where have you been?"

"I was checking on Barbara over at the show," I replied as Lamar Alexander excused himself and walked over.

Putting an arm around me and turning me away from the table, he whispered, "You could wind up just like her if you don't get with the program. You've got programs to hand out. But right now, you're interrupting my dinner. Have you had anything to drink?"

"No, Sir," I replied, traumatized at the magnitude of his threat.

Lamar Alexander instructed me to leave immediately, order a grasshopper from the conservatory bar, and wait for further instructions.

It was a matter of routine for me to order a "grasshopper" from Opryland Hotel's conservatory. The ice cream "drink" was specially made -- always with a hypnotic drug in it. As sometimes happened, the waitress was unfamiliar with the process, and conservatory harp player and CIA operative Lloyd Lindroth interceded. The drug had the same effect as that administered at the D.C. NASA programming center by Bennett, and my mode was robotic compliance.

After the drug kicked in, Lloyd Lindroth instructed me to proceed to the main ballroom of the Hotel, where Lamar Alexander would be meeting me. The outer lobby of the ballroom was decorated in wall-size murals that extended to the top of the gothic ceiling. A life size steam engine depicted on the far wall appeared to be racing toward the grand staircase. I had seen the murals numerous times before, but never had they seemed so real as they did to me that night on the NASA drug. The heavy double doors leading to the ballroom caused me to feel very small as I pulled with all my strength to open it. Inside, the room was a sea of black suits and ties, and I was relieved when Lamar Alexander ushered me back out into the lobby.

Alexander positioned me near the train mural as a cryptic indicator to those in the know that I was a "trained" mind controlled slave. I was provided a box of brown envelopes packed with the Education 2000 information I was to hand out to the governors. Alexander instructed me on exactly what I was to say in conjunction with the message Bennett had programmed me with in D.C. Then he returned to the ballroom, where he apparently acted in the capacity of a pimp.

"Are you waiting on the train?" a paunchy governor asked.

"No, Sir," I answered. Then, as instructed, I said, "But I do have a packet of information with your name on it. Shall I take it to your room for you?"

"Oh? And what is my name?" he asked.

"Governor," I responded. There actually were no names on the envelopes. "Astute," he responded. "And what is it you have for me?"

"This packet," I answered, handing it to him. "And anything else you want compliments of Lamar Alexander and (tapped) Secretary of Education, Bill Bennett."

According to some of the men, Alexander had cued them as to my position. Others, such as then Governor of Pennsylvania, Dick Thornburgh and Ohio Governor Dick Celeste already knew me.

"I've got a packet of information with your name on it..." I was saying as I bent over to lift one from the box.

"I don't think so," Governor Blanchard of Michigan interrupted. "Bill (Bennett) wouldn't stoop so low as to insult me that way. I'm doing the same thing here you are, but from a very different approach. The figures I offer reflect the success of Education 2000 in the Michigan school system."

I recognized Governor Blanchard, and was well aware of Michigan's ranking first in the nation in education. "Speaking of which," he continued, "I believe I see your mother more often than you do these days since she is working in the schools. That little sister of yours (Kimmy) is a prime example of what proper instruction can produce. Your little sister is coming to Mackinac to further her skills. Your whole family is a prime example of how good Education 2000 works."

I finally met up with Bonnie again in Lamar Alexander's room as the night came to a close. "Bonnie, how's that snake of yours?" he asked. Bonnie, who had been filmed pornographically by CIA commercial photographer Jimmy Walker with Dick Flood's snakes, had a pet boa constrictor.

"Great!" Bonnie laughed. "How's yours?" "Constricted," he replied.

Bonnie unzipped his pants as she admittedly had done numerous times in the past, playfully saying, "Let it loose!"

Lamar Alexander began removing his pants. Referring to me in Project Monarch terms he said, "When I first saw you, you were a worm with no hint of

being a butterfly."

"Daddy (Alex Houston) said she was a diamond in the rough," Bonnie volunteered.

"She shines now." Turning to me he said, "I know you are a shoe shiner, and mine need a shine."

Bonnie, also familiar with the Stockyard booth and Lamar Alexander's meaning, laughed when he said, "Why don't you both take a foot."

Task complete, I went to Byrd's nearby room as instructed. He was in the bathroom preparing himself for bed. "Louise had her feathers ruffled over Barbara's collision with destiny and I had to smooth them down a bit." Drying his dough grey hands on a towel, he turned to me and said, "Looks like you've had your wings spread a bit tonight."

"I wore a path up and down the stairs," I stated.

Much to my relief he said, "I'm not going to fiddle with you further. I just wanted to give you something to remember me by -- Bye." He compartmentalized my memory with his stun gun.

Soon thereafter, Kelly and I were transported to Mackinac Island, Michigan to meet with Canadian Prime Minister Brian Mulroney at then-Governor James Blanchard's mansion.

Houston led Kelly and me to a horse drawn carriage as quickly as we stepped off the ferry boat onto the timeless, antiquated island. I noticed that the Canadian flags were again flying at the Grand Hotel, but was of no mind to question. Kelly sat quietly beside me, apparently drugged as our carriage took us through the woods to the Governor's mansion.

The guests in the mansion were reminiscent of the recent Tennessee Governor's convention: Michigan Governor Blanchard, Ohio Governor Dick Celeste, and Pennsylvania Governor Dick Thornburgh. Guy VanderJagt and Jerry Ford were also present. Mulroney appeared to be the guest of "honor."

He reached out his hands and greeted me, "I told you I would see you somewhere in time! I slipped time, space, and distance to be here this evening. You and I have some ground to cover."

"Yes, Sir. President Reagan's Global Education Secretary Bill Bennett has sent me to deliver this education packet directly to you." I was to deliver a large, brown envelope of documents similar to those handed out at the Governor's Convention.

Blanchard excused himself. "I've already heard the schpiel," he said as he turned to his other guests, leaving Mulroney and me alone.

"Global Education is the wave of the future," I recited as programmed. As the world gets smaller and smaller due to higher technology spanning the globe, our children must be educated in the ways of the "worldo. Education as it is, barely equips them for life in their own backyard. We need to become involved in our children's education for the sake of their future and our legacy. Global education is the way. The only way. Look into it..." I handed him the envelope. "...Peer into the future."

Mulroney uncrossed his arms long enough to accept the envelope, which he casually tossed on a chair. "I am interested in the children, the legacy we leave them, and how we shape their future by the way we record our history in their test." Using Order of the Rose cues, he signaled me to photographically record his words for future delivery. "Tell Mr. Bennett(sss)," he hissed, cryptically revealing his knowledge that Bill and Bob Bennett worked together using reptilian-alien themes, "implementation is high. I'm already sold on Global 2000, and have additional points I would like for them to consider. Headsets at every computer station for openers. Double the impact with dual learning. We're being thrust forward at warp speed, and the generations of the future may need an added booster to bring them up to speed. A united global effort using your education package as a basis is destined to bring the future into a clear and present reality."

Business complete, Mulroney triggered my sex programming and led me upstairs to the bedrooms where Kelly was robotically waiting, entranced under Orders of the Rose.

---

[1] I have witnessed girls die of suffocation from this practice even though 3 to 5 minutes without breathing is common.

[2] While Bonnie was not raised in Project Monarch, Houston's pedophilia and stage hypnosis techniques rendered Bonnie unable to control her own actions. Bonnie is a multiple with a record of prostitution in need of therapy and care.

[3] Irby Mandrell openly discussed Senator Byrd's direct involvement in the Project Monarch government mind controlled victimizations of his incestuously abused daughters with Houston. "Having babies can be a lucrative way to feather your nest -- that's what the Byrd taught me." Mandrell continued, "Louise was a little withdrawn, and she needed to come out of her cocoon and spread her wings. I ran the idea by Byrd, and he said 'If she doesn't have a talent, let's make her one. What is a band without a fiddle?' And viola, there she is. Another star on the rise launched from NASA City, USA (Huntsville, Alabama)."

[4] Friendships between mind controlled slaves are usually forbidden, and conversations are kept to a minimum lest cross programming triggering occurs. Throughout the years, my own relationship with the Mandrells was limited to a superficial basis, whereas Irby Mandrell employed Houston's hypnotic abilities to maintain mind control over his daughters while touring.

182

CHAPTER 22

MY CONTRA-BUTION

U.S. and Mexican relations were flourishing in the successes of NAFTA's groundwork, while political differences pertaining to Nicaragua remained a minor point of contention. Since the Catholic Vatican's Intelligence arm of Jesuits were working closely with U.S. Intelligence to usher in the New World Order, they used their established influence in Mexico and Nicaragua to provide a common ground for "diplomatic relations." My duel mind control victimization by the CIA and the Jesuits since childhood, and my previous "diplomatic relations" in Mexico thrust me into the role of messenger and prostitute to Nicaragua's Daniel Ortega.

Were President Reagan's Nicaraguan Freedom Fighters fighters OF freedom or FOR freedom? My mind controlled existence rendered me incapable of pondering such questions. Nevertheless, I had a programmed "passion burning in my bosom" for the Contras as was patriotically instilled through torture, when I embarked on my "peace keeping mission" to Nicaragua for Reagan late in the summer of 1985.

I boarded NCL as usual to reach my appointed destination. Since Nicaragua was not a port of call for NCL, I flew from the Yukatan of Mexico to a remote military airstrip in Managua. It was in this small mountain top clearing that I met with Contra rebel forces Commandant, Daniel Ortega, as had been arranged through the Vatican.

I was dressed seasonably in shorts, with my long, blonde hair tucked back in a french braid. Ortega's attire, too, was reflective of the casual air to our meeting. His tan military uniform had worn thin, and was free of any protocol insignias. The dark, rose colored sunglasses he peered through apparently had not changed his somber view of the "noble cause" he claimed to represent. A man of few words, he greeted me with an order, "Come with me." I rode with him in silence as he drove a jeep the short distance across the airstrip to a small, neat, two story white frame house.

As we came to a stop in front of the house, Ortega said in a sad slow voice, "I have needs like any man. But I feel like a whore myself for accepting your President's offer."

His bedroom was clean and functional, with numerous assault weapons scattered around. I did not see any modern conveniences or personal effects, but Ortega seemed to be at home in his surroundings.

Ortega's demeanor was that of a man who had abstained from sex longer than most in his political position. As he slowly unbuttoned his shirt, I noticed a Catholic medallion with the secret Jesuit ascension/dissension symbol on it, a common accessory among Jesuit spooks. He sat in a wicker chair as I followed his silent lead in gratifying him orally.

While he chain smoked cigarettes, I sat in front of him on the floor, and relayed Reagan's message to him as programmed. I began, "President Reagan has sent me as a messenger of peace."

He casually interrupted, slowly looking me up and down. "I'd like to have a piece in a few more minutes."

I continued, "Your people have endured many hardships throughout their existence. He (Reagan) only wants to help. The American people want to see peace and freedom in your land. Mexican and U.S. relations are growing stronger by the day, and it is imperative that we resolve your conflict in order to resolve our own with the Mexican government. We

183

have come to the agreement with Mexico that the Nicaraguan conflict must be resolved for the sake of your people as well as our own. I am here on a peace keeping mission representative of Vatican based common ground shared by both Mexican and American governments, to enlighten you to our peaceful intentions. The unified effort of Mexican-American Catholic missions is to promote peace in your region, while only enhancing your culture. The world is rapidly turning toward world peace, and Nicaragua is way behind the times -- from technology and education to government ideals and religious convictions. Pope John Paul is praying diligently for peace in your region, and has joined forces with President Reagan, Mexico, and even the Soviet Union to ensure that peace. He (the Pope) knows your goals, he knows your motives (I leaned forward, almost whispering from my own instilled belief), he knows your soul. We can all work in tandem to achieve that peace. Nicaragua, small though it may be in relation to the rest of the world, is a significant stepping stone toward unifying world powers. It can no longer be a source of contention and disagreement. Your people must be free. Free to worship God through your holy Catholic church. That is first and foremost on President Reagan's agenda, as well as the Pope's and President de la Madrid's. A New World Order is coming into being with or without you, it is an inevitable process that cannot be stopped. A whole new world of peace awaits us all. I can see you are a peace loving man. It emanates from your being. Blood has flowed across your land so heavily that your people are drowning in it. Together we can cauterize that wound. Replace blood flow with cash flow. Americanization can upgrade your technology at a rapid rate. Your people could compete in world markets by the turn of the century. Your future global position has already been determined by geography alone. Flow with it. Lead your people out of poverty. Educate them in a manner conducive to their destined position in world markets. Free them from their struggles that have held them captive for so long. Allow the church bells to ring with good news of peace, prosperity and freedom. You can achieve all of your goals for your country's advancement with our help."

Ortega thoughtfully finished smoking a cigarette, and lit up another as he confidently replied, "Tell your President that I have seen his freedom and listened to his words projected through yet another example of it. He paints a beautiful picture suspended within his framework. A picture can appear serene to its beholder while it is being gazed upon. I cannot worship a graven image, and the picture he paints is just that. We have fought too hard and too long, spilling sweat and blood across this land in our determined effort to maintain human values instilled in us by our forefathers, who gained their profound wisdom from the original Catholic missionaries. These values are the same as those portrayed in President Reagan's painted picture -- only ours are real. His have only surface value, like any other painting. If I were to concede, I would only be framed within the picture he paints, hung on his wall like a trophy. I will not mislead my people, in spite of his offers of wealth and position. I am true to my convictions, and when he is true to his, then we will meet on common ground and have something of substance to discuss. For now, words are only a waste of our time."

Ortega put out his cigarette, and pulled back the covers on his bed. "I'll take you somewhere pleasant." He took a well used opium pipe/bong off his dresser and handed me a nozzle. I had been trained to accept any drug given to me with the only exception being the strictly forbidden marijuana. I hesitated until Ortega assured me it was opium. As the drug took affect he said, "This could be the way to world peace." Sex with Ortega was at very least free of pain and perversion. Unlike most I was forced to have "diplomatic relations" with for the Reagan Administration, he fell asleep when he was through due to the difference between opium and cocaine.

The honk of a jeep's horn outside awoke him. As I prepared to leave, he said, "Wait." He took a small, 1/4 inch or so ball of black opium from his personal stash, wrapped it in the cellophane from his cigarette package wrapper, and said, "Give this to your President and tell him that you and I found more peace with this substance than he'll ever impart on the surface of his painted globe." As he closed the door quietly behind me he said, "Come back and see me when you have more to offer."

I was immediately returned by plane to Washington, DC where my "mission" had originated. This time I was taken directly to Bush's office where I delivered Ortega's message verbatim. Eliminating most of the dialogue, Bush instructed me to deliver a partial message to Reagan. Unable to perceive message content and people beyond my "Need to Know" mind controlled limited view, I had no concept that Ortega's message would have a negative impact. It never occurred to me that Ortega had proven himself to be as much a hypocrite as he purported Reagan to be by using me as a prostitute and messenger of bad news knowing full well that I had no free will with which to make the message more palatable. Bush's revision of Ortega's message added fuel to a proverbial fire that I didn't even know was burning when I delivered the message to Reagan.

Bush was with Reagan and I in Reagan's secondary office (to the Oval office) of the White House as I relayed the message as instructed, "Daniel Ortega is a peace loving man, who seeks the same resolutions that we do. But he told me to tell you -- (I dug in my purse for the opium) that he and I found more peace in this substance -- (I handed the opium to Reagan) than you'll ever impart on the surface of your painted globe."

Bush smiled as Reagan's face instantly turned beet red with rage. Bush then reacted and spun up out of his chair, took the opium for himself, and told Reagan, "Settle down. There's more. It seems the only peace she spread was between her legs." He headed for the door, saying, "I would reconsider my position if I were in your shoes -- considering what's filling hers." Bush dropped his gaze down the back of my legs to my shoes as he continued, "Its running down both sides of her legs."

Obviously I wouldn't be subjected to sex with Reagan that day. I was quickly excused and flown back to Mexico, where I resumed my NCL cruise. With my memory of the event compartmentalized through high voltage, I believed at the time that I had never been gone at all.

CHAPTER 23

WHIRLED VISION

In the fall of 1985, the same part of me that met with Ortega was walking with (Reagan appointed) CIA Director William "Bill" Casey through the arboured rose garden of his Long Island estate. Casey began by manipulating my Jesuit/Vatican programming base personality with the expertise indicative of the current union between Catholic and CIA operations. Casey, whom Reagan referred to as a "man of Vision," was forming my Jesuit mind control programmed "understanding." "I have a World Vision,[1] one of peace. By removing the more violent factions of societies world wide and replacing them with faithful leaders of one world government, and the one world church, global unification is eminent. It is a beautiful vision, and it came to me in my dreams. God has moved me to move men. I've moved them here and I've moved them there -- now it's time to remove them. My World Vision encompasses the globe and puts to rest any and all tensions, strife, overpopulation, and starvation. My vision is a World Vision, and the churches see it my way as evidenced by their support of the cause."[2]

Referring to my mind controlled involvement in Haitian operations via NCL, Casey further defined 'the cause,' "Your heart felt mission in Haiti has helped in my World Vision quest for her people to abandon hedonistic voodoo and turn their eyes to God and Godly ways. By their own design, they have created an atmosphere of evil whereby a plague will be visited on their land. The Lord has so moved me to move men who share our goals into place, and re-move those who stand in the way of peace. It is for this reason that your mission in Haiti must be brought to a close. Baby Doc, in his tireless devotion to saving the demonically possessed cannot bear the burden of watching his people die the wretched death unleashed upon those doomed for hell. We are left with no alternative but to heed the word of God and spare him from annihilation. For this reason, we will send in the missionaries (Jesuit Mercenaries) to inoculate the population with a vaccine that will spare only the good of heart by virtue of its design. All attempts to maintain Haiti within the loop of financial gain will cease. Tourism must be stopped for the sake of the innocents visiting a plagued land. Despite our differences, Baby Doc has complied with the Vatican's orders to the best of his abilities in his demon infested land, and must resign his post. We owe it to him to transport him to safety. It is our duty as Americans and followers of God to obey the commands of our Lord and master and enforce the World Vision. It is your duty as an American and follower of God to instill the understanding that God has spoken, and a plague is imminent. Baby Doc is being prepared for transition and awaits word of direction. You will provide him with that word."

With my perceptions distorted and Catholic Jesuit programmed "understanding" instilled, I was prepared to "religiously accept" any and all I was told. I believed that the revolution in Haiti was a holy war, never capable of realizing it was a test run battle for the minds in this 4th world country.

The devotion I felt toward the Haitian people was more than a religious understanding of these alternately Catholic-Santeria[3] voodoo worshippers. I was actually subconsciously recognizing other tortured mind controlled slaves in this human created hell called Haiti. Consciously, I now know it

186

was due in part to the visible stun gun/prod marks, plastic ever-present smiles that never quite reach their dead appearing eyes. The children clung to their wide eyed mothers, as they performed their tasks in robotic servitude. I had recognized these characteristics in other slaves throughout the years, but never had I seen a whole country entranced. My compassion for the Haitian people penetrated into the realm of the spiritual, into a part of me that mind control and manipulation of religion could never touch.

Casey and I had been walking through the garden, guarded by more armed men than the President. It wasn't that I was a threat, I couldn't even think to save myself. It was that Casey and his World Vision were a threat to humanity that so many guards were needed. The men appeared to be U.S. Secret Service officers according to their attire, weapons, and earphone headsets. One guard conspicuously placed his hand to his headset, listening as though it were remote control. He walked briskly over to Casey, who signaled me to leave with an escort who instantly arrived at my side awaiting instruction.

"Take her to my chambers," Casey told him. "Clear her mind. I have something I need to instill." Robotically I followed my escort into Casey's office library. The room was barren, dark, and hot -- just as described in a book I had been given to read in keeping with You Are What You Read programming. It produced a sensation of having somehow stepped into the novel *Chameleon* by **insider** William Diehl. The mind scramble of the book and reality instantly commenced.

"It's warm in here," the agent said, unbuttoning my white eyelet blouse. "Bill (Casey) likes to keep it this way in case-he (Casey) gets a chill and his blood runs cold. Chameleons[4] are naturally cold blooded. Make yourself comfortable while I turn up the heat. Mr. Casey doesn't want to hear a peep out of you, so I'll warn you now -- be Silent." He deliberately triggered and activated the Jesuit programmed part of me that believed in my Vow of Silence.[5] "The walls have ears and the plants have eyes, so your silence is tantamount to success. I'm going to leave you to reflect in Silence. Bill will be along any minute."

Had I been capable of "reflecting," I would have questioned the validity of Casey's dramatic position of "religious overtones" on Haitian policy. Like Reagan's, Casey's sincerity did not ring true considering the fruits of his labor. But then, I could not consider any more than I could reflect, and I sat in a state of what felt like suspended animation awaiting my instructions. I could not anticipate nor dread what was about to happen as futuristic thinking was left in the hands of my controllers. Had I realized the scramble of reality with William Diehl's book, I could have "psychically" predicted what happened when Bill Casey strolled in.

Casey walked over to his highly polished dark wood desk and opened the top drawer. Casey's desk was one of the few furnishings in the large, airy room. The dark polished reddish wood paneling seemed even darker with the midnight blue carpeting curving slightly up the wall. Heavy, gothic maroon velvet drapes blacked out the sun from the windows behind his desk.

"I can see quite clearly that you have taken a Vow of Silence. Maintain it. Maintain it and Lisssten," Casey hissed, using preset triggers. He reached into the drawer and took out a foot long, maroon box with a diamond embossed on the top.

"I received a box, quite anonymously as I do from time to time," Casey said in keeping with the book scramble. "The box has your name on it. I expected to open it and find the usual pierced chameleon and found, instead, a weapon intended for one."

He opened the box in front of me. Inside, laying on a bed of cotton, was an elaborate dagger with a handle of the same rose crystal from which the crucifix Byrd had presented me on "our wedding night" was made. My first personal meeting with Casey promised to be torturous as I recognized Byrd's participation in the grisly ordeal.

I listened, deeply tranced, as Casey said, "Is it a knife or a crucifix? I can't tell. Both symbolize martyrdom as far as I'm concerned. Note the rose pattern cut into the crystal. Now, I wonder who would have sent me this to give to you."

Even under mind control I knew, as I was supposed to, that Byrd had provided him with the knife. My worst fears were confirmed when Casey began using Byrd's hypnotic induction, "In like a knife, sharp and clean, I'll carve out what I want." Casey sliced through the front of my bra, exposing the area between my breasts where Byrd routinely cut me with his pocket knife. He pierced into my breastbone deeply so that I believed I would split, and indeed did split off a personality fragment compartmentalizing this event. Using standard Jesuit based infinity program, Casey instructed me and programmed me with messages that I would deliver as though my life depended on it.

"You must go to the Citadel and warn our Dominican brothers of impending doom to their neighbors in Haiti. From the Dominican side (of the Haitian island) you will be flown to Port Au Prince where you will meet with Baby Doc (Duvalier) at his Palace. He is already receptive to your word, and knows that my words are your words and your word is Silence. You must tell General Cedras his Order is from The Rose." Casey touched the white rose in his lapel, signaling me to photographically record his words verbatim.

When he was through programming me with his message, Casey told me, "As quickly as you complete this mission, you must depart Haiti, never to return again." Casey used excessive high voltage to compartmentalize my memory. I recall being nauseated and ill from his stun gun as I departed his Long Island compound/home via ferry programmed with messages to Cedras and Baby Doc.

Haiti had recently been dropped from the NCL itinerary as a Port of Call, but the Dominican Republic side of the island remained open to tourism. When Houston and I debarked the NCL ship in Puerta Plata, we walked past a World Vision cargo ship that was being unloaded at the dock. I recall that a soft ocean breeze gently lifted the hem of my white, gauzy dress as I weaved my way through the dockload of World Vision freight to a waiting automobile.

Religion and politics apparently mix in the Dominican Republic as evidenced by the inseparable mixture of Catholic Missions, old forts, statues of Christopher Columbus, and Catholic Shrines. As we drove past the mountain tramway that takes tourists up and down to the rustic Citadel and Catholic Shrine at the top, Houston perpetuated the "Chameleon" book scramble. Dually referring to Cedras and the short donkey ride from the tram to the Citadel depicted in Diehl's book, Houston threatened to put me on the rickety tram saying, "Some Jackass will see you at the top."

In an area reserved for covert activities, out of view of tourists, I met with General Cedras in his Citadel office. Dressed in the eerie Jesuit dark hooded robe, Cedras completed Casey's "Chameleon" book scramble scenario as we walked through the ancient structure to his office. Cedras' demeanor made him appear more as a militant than a "spook," despite the corny monk's attire. With his hood down his back, Cedras' sharp, craggy features and darting steel blue eyes kept my full attention. I had seen him at a monastery in Santo Domingo as ordered before,[6] when Haiti was still being used by the CIA for Operation Watchtower to transport cocaine and Contra weapons from Cuba.

Alone with Cedras and properly signaled, I began photographically reciting Casey's message, "I have word of warning from the Vatican by way of the honorable and faithful William Casey. He sends word of impending doom that is to befall your neighbors on the darkside in Haiti. Voodoo manifest itself in mysterious ways while the way of the Lord is clear. Evil must be stopped at all costs. The cost shall be in terms of human casualty, as a plague is being visited upon the land. Those who fornicate with devils shall be infested with the plague. Woo unto them who have stood in the path of World Peace. By God's design the New World Order shall come into being with or without the Haitians. All American operations in Haiti are now destined for your ports. Your people (the CIA-UN operated Dominicans) will flourish in peace and prosperity while the dark side (Haitians) drown in the blood of this holy war that they have brought upon themselves. Close your borders swiftly and maintain guardians at the gate lest the Haitians infest your land with their evil plague. Inoculation of the masses shall be masked in the body and the blood shall carry the doom. As more and more Haitians turn to God in their final hour, the communion they partake will be Satan's own. With their God as the scapegoat, your Island in the Son (sun) will be freed of the vile and wicked. I have seen a vision, a World Vision, and it is through communion with the ancients that we have been granted the Keys to the Kingdom[7] to unlock the gates of hell. The holy water sent herein has the blessings of the Vatican and must be sprinkled like rain upon the Haitians. Our God reigns, and he rains rivers of blood upon the Haitian masses, and he reigns supreme upon your mission. Your mission is clear. You serve communion and let God sort them out. Those who serve the body of Christ are covered by the Vatican, those who serve voodoo evil shall be covered in the blood of their own. It is clear our God reigns. Let the games begin."

Combining the cryptic language of Cedras' CIA and Jesuit operations, Casey had weaved numerous cryptic commands into his message. Had I been inadvertently accessed, the instructions would make little sense to those not cued to the language. Cedras was listening religiously, fully grasping the magnitude of Casey's instructions. I concluded the message, "The holy water with the Vatican's blessings will arrive at 1 PM today by way of World Vision. The blood shall host the plague."[8]

I was relieved to depart Cedras' presence without being subjected to his usual perverse sexual brutality. This would be someone else's job this time, as my programmed trance was maintained until I delivered Casey's message to Baby Doc Duvalier on the "dark side" of the "Island in the Son."

Houston took me to the small CIA operated air port at the foot of the mountain where I boarded a small white airplane destined for Port Au Prince, Haiti. When we landed, the pilot walked me over to Baby Doc's Tonton guards, and ordered that I be taken to the Palace. He spoke in rapid Haitian French, and lifted my symbolic rosy cross necklace for emphasis to the guards. Reinforcing my instilled belief that the Catholic emblem would protect me, the guards treated me with the respect that apparently was reserved for identified Jesuit spooks. I was driven by white Mercedes to the Haitian Presidential Palace. Looking even more conspicuously out of place in contrast to stark poverty than his fleet of Mercedes, Baby Doc's Palace was decadent. I stood reverently in the foyer waiting for my arranged meeting to begin, unable to question Baby Doc's luxurious surroundings in view of the despair and starvation around him.

I had met with Baby Doc throughout the early '80s in the capacity of a Project Monarch prostitute. All Haitian based U.S. covert operations were run by a bed ridden old man referred to as "Ol' Charlie," who resided at the El Presidente Hotel until his death in the mid '80s. During my tenure as a mind controlled messenger and prostitute in Haiti, I had been forced to attend a voodoo ceremony for my (and others') traumatization purposes. I was ordered to perform oral sex on Baby Doc as his dark windowed Mercedes slowly proceeded through the crowds of Haitians on their way to the ritual. With my Haitian missions previously established with Ol' Charlie for business and Baby Doc for prostitution, my meeting Baby Doc for business was unprecedented.

"What brings you here?" Baby Doc spit the words at me in English. I had been led into his library by three armed guards. "I have no need of a Catholic whore."

Baby Doc's applicable knowledge of the English language was limited by his intellect whereby an aide filled the need for an interpreter as I delivered Casey's message.

"I come in the name of peace. I have a message for you from William Casey, sanctioned by the Vatican. The Pope is in agreement with U.S. policy in Haiti. He has seen a vision, a sign from God. The vision is a World Vision, whose people are reaching out to yours with charity in abundance. The goods and services provided require only that the people of Haiti anoint the sick, feed the hungry, and clothe the poor through his servants of World Vision. Their mission will separate good seed from bad and restore peace in your region. The peace that shall be visited upon your land amongst your people is eminent, but not before the rivers run red with the blood of the wicked. The vision is plague, and your people will fall in the streets pleading for mercy, and you will not be here to hear it. The time has come for you to leave. It is God's will that you escape the plague with blessings from the Vatican, never to return to your homeland. Prepare for your exodus today for tomorrow holds a promise of doom. Using your prophetic wisdom, warn the masses of impending doom and arm them with World Vision. The vision is one of peace[9] for those who flock to the tents and churches for salvation. Your destiny is clear, and the Vatican has cleared the way for your departure."

With Casey's message delivered, Baby Doc's Tontons returned me to the same airplane I had left a short time before. I flew in silence, unable to think to comprehend the magnitude of what had just transpired. Events to a mind controlled slave are all perceived as first and last times. Therefore, Casey's instructions that I would "depart Haiti, never to return again" seemed business as usual to me. Flying over the mountains that separate Haiti from the Dominican Republic, I noticed the gentle people below bathing in the waterfalls, toilessly washing their bright clothes on the rocks, and primitively hauling goods in the baskets balanced on their heads. An occasional goat ran across the barren land, and the children, bellies swollen from starvation, played with sticks and vines. With my mind controlled and spinning with misperceptions, my whirled vision, like Ortega's rose colored glasses, prevented me from seeing the reality of New World Orders."

[1] World Vision was/is a Jesuit controlled organization that led churches to give them money under the guise of spreading world peace. What they were not saying, was what the money was actually funding -- a world peace plan under mind control.

[2] Perceptual distortions of the virtues that good people hold most dear is one reason for the proliferation of criminal activity within such organizations as World Vision. There are those within affected factions of such organizations, the Catholic church, and even the U.S. Government that operate under distorted perceptions referred to by the CIA as a "Need to Know" basis -- and they "Need to Know" that their minds, religion, and/or perceptions are being deliberately manipulated.

[3] Since the Catholics had joined forces with the United Nations to overtake the world through mass mind control, the Jesuit influence on Haiti was complete. By maintaining much of the ceremony, placing literal interpretation on "eating the body and drinking the blood," and providing a mirror reversal of good and evil, Catholicism and voodoo, like Catholicism and the United nations, became one in the same.

[4] The term "Chameleon" is a term used to describe spies who are expertly trained to blend into any environment at any time unnoticed -- just as an MPD mirrors the one they're with.

[5] The Jesuit Vow of Silence was installed through the Rite to Remain Silent of my childhood. Now I know, like so many others in Intelligence, that "Silence Equals Death." Knowledge is our ONLY defence against mind control.

[6] Byrd had told me that Cedras was "a strategically placed chess piece that the CIA, Jesuits and U.N. moved around" to usher in their New World Order.

[7] "Keys to the Kingdom" was defined by Bill Bennett in accordance with Jesuit programming as follows: "At the onset of Christianity, the Apostles compiled all the information that they had obtained from Christ and built the Holy Catholic Apostolic Church. Christ intended it to be the one world church then -- the truth, the light, and the way. The secrets were kept in the ark of the covenant, and passed down generation after generation. And generation after generation Christ caused for more to be written -- the fruits of his labors expounding on the truth. Now the ark has become archives -- a wealth of information. This information is accessible to very few, the very few who hold the Keys to the Kingdom."

[8] Interpretation of the final message is left to the minds of the masses who can still discern truth. My conclusions are "clear," based on conversations overheard and my experience as a White House sex slave. Although Byrd and Reagan, among others, had prostituted me to officials in AIDS infected countries, they used no protection against "the plague" when having sex with me.

[9] There can be no world peace without peace-of-mind, and there is no peace-of-mind under mind control. Haiti, once a prototype of New World Order controls, has now been used up and discarded by the CIA and Jesuits. U.N. "peace keeping forces" have created a smoke and mirrors illusion of "peace" by keeping it FROM the Haitian people.

CHAPTER 24

A-HUNTING WE WILL GO

On December 4, 1986, I turned 29 years old. Usually mind controlled slaves were discarded, "thrown from the Freedom train," at 30; but I argued with Houston when he told me my government abusers only had one year left to "use me up." I had had no conscious awareness of the passing of time, and believed I was still only 24. Regardless of what I believed, my abusers did their best to "use me up" physically and psychologically before even a month had passed.

I was in Washington, D.C. on a routine trip, which included being prostituted to President Reagan. "Uncle Ronnie's" cheeks were flushed from excitement and cognac as he told me, "I always take two weeks off for Christmas to go back to California." Reagan interrupted himself to break into an old Hollywood style song and dance, "California here I come. . ." The White House, he claimed, had always been confining to him, and he appeared genuinely excited about his upcoming trip. "I look forward to this trip every year because I get to see old friends. Oh, I still work while I'm there -- the President's work is never done -- but at least I'm there. Its about time you see where I call home." Then, quoting the Wizard of Oz, he said, "'There's no place like home.' And you're about to see why. Say it with me, 'There's no place like home. There's no place like home'." Then he instructed me in Oz cryptic, "Click your heels. There's no place like home."

Blue-white light seemingly exploded in my brain, like being hit with deadly low voltage AC electrical current. Reagan was "setting the stage" for an attempted mind scrambling time slip, to be reactivated at an upcoming meeting I would have with him in Bel Air, California.

The motor home was packed to the walls, and the walls were packed with cocaine as Houston, Kelly, and I departed on our long drive to California. Houston had planned several "tourist stops" along the way that proved as nightmarish as the California ordeal itself.

In Las Vegas, Nevada, Houston kept Kelly and me busy prostituting us to everyone he knew "in the know" and in attendance at the Country Music Association's annual convention. Weary of being sent from room to room, I was back in the lobby literally trying to catch my breath when I saw Michael Danté. He was dressed in an expensive light gray silk suit and dark glasses, looking more like a fed than a mobster, leaning on a post, waiting for me. "Our love" he professed over the phone for mind conditioning purposes was certainly not apparent now. "You're late," he growled as he looked at his watch. He ordered me into the Ladies' Room to activate programming by having me "lose myself" in the infinity mirrors that lined the walls. With my mind set like he wanted, he then used and directed me in commercial pornography. Later, he did the same with Kelly.

At the Grand Canyon, Houston traumatized Kelly and me in preparation for the upcoming events in California. While hiking down the canyon, Houston attempted to anchor hypnotically all of the trip's events behind the death and insanity programming to which he was subjecting us. When we stopped for a late afternoon lunch in the Canyon, Kelly collapsed in a state of shock, unable to eat. Houston was pleased because he "got to eat it all himself." I was, as usual, undergoing the food and water depravation. I was so thirsty, I could not think to eat. Kelly's condition magnified my own terrified state, and I did all I could to keep Houston from supposedly pushing her over the edge. I carried her for hours all the way out of the canyon, without pausing to rest. In my own mind I wanted to believe I was actually able to protect her. The fact was, Houston was wearing me down physically to ensure that I could not protect her at our next destination: Lake/Mount Shasta, California.

George Bush was highly active in both the Lampe, Missouri and Shasta, California retreat compounds. Just like Lampe, Shasta's cover was country music. According to everyone I knew, singer and songwriter Merle Haggard supposedly ran the show at Lake Shasta, diverting any and all attention from the nearby Mount Shasta compound. Shasta was the largest covert mind control slave camp of which I am aware. Hidden in the wooded hills, military fencing corrals an enormous fleet of unmarked black helicopters and more mind controlled military robots than I saw in all of Haiti. This covert military operation served its own agenda, not America's. I was told and overheard that it was a base for the future Multi Jurisdictional Police Force for enforcing order and law in the New World Order. In the center of the high security compound, was another well-guarded military-fenced area that was regarded as a "Camp David" of sorts for those running our country. George Bush and Dick Cheney shared an office there, and claimed the outer perimeter woods as their own hunting ground where they played "A Most Dangerous Game." Predicated on conversations I overheard between the two, it was this world police military background that earned Dick Cheney his cabinet appointment as Secretary of Defense[1] with the Bush Administration.

Houston stayed at Haggard's Lake Shasta resort while Kelly and I were helicoptered to Mount Shasta for our scheduled meeting with Bush and Cheney. The helicopter pilot directed our attention to the military fencing surrounding the outer perimeter of the compound. Rarely did pilots ever speak to either of us, but this one smiled wickedly as he told us we would need to know the outer limits for A Most Dangerous Game.

As soon as we arrived at Bush and Cheney's inner sanctum, noticed George Bush, Jr. was with them. It was my experience that Jr. stood by his father and covered his backside whenever Bush would become incapacitated from drugs or required criminal back up. It appeared that Jr. was there to serve both purposes, while his father and Cheney enjoyed their work-vacation.

Hyper from drugs, Cheney and Bush were eager to hunt their human prey in "A Most Dangerous Game." They greeted me with the rules of the game, ordered me to strip naked despite the cold December winds, and told me in Oz cryptic to "beware of the lions and tigers and bears." Kelly's life became the stakes, as usual, which resurrected my natural and exaggerated programmed maternal instincts. Tears silently ran down my cheeks as Bush told me, "If we catch you, Kelly's mine. So run, run as fast as you can. I'll get you and your little girl, too, because I can, I can. And I will."

Cheney, daring me to respond, asked, "Any questions?"

I said, "There's no place to run because there's a fence -- the kind I can't get over. I saw it."

Rather than physically assault me, Cheney laughed at my sense of "no where to run, no where to hide" and explained that a bear had torn a hole in the fence somewhere, and all I had to do is find it. He lowered his rifle to my head and said, "Let the games begin. Go."

Wearing only my tennis shoes, I ran through the trees as fast and as far as I could, which wasn't very far at all. Bush was using his bird dog to track me, the same one that had recently been used with me in bestiality filming as a "Byrd-dog" joke on my owner, Robert C. Byrd. When caught, Cheney held his gun to my head again as he stood over me, looking warm in his sheep skin coat. Bush ordered me to take his dog sexually while they watched, then he and Cheney ushered me back to their cabin.

I pulled on my clothes and sat in the office part of the cabin awaiting instructions. I had no idea where Kelly was, nor do I in retrospect. Bush and Cheney were still in their hunting clothes when the programming session began. Bush said, "You and I are about to embark on a most dangerous game of diplomatic relations. This is my game. You will follow my rules. I will have the distinct advantage of hunting you with my Eye in the Sky (satellite). I'll watch every move you make. As long as you play the game by my rules and make no mistakes, you live. One mistake and I'll get you, my pretty, and your little girl, too. You die, and Kelly will have to play with me. I prefer it that way. Then it will be her most dangerous game. The cards are stacked in my favor because, well, it is my game! Are you game?"

There was no choice. I responded as conditioned, "Yes, Sir! I'm game." The parallels to the Most Dangerous game that had just occurred in the woods were deliberate and intended to make retrieval of memory "impossible" due to cryptoamnesia scrambling.

"Good. Then let the games begin. Listen carefully to your instructions. You have no room for error." Cheney flipped his "game timer" -- an hour glass. Bush continued, "This game is called the King and Eye, and here's the deal. You will be establishing stronger diplomatic relations according to order between Mexico, the U.S., and the Middle East. Your role will require a change of face at each new place. I'll chart your course, define your role, and pull your strings. You'll speak my words when I pull your strings. There is no room for error."

Cheney was half lying across the plain military issue style desk in an apparent drug stupor as Bush talked. Still wearing his hunting coat and hat, Cheney aimed his rifle at me from the desk and threatened, "Or a-hunting we will go." Bush finished Cheney's threat by singing, "We'll catch a fox and put her in a box and lower her in a hole."

Bush looked at Cheney and burst out laughing. The sight of him dressed in his hunting clothes with a huge bore double barreled shotgun to his shoulder inspired Bush to tell him he "looked like Elmer Fudd."

Cheney, imitating the cartoon character, said, "Where is that waskily wabbit?"

Operation The King and Eye would involve Reagan's #1 envoy Philip Habib (who cryptically played the Alice in Wonderland role of the White Rabbit with slaves such as myself) and Saudi Arabian King Fahd. So when Bush referred to the two as "Elmer Fahd and the Waskily Wabbit," he and Cheney laughed until they cried. Since both were already high from drugs anyway, they had a great deal of difficulty maintaining composure long enough to complete my programming.

---

[1] Dick Cheney has no official U.S. military history to justify his position as our nation's former Defense Secretary under President George Bush.

CHAPTER 25

BUSH BABY

It was late evening when Bush and Cheney finished programming me with numerous messages pertaining to the immediate opening of the Juarez, Mexican border to free (drug and slave) trade. They then took me downstairs to the living quarters of the western cedar and redwood structure where Kelly soon joined us. George Bush, Jr. deposited my obviously traumatized and withdrawn child at the door. Referring to the Most Dangerous Game she told me in a quiet, defeated and sad voice, "I was caught same as you."

In retrospect, I do not know if she was actually hunted (I can only hope she was not). Regardless, this reinforced the fact that I had been caught and therefore was "responsible" (when in fact I was not) for everything that happened to Kelly from that point on.

The decor of the residence area reflected Cheney's primitive, rustic, western preference. Like his "ultra secret" Pentagon Bunkhouse, use of leather was in abundance. The main room was small, but appeared larger due to an infinity mirror on one wall. The room was decorated in mirror fashion with one side looking like the other. Centered between two facing black leather sofas was a coffee table littered with drugs and paraphernalia. Bush and Cheney were sitting in matching black leather recliners angled towards the large stone fireplace where a fire was blazing, illuminating and heating the room.

Heroin, Bush's drug of choice, was in abundance and Cheney joined him in using it. The smorgasbord of drugs laid out supposedly included opium, cocaine, and Wonderland Wafers (MDMHA-XTC a.k.a. ecstasy), which indicated to me they intended to celebrate their vacation with abandon. I had seen Cheney stumbling drunk before, but this was the only time I saw him use heroin and give it to me. Kelly, too, was subjected to the drugs.

Bush attempted to sell Cheney on the idea of pedophilia through graphic descriptions of having sex with Kelly. Both were already sexually aroused from drugs and anticipation. Cheney demonstrated to Bush why he did not have sex with kids by exposing himself to Kelly and saying, "Come here." Upon seeing Cheney's unusually large penis, Kelly reeled back in horror and cried, "No!" which made them both laugh. Bush asked Cheney for his liquid cocaine atomizer as he got up to take Kelly to the bedroom. When Cheney remarked how benevolent it was of Bush to numb her with it before sex, Bush replied, "The hell it is. It's for me." He described his excited state in typical vulgar terms and explained that he wanted it to spray cocaine on his penis to last longer.

Cheney said, "I thought it was for the kid."

Bush explained, "Half the fun is having them squirm." He took Kelly's hand and led her off to the bedroom.

Cheney told me that since I was "responsible" for Bush's assault on my daughter by being caught in A Most Dangerous Game, I would "burn" (in hell). He burned my inner thigh with the fireplace poker, and threatened to throw Kelly in the fire. He hypnotically enhanced his description of her burning to traumatize me deeply. As he sexually brutalized me, I heard

Kelly's whimpers coming from the bedroom. As her cries grew louder, Cheney turned on classical music to drown out her cries for help.

At 4:00 A.M., as ordered, Bush Jr. (and his helicopter pilot) came to retrieve Kelly and me. We were flown (by helicopter) back to the Lake Shasta area where Houston and the motor home awaited us. Bush's assault of Kelly proved to be a mind shattering experience for me, and physically devastating to Kelly. She was in dire need of medical attention and was unable even to move. Houston threatened to stop the motor home in the Yosemite area and throw me from a steep cliff if I didn't settle down. His threats and commands could not control my hysteria, as much of his control programming had inadvertently shattered. Fearful he would lose both his "money makers," Houston permitted me to telephone Kelly's doctor and begin administering medicines. As for me, he arranged for assistance in picking up the pieces in order that I complete my primary purpose in traveling to California, i.e. meet with Mexican President Miguel de la Madrid and finalize plans to open the Juarez border.

CHAPTER 26

NEW WORLD ORDERS

There was "no time to lose" in bringing me back around to a functioning level. I knew I had work to do. Although I was to be "used up" by my 30th birthday, I do not believe it was Bush and Cheney's intention to expedite the process so quickly. Apparently it was their incompetence due to over- indulgence of drugs and subsequent abuse of Kelly in my presence that destroyed parts of my maternal based programming. Regardless of their "excuse," Houston drove us to San Francisco, California where Temple of Set (Satan) founder U.S. Army Lt. Col. Aquino made some emergency "repairs."

I was not taken to a hospital or a mental institution, but to a brain/mind research and development lab on the U.S. Army Reservation at Presidio. There are many facilities such as this one across the country at various CIA, military, and NASA compounds where hyper advanced government knowledge is put to the test, developed and modified. Those I met who had expertly learned the scientific mechanics of the brain in conjunction with the ins and outs of the mind used their gained secret knowledge to manipulate and/or control others. The only thing Mark Phillips, Byrd, and Aquino had in common was the belief that "secret knowledge equals power".[1] Byrd explained to me that New World Order "powers were strengthened" by allowing the mental health community only partial and/or deliberate misinformation through their organization lobby, The American Psychiatric Association (APA), concerning treatment modalities for severe dissociative disorders being created through mind control! Perpetrators believed that withholding knowledge and the proliferation of deliberate misinformation allowed them control over their secrets, and subsequently over humanity. They may be correct if no one can or will react to the information presented in this book.

Intended or not, I overheard a conversation pertaining to death and the mind between Aquino and a lab assistant as I lay on a cold, metal table in a deep hypnotic state. Aquino was saying that I had come close to death numerous times which "increased my ability to enter other (mind) dimensions en route to death." I had listened to Aquino talk at length about such concepts before, as though he were trying to convince himself of some interdimensional time travel theory. "Whether in principle or in theory, the results are the same," he claimed. "The concept of time is abstract in itself." Hypnotic talk of past- present-future set my mind in a spin that, when combined with *Alice in Wonderland*/NASA mirror world concepts, created an illusion of timeless dimensions. I now know that the only "dimensions" I experienced were elaborate memory compartmentalizations of real, earthly events by real, earthly criminals, and certainly not by aliens, Satan, or demons.

After moving me from the table to an elaborate box, Aquino then shifted my mind to another area of my brain, claiming to have taken me into another dimension by way of "death's door." This was accomplished while I was subjected to sensory deprivation combined with hypnotic and harmonic re- programming. The seemingly coffin like structure was transformed in my mind to a crematorium, where I endured the sense of increasing heat while "I slowly burned" through hypnotic suggestion. Aquino then "pulled me through death's door" and into another dimension "void of time." Parts of my programming were "recreated for the recreation of world leaders," i.e. U.S. President Reagan, Mexican President de la Madrid, and Saudi Arabian King Fahd.

In my next recollection of awareness, Houston, Kelly, and I were in Hollywood, where Houston claimed the motor home "broke down" -- an over used attempted memory scramble. He sent me down the street to telephone Michael Danté, who lived nearby in Beverly Hills. Danté was expecting Kelly and me to join him in his Beverly Hills mansion for several days as had been previously arranged by our handler Alex Houston. Kelly and I waited at the phone booth as instructed until Danté arrived to pick us up in his midnight blue Ferrari. As soon as I sat down, Danté said, "I got something for you, Baby. Give me your arm." Heroin was a common "vice" he shared with Bush, and he shot me up with the drug right in front of Kelly.

Later that evening at his house, Danté told me that he refused to "handle damaged goods," and that he would not be my next handler as previously planned. Not only was I "not fit to live with" him, but I was not "fit to live" at all. I am not certain what he meant to accomplish by these threats, but I know in retrospect that this was not his decision to make. Besides, I never perceived existence with him and his professed "love" as a "future" anyway. Instead, he said he would go along with the original plan long enough to "acquire Kelly."

The next day, hours before I was to meet with de la Madrid, L.A. Dodgers baseball team manager Tommy LaSorda, George Bush, Jr., and star pitcher of Jr.'s Texas Rangers, Nolan Ryan (who was also a banker) were at Dante's house working out the details of money laundering and bank transactions for the eminent opening of the Juarez border cocaine, heroin, and white slavery route. The common bond of covert criminal activity overrode any professional baseball conflicts between them. All three were in town to be in attendance at various gatherings and parties of Reagan's, who would be arriving in a matter of days. And all three appeared to have an understanding of my function as Reagan's "Presidential Model" mind control sex slave.

Danté was gathering the necessary clothes and props for the evening rendezvous with de la Madrid. LaSorda, Nolan Ryan, and Jr. were standing in the entrance way of Danté's house attempting to activate my "Baseball Mind Computer" programmed personality fragment that had inadvertently been shattered by Bush and Cheney's traumas at Shasta. Danté told them, "She knows more about baseball than you and Tommy [LaSorda] put together. Go ahead and ask her something. Anything."

Much to LaSorda's amusement, Nolan Ryan asked, "How many times does Fernando Valenzuela (Dodger pitcher) touch his hat if he's going to throw a srewgy (screw ball)?" I could not respond, although I had once known more statistical data than would ever be in print.

Jr. hollered, "Hey, Danté. What's with your baseball computer here, huh?

Are we supposed to say a magic word?"

"I don't know," Danté responded. "Could be drugs. Her sex is working fine, though. Give it a whirl."

Jr. declined, saying, "No thanks. The Baseball Computer sucks enough. Listen, we'll see you later." Jr. had never shown any interest in me sexually. Like his father, he had only shown sexual interest in Kelly, who had been away with him most of the day. As he turned to leave, he stroked me under the chin and cryptically said, "Have a Ball tonight."

LaSorda, who had not been on his Ultra Slim Fast sponsored diet yet, said, "Speaking of balls, mine could use a little attention here." He unzipped his pants.

Danté told me, "We gotta get dressed. Three minutes." Three minutes was a trigger for me to perform a specific oral sex act. I knelt on the floor and pushed up LaSorda's enormous belly, resting it on my head as I groped for his penis as ordered. Danté's two Great Danes came in as Jr. and Nolan Ryan left. I had been forced to participate in a bestiality film with these sex trained dogs earlier that day, and I had to fight them off as I sexually gratified LaSorda before getting ready for "the Ball".

---

[1] Mark Phillips explained to me that, by revealing their "secrets" their power would diminish. "Good always prevails through positive application, whereas the bad guys are hindered and slowed in their criminal endeavors through having to cover-up their negative actions with lies to support lies. This inevitably allows the truth to emerge," Mark said.

CHAPTER 27

HOTEL CALIFORNIA

Danté threw me a short, red slinky dress with rhinestone straps and a pair of "glass slippers" to wear to "Cinderella's Ball." The shoes, like Oz ruby slippers and Philip Habib's "magic lightening bolt" shoes, were to trance-form me into the personality fragment that had been pre-programmed for the event.

Danté escorted me to the party/"Ball" where I was to meet with Mexican President de la Madrid. Dante had been bragging about his "second home in Malibu" ever since I first met him, and the place was opulence personified. I do not know who actually owned "his" second home in Malibu, California, but Reagan's influence was evident in the decor. From the front, the white stucco house gave the illusion of being two story. The view overlooked a secluded Pacific bay, and revealed three levels built into a cliff. Through the smoked glass wall panels that spanned the back, the three stories, lavishly carpeted in red, white, and blue provided a patriotic view. All levels had a beige-white interior decorated in gold and crystal. An enormous chandelier hung from the cathedral ceiling, illuminating all three levels at once from the greatroom which overlooked the bay.

I was told that Uncle Ronnie (Reagan) would be arriving the next day. It was my "patriotic duty" to attend de la Madrid's welcome party and "wear down any resistance he may have" in order that Reagan's business meeting with him would "go smoothly." This was not the first time I heard this excuse for being politically prostituted, nor would it be the last. In reality, I was to do the initial dirty work, delivering messages, and encourage de la Madrid to use drugs and party with abandon. The diplomatic relations between the U.S. and Mexico were already strong, but this phase of the operation required total commitment from de la Madrid.

Danté and I waited at the top of the staircase as de la Madrid, accompanied by two body guards, climbed to the red level of the house. I greeted de la Madrid, "Welcome to the U.S. and (seductively) welcome to the Hotel California." His deep throated laugh indicated he had been cued to the ramifications of my cryptic statement. "Hotel California," taken from a popular song by the Eagles, stated "you can check out any time you like, but you can never leave." To de la Madrid this confirmed the permanency of his involvement in the criminal covert operations in which he was conspiring. Blackmail was openly initiated to ensure that each criminal participant understood that if one fell, they all fell. Maintaining "dirt" on each other through this Mafia style method was seemingly the only way these criminals implementing the New World Order kept each other "honest."

De la Madrid and I went into a nearby bedroom, followed by Danté and the body guards. Danté then activated the programmed message instilled at the Shasta resort from Bush to de la Madrid. I recited, "If you please, Sir, I have a message to deliver to you from the Vice President of the United States. Welcome to our Neighborhood. As you know, Salinas and I have worked out the details towards implementing our plan to open the Juarez border tomorrow. In preparation and celebration of this accomplishment, this little party tonight will bring you face to face with a trusted few who are integral parts of this endeavor, and give you the latitude to see first hand the friendship and honor among the (government involved Mafioso) family members. I regret that I could not be here in person to greet you, but Ron [Reagan] can show you the ins and outs of the organization better than I. The transaction numbers have been recorded, and are available to you for cross reference purposes and to uphold the integrity of the players involved on your end of the Juarez border. Your commitment today ensures you of a higher economic standard of living for your people, increased relations with the U.S., an influx of American industry, and a position of high esteem in the New World Order. With your 'Seal of Approval' we can dissolve the Juarez border and make way for a future of prosperity for Mexico. For now, relax and enjoy your stay."

One of de la Madrid's guards was shuffling through some papers from a briefcase, and he told Danté he would like the bank transaction numbers. Danté switched me to "You Are What You Read" Passbook programming, and I delivered the numbers intended for the border guards to de la Madrid as ordered. A computer of sorts was used to calculate and confirm the numbers. Aware that the meeting was being filmed by one of Danté's high tech "hidden" cameras, de la Madrid held up a paper wrapped ball of Mexican heroin. Speaking directly at the camera, he cleverly said, "A token of appreciation, Mr. Bush. Something for your private stock. The finest heroin available. Enjoy."

Danté strode across the room and said, "I'll take that and see to it that he gets it myself."

"I'm sure you will," de la Madrid laughed. He then put all but one paper back in the briefcase. I was instructed to present the elaborately embossed Mexican Presidential Seal (of Approval) to pre-appointed Juarez border guards as proof of de la Madrid's commitment, then deliver it directly to Bush for his file on the future NAFTA agreement.

Prepared to present a modified Hands-On Mind Control Demonstration to de la Madrid, Danté said, "You've heard from a Carrier Pigeon (messenger). You've seen her in a mode to accept program. And now I will demonstrate some of her sexual modes."

"That will not be necessary," de la Madrid told him. "I have been given a handful of keys that I would like to use on my own, including the one to destroy all memory. Not that it matters when we are monitored (he gestured toward the camera), but nevertheless I was instructed to do it." Danté did not seem to know this was not the first time I was sexually prostituted to the Mexican President.

"She rides a horse well," Danté said, referring to both the rare practice of heroin to supposedly block my memory of this event, and a Reagan inspired sex act. Danté stuck a needle in my arm. "May I recommend a ride for you?"

"I am on one now that I would like to maintain," de la Madrid answered, referring to cocaine use and his running nose. Danté laid out several generous lines of the white drug on a black mirror. He stroked me under my chin triggering Reagan's sex Kitten personality, picked up Bush's heroin, and ushered the two guards out the door.

De la Madrid, fully aware of my pornography exposure, said, "You like cameras? Let's give them something to watch." He snorted two more lines of coke, undressed, and further activated my sex programming with the verbal and physical keys and triggers Reagan had previously provided him. At one point he enthusiastically commented that "if I have my way, the Free Trade Agreement will include a few top of the line (he snorted another line of coke for emphasis) 'models' (vaginally) carved and trained like you." De la Madrid had long been obsessively fascinated with my vaginal mutilation carving. He was perversely excited at the prospect of the Juarez border joint venture drug deal including protected "free trade" of mind controlled slaves. He reiterated his desire the next day during a meeting with Reagan.

CHAPTER 28

"FREE TRADE" OF DRUGS
AND SLAVES AT THE JUAREZ BORDER

The next day, Danté drove me to a Bel Aire mansion high on a hill where another party was underway. As I joined those who had gathered on the manicured lawn, I recognized many of the same Mafia people who had been at the Malibu retreat a.k.a. "Hotel California." This was a welcome party for President Reagan, who had just arrived. He was walking across the yard toward me with his friend, Jack Valenti, who was the president of the powerful Motion Picture Association of America. Reagan looked his role amongst his mobster friends, his beige coat with fur collar draped over his shoulders revealing a dark grey pinstripe suit underneath. In retrospect, I remember him as dressed like the one mobster I did not have to meet, John Gotti. As soon as my eyes met his, I was knocked to the ground by a familiar blue-white blast (high voltage) like the one I had recently experienced in D.C.

When I came back around and my eyes refocused, Danté was holding me up. Reagan said, "Well, hello Kitten."

"Uncle Ronnie, how'd you get here?" I asked in child like innocence.

"The rainbow, Kitten, the rainbow," he answered in Oz cryptic. "I told you I was coming home. There's no place like home, and you said it with me. So, here we are. I keep a little piece of the rainbow in my pocket so I can get back over it (to D.C.) anytime I want to. I make a wish, and click my heels, and I'm gone."

For the moment, Reagan succeeded in confusing my mind with Oz cryptic metaphors, reconfirming to my child personality that he was indeed the powerful Wizard. As we went inside for a brief meeting, my personality was deliberately switched to the one that had dealt with de la Madrid the night before.

The gray-white stucco house was decorated in plush Presidential blue carpeting and deep cherry wood tones. The "office" was small and further crowded by those of us present for the meeting. De la Madrid was comfortably seated, as was Jack Valenti. I was not privy to Valenti's exact role in opening the Juarez boarder. I only know that he was well educated to the particulars of this meeting. Danté and I remained standing since we would be leaving as quickly as I heard what Reagan, who was shuffling papers and pacing the room, had to say.

"Well, Kitten," Reagan said to me, "this is your death sentence: You'll go out in a blaze of glory." I was not surprised to receive confirmation of my imminent death by Reagan. I had heard about death by fire from seemingly everyone involved in establishing "free trade," through Mexico, of our nation's children for drugs. Reagan's use of patriotic metaphors and puns while matter- of-factly informing me he ordered my death was reflective of his often displayed lack of respect for human life. What reflected his character even more were the crimes he was involved in that prompted him to cover-up through "sentencing" me to death. I had witnessed the criminal foundations of NAFTA, which in turn could threaten the successful implementation of the New World Order should these secrets ever be revealed. Initial "Free Trade" including drugs and white slavery extended beyond the U.S./Mexican border. It routed U.S.

traumatized, robotic, mind controlled children into Saudi Arabia, while building up weapon stockpiles in

Nicaragua and Iraq. Although I was considered to be no threat, predicated on the (erroneous) belief that I could not be deprogrammed to regain my memory of these events, my death would provide extra insurance to those involved. I was nearly "used up" anyway, and recording my death via "Snuff Film" was agreed upon as proof to De la Madrid and other leaders at risk, that I had indeed been silenced through death.

I could not think to respond to Reagan's "death sentence". Danté wanted to make sure I grasped the point as he graphically expounded, "The next time I ignite your [sexual] flame, Baby, it will consume you, body and soul. And you will burn, Baby, burn. And I'll take your ashes and scatter them to the wind. I'm going to blow you away. On film."

Upon hearing something cryptic to which he could relate, Valenti laughed at Danté's twist of words. Referring to the old porn blue pencil editing term "Blue movies," he added, "Blue blazes."

Danté laughed with him. "We'll call it 'Who In Blue Blazes Was That?' Or, how 'bout 'Cream-Ate'?"

De la Madrid noticed Reagan was not laughing and said, "That's like crashing a Mercedes to film a stunt." He leaned forward in his chair closer to Reagan, lowered his voice and said, "It is my desire to have seven just like her roll off the assembly line and shipped to me prior to the agreement's completion."

Reagan agreed, responding, "Those (blonde haired, blue eyed) fine kids on the relay to Saudi Arabia are top of the line, but they don't have what she's got." "Two faced Ones are hard to come by," de la Madrid quipped, referring to

my vaginal mutilation and Presidential programming code. He cut his eyes over to me, touched himself and cryptically continued, " -- from one perspective, anyway. And I like having 'One' I can 'count on'."

Reagan chuckled while Danté shifted his feet and unfolded his arms long enough to cough-laugh. Valenti seemed to be bored of clichés or was missing many of the cryptic double meanings, but judging from the tone of the meeting, that was just as well. "I'll mention it to Bobby (Byrd) and delegate your order to him," Reagan told his Mexican counterpart. "It should be relatively simple to slip one in for you every few shipments or so once the Juarez border is open to such free trade activities as planned." Reagan spoke as though he were distracted and thinking of something else, even when he looked my direction.

"If you please, Sir," I began, "I have the Presidential Seal of Approval and am prepared to fulfill my role." Danté looked at his watch, aware that I was scheduled to be at the Juarez border by the "stroke of midnight." Reagan walked over to see the paper I had received from de la Madrid the night before. "OK. Well, fare well, Kitten," Reagan said, as he kissed my cheek. He added in Oz cryptic, "I'll see you on the other side (of the rainbow in D.C.). Click your heels. . ."

My world spun black. Someone had hit me with a powerful stun gun and I was down, feeling as though Danté was half dragging me as he led me to his car, which was already idling in the circular drive. We soon pulled up to the motor home at the gas station on Hollywood Boulevard, where he had picked Kelly and me up several days before. Kelly was already in the motor home, vomiting sick and horribly traumatized. She had been convinced by someone that I had been killed. Houston attempted to create a hypnotically induced "time slip," acting as though I had only been gone a few minutes. We drove quickly, stopping only for fuel in order that I be in Juarez at the appointed time. There I robotically presented the Presidential Seal of Approval to the proper officials as programmed, officially opening the border to "Free Trade" of crimes against humanity. Houston and I had hurried across the Juarez border where we were met by the Mexican official in charge. The guard looked to be in his late 40s, with classic rugged Mexican features. He stood approximately 5'11', had black hair, an unkempt moustache, black beady eyes and a paunchy belly protruding over his short, squat legs. He spoke excitedly in Spanish, with a harsh, cold tone to his voice as he spit out the necessary words in English, "Give me the Seal." He snapped his fingers, impatiently hurrying me. He took the Presidential seal and knocked me face down on top of a small, barren metal desk while he closely inspected the document. Even Houston was unusually quiet while this particular uniformed guard paced the small tower room, sweating profusely while he talked on his walkie talkie. Finally, he accessed and verified the bank transaction codes provided through whom he said was George Bush, Jr. He concluded the encounter by taking a stun gun from his belt and jolting me with it, supposedly to erase my memory.

I was nauseated and weak from high voltage and the ordeal as Houston and I made our way back across the border. My empty stomach rolled, prompting Houston to lie, "I told you not to drink the water." In reality, I had had nothing to drink since the champagne at the Hotel California, and I hadn't eaten in days. I was thoroughly exhausted when we reached the motor home in El Paso, but Houston was sexually aroused from cocaine and the criminal events that merged Mexico with the U.S. at the Juarez border.

CHAPTER 29

THE LIZARD OF AHS

After the opening of the Juarez border, I was kept actively busy according to the plan to "use me up" before my 30th birthday death sentence. I was subjected to a brutal (near death gang rape) "celebration benefit" at an identified Masonic Lodge in Warren, Ohio to "celebrate the free trade benefits" gained by involved east coast politicos. Centers such as the nearby Youngstown "Charm School" went into mass production of slaves to mule drugs or be part of the mind controlled sex slave "trance-sport operations." Mexico was not the only country reaping the economic benefits of criminal free trade.

After Kelly's ordeal in California, Dante' and Houston were criminally exploiting her for literally "all she was worth." Subsequently, she missed an extraordinary amount of schooling. When she was in school, she was experiencing difficulty with her peers. These factors prompted plans to send her to a local Catholic school the next year, where her unusual behavior would be overlooked and covered up.

Soon thereafter, Senator Byrd came to Nashville to fiddle at the Grand Ole Opry and, as my handler Houston remarked, "fiddle around with me" at the Opryland Hotel. Byrd explained that close association with me had become volatile due to my roles in Iran-Contra and NAFTA, and therefore he would be distancing himself from me. He spent most of "our last night together" working on his memoirs for a voluminous book on the U.S. Constitution he was writing [now published at tax payers' expense], which focuses on his long winded Senate (filibuster) speeches.

Byrd attempted to strengthen my programmed "loyalty bond" to him to keep me quiet "until death do us part." He told me, "If it was up to me, I would let you live." He talked at length about how our time together had been infringed upon by both de la Madrid and Reagan. Bitterness over their stronger controls on me was evident as he mocked their self appointed roles as the Wizard and Lizard of Oz. De la Madrid's fascination with U.S. mind controlled slaves reportedly inspired him to combine Bush's lizard-like alien themes and his reputed Mayan roots/lizard man theories with Reagan's Oz themes to claim the role of Lizard of Ahs. From Byrd's ramblings, it appeared that his mockery of their roles was due to their having decided "how" "his" slave would die, and had nothing to do with caring that I would be killed. Byrd maintained his "bonding" programming charade all night. He played his fiddle and sang "to me" in place of his usual torturous whipping and brutality. Sex was, for the first and last time, painless.

Byrd had not distanced himself too far from me, though, where government operations were concerned. When I was "over the rainbow" in D.C. during the summer of '87, it was business as usual with Byrd. I was escorted to Goddard Space Flight Center, where Byrd was waiting for me in a sterile hallway near the brass-trimmed, mirrored elevators. He was loaded down with items, which he deposited on a small table as he greeted me. He picked up a NASA ID badge and clipped it on my nipple, the metal teeth biting me with their serrated edges. When I (softly) cried out, he said, "Oh, OK. I'll wear it," removed it, and clipped it on his white lab coat. He handed me a NASA lab coat like his and a white hard hat.

His hard hat suggestively and "humorously" said HARD in bold red letters. My hat said NASA, in a mirror reversal of the standard bold red lettering. When I read it in a mirror, it appeared as though I were on the wrong side of the mirror and needed to step through (according to Alice in Wonderland/NASA programming). It also clearly indicated to those-in-the- know that I was under mind control. Byrd looked at his pocket watch prompting a wave of terror in me, and said in Wonderland cryptic, "We're late. As the elevator drops down the rabbit hole, we'll reverse time in order to get there a few minutes early."

Byrd spun me around to face the elevator's mirrored doors saying, "Look deep into the mirror and be all that you can be by becoming infinitely lost in all that you see." Byrd timed his hypnotic induction so that when he ordered, "Step through the mirror," the doors opened and we stepped through.

As the elevator supposedly went "down 99 (taken from Aquino's corny reversal of 6s) levels to the depths of hell," Byrd told me the earth "spins faster and faster at the core, causing us to spiral downward in a tornado effect." I dropped deeper in my hypnotic trance. The elevator doors opened to what appeared to me as an exact replica of the floor we just left. However, this floor's hallway led to a computer room and sanitized-looking lab area. Several of the scientists working there were amused by our hats, prompting Byrd to ham up his comedic act. Byrd ignored the fact that these NASA workers, like many others, may have deliberately stroked his entertainer's ego because they relied on his appropriations for funding.

Byrd made me robotically announce to the workers, "He's taking me to your leader."

"I'm the Commander, here," the apparent director of the underground lab said. The workers again busied themselves as he stood, arms folded defensively across his chest, while his bespectacled intelligent eyes darted the room surveying the situation. The Commander had a few grey strands salting his short dark hair, yet his build was surprisingly youthful and trim for his age. He and Byrd apparently knew each other quite well. Byrd strode over to him, dragging me along. "Tom," Byrd called to his 50ish 6'1" friend. "This is your specimen of the day that I promised I would deliver. I will be most interested to see what "youo can deliver since diplomatic relations with Mexico depends on it. Not that I want to increase any pressure you may feel, but we need seven more just like her to stuff in the mouth of his royal Lizardry (de la Madrid) to keep him from spilling his guts on the project."

"It's just as well, my friend," the Commander said, stroking his chin without uncrossing his arms. "That way he can't talk without implicating himself."

"That's the way the Chief feels about it," Byrd agreed. "He's already in deep anyway, but this order [for slaves] hits him closer to home since they'll be serving him personally."

We walked to a clinical, sanitized area that had a maze of small rooms where I was undressed and prepped for the lab. A nurse of sorts injected me with the NASA "Tranquility" drug and instructed me to put my lab coat back on. "Walk this way," she ordered as she led me down the hall, swinging her hips in an exaggerated manner. I immediately complied. The Tranquility drug had no recreational affects but produced an attitude of peaceful compliance to all orders given. As we approached the theater-type lab, a small group of men who would be in attendance were talking with

Byrd and the so called Commander. They looked at us and laughed at my literal compliance to walk like the nurse.

I was then led by the Commander to a "backstage" entrance, which was actually a glass encased lab surrounded by seats in ascending rows. Scientists in NASA lab coats looked down on the lab table where I lay as the Commander wired me up to a computerized machine. A camera was positioned high in one corner of the room, filming all that transpired. I was aware through conversations between Byrd and the Commander that de la Madrid had requested a video of the latest advancements in mind control technique being used to create his seven slaves. In reality, the camera was filming scientific methodisms salted with "comic" misinformation as a humorous "no" to his request.

Since I was considered "used up" and my death was imminent, the Commander told the scientists to "feel free to fuck the lab specimen." "But first," he said, "before you satisfy your mental and physical curiosities sampling the President's [Reagan's] wares, we must satisfy El Presidente's [de la Madrid's] perverse intellect with a little space humor." He turned to one of the technical workers and said, "You're going to have to edit this tape for de la Madrid's benefit and take this part out while we prepare her for an 'off color' chameleon joke."

A live lizard encased in a glass test tube of sorts was inserted in my vagina. The camera was focused on the area while my legs were spread in a birthing position. Acting as though I had conceived while having sex with de la Madrid, the Commander said, "Now for the finished product, which in layman's terms equates to the reproductive offspring of a Lizard breeding machine." He dramatically snapped on a rubber glove and probed me as though he were giving me a gynecological exam. In fact, he was opening the trap door of the Lizard's tube to turn him out. Very slowly, the sluggish lizard poked his head out of my vagina and crawled out onto the metal table. "This concludes all of the experimentation demonstration of the cloning of a Presidential model," the Commander said.

I apparently had been selected as the prototype for the seven programmed slaves de la Madrid had requested. De la Madrid was interested in NASA programmed slaves that would be vaginally mutilated like I was. He was sexually obsessed with the hideous carving. I have no way of knowing what, if any, technological advancements were actually provided to de la Madrid via the film. I only know that deliberate misinformation tainted the methodologies depicted, and that I had never experienced programming or testing before or at the time by any such methods.

This video created for "his Royal Lizardry" was one of many cryptic lizard themes that NASA used in its Mexican operations. All of my programmed roles in Mexico involved the prolific local iguana lizards. De la Madrid had relayed the "legend of the Iguana" to me, explaining that lizard-like Aliens had descended upon the Mayans. The Mayan pyramids, their advanced astronomical technology, including the sacrifice of virgins, was supposedly inspired by the lizard aliens. He told me that when the aliens interbred with the Mayans to produce a form of life they could inhabit, they fluctuated between a human and Iguana appearance through chameleon-like abilities. "A perfect vehicle for transforming into world leaders." De la Madrid claimed to have Mayan/alien ancestry in his blood, whereby he transformed "back into an Iguana at will." De la Madrid produced a hologram similar to the one Bush did in his You Are What You Read initiation. His hologram of lizard-like tongue and eyes produced the illusion that he was transforming into an Iguana. While in Mexico, I was always ordered to wait by rocks where the abundant Iguanas sunned before being "trance-ported" to my scheduled meetings with "his Royal Lizardry," the Lizard of Ahs.

CHAPTER 30

IN THE INTEREST OF TIME AND SPACE

Senator Patrick Leahy (D-Vermont), who served as vice chairman on the U.S. Senate Intelligence Committee in 1985-86, was a "friend" of Senator Byrd. Leahy's position on Byrd's Senate Appropriations committee, coupled with his former position in Intelligence, afforded him an inordinate amount of power and influence. While I had cause to have contact with Senator Leahy on numerous occasions, Kelly was apparently more familiar with him than I. This was evidenced by our meeting with him in Vermont in the late summer of 1985.

Alex Houston was booked to "entertain" at the State Fair in Rutland, Vermont. The entire trip proved to be a whirlwind of covert activity for me, during which time I obtained a packet of papers from an unidentified operative with orders to hand deliver them to Senator Leahy. Kelly had been kept as busy as I, since Boxcar Willie and other CIA operative pedophiles were in abundance at the fair in Leahy's home state.

President Reagan had given me specific orders to carry out while in Vermont, which included delivering a message to "Patrick" for him. He also told me, "When you go to Vermont, be sure and go by ("buy") LL Bean."

Literally interpreting what he suggested, I asked, "The whole store?"

"No," Reagan laughed. "I meant stop by there. I didn't mean buy the whole store. I already own it. Just buy a few things, like an LL Bean Swiss Army Knife."[1]

When Reagan said he "already owned" LL Bean, I thought he was referring to the amount of shopping he did there. He wore LL Bean shirts, sweaters, and slippers; slept on LL Bean flannel sheets in his LL Bean pajamas; and carried his "Presidential" black LL Bean Swiss Army Knife, with which he cleaned his fingernails. But I learned the real significance of Reagan's statement when I "stopped by" the Vermont LL Bean outlet on the final day of Houston's lengthy Vermont State Fair engagement.

The LL Bean outlet, located near the top of supposedly the highest mountain in the pristine forest, appeared to be a store front for CIA covert activity. When I asked the 'clerk' assigned to Kelly and me for a black Swiss Army Knife, his response was indicative of familiarity with government covert operations. Using the old familiar statement (trigger), he ordered Kelly and me to "Walk this way," as he led us through a storage area and out the back door. There, a black, unmarked helicopter was waiting on a pad for us.

The pilot flew us a short distance to the top of a mountain, where we landed in a clearing next to a house that appeared to have no other access. The place was run like a fortress, and two guards in suits met us as Kelly and I emerged from the helicopter. The guards escorted us into the house, keeping Kelly while I met with Senator Leahy.

I walked into an office-type room that had a panoramic view of the wilderness, where Leahy was leaning against a highly polished wooden desk. He was wearing an orange flannel shirt that lost its purpose in crispness. It was my experience that Leahy's surroundings, like his appearance, were as sanitized as possible.

I delivered the documents and message as ordered. Leahy then proceeded to explain that he was aware that my death was immanent due to my groundwork

participation in NAFTA, and that subsequently Kelly would be traded to the West Coast pornography operation. Not only did he obviously want to join in on "using me up" before my 30th birthday, but he had "tracks" to cover-up where Kelly was concerned.

Most of my traumatic encounters with Leahy were alien-themed, but he often relied on my Catholic upbringing to drive his points into my mind. From my perspective, Leahy was unquestionably one of the most intelligent criminals of this entire Shadow Government. His carefully contrived chameleon-like characteristics provided him the latitude of appearing to share the principals and beliefs of whomever he was masterfully manipulating on both a national and international level. He won Reagan's respect through their shared diplomatic ties to the Vatican, and his Irish-Catholic heritage. While he appeared publicly to oppose Byrd on Senate Appropriations issues, they actually worked together behind the scenes in their shared world dominance efforts. Again from my perspective, Leahy was a loner who had his own agenda and answered to no one I knew. Leahy's intelligence was often manifested to me by triple depth meaning to his words and actions. Everything he did was for a deeper purpose, and this trip to Vermont proved to be no different.

Kelly and I had been given what felt like a sophisticated variation of the NASA CIA-designer drug, Tranquility, which turned us into the robotic mind controlled slaves that Senator Leahy preferred. As the drug was overtaking me, I attentively listened to what Leahy was saying.

"God condones that one," Leahy said, referring to both my role in NAFTA and his pedophile abuse of my daughter. "Of course, God is not the one you need to be concerned with. He is a passive God. One who's passed on and lives only in a Bible. The God you need to be concerning yourself with is the all- seeing, all-knowing God. That great big Eye in the Sky. It sees all, records all, and transmits the information right where its needed. Let me give you some sound advice -- Keep your mouth shut and none of this need be known anywhere. Only your Vice President [Bush] will know for sure, and he's been keeping secrets all his life. I'm not suggesting George Bush is God. Oh no, he is much more than that. He is a semi-God, which means he is straddling the heavenly and earthly planes in order that he take action on what he sees with his ever watchful Eye In The Sky." Content with his metaphorical manipulation of my literal mind, he finished, "Now, that's enough fore-play. Go get the kid."

Kelly was standing quietly and robotically just outside the door with the two guards. They ushered us down the hall, through an ornately carved door, and into Leahy's bedroom. The room was highly effeminate for a man, decorated in pastels, white eyelet, and huge billowy pillows. When the Senator walked in, Kelly groaned, "Noooo, not you again." Leahy signaled Kelly with his hand, thus switching her into total silence and submission. Then, accessing specific personality fragments that previously recompartmentalized in my mind from Bush's and Byrd's sexual abuse of Kelly, Leahy began undressing. His pale skin looked even whiter against the white eyelet sheets, which seemed to accentuate the perversity of his pedophile actions with my daughter that I was forced to watch. His torturous abuse complete, Leahy ordered Kelly and me to follow him downstairs to his "torture lab."

I had seen and experienced basement "spy conditioning" torture chambers before both in the U.S. and Mexico, and Leahy's "torture lab" looked more like a

NASA lab. His access to the latest advancements in electronic/drug mind control technology was consistent with his ability to use it. I was immediately strapped to a cold, chrome and stainless steel table by the two guards. Leahy began reciting, "Cross your heart and hope to die, Stick a needle in your eye." A wirey "needle" was pushed slowly into my right eye while Kelly was forced to watch. This entire ordeal was directed for trauma purposes primarily at Kelly since Leahy figured I would be dead soon anyway. "If you holler, if you cry, Kelly will be the first to die. Pray to God and Bush will hear, because his Eye now has an ear." Leahy interrupted his poem to explain that I was now a "computer-eyesd" link-up to Bush's Eye in the Sky, with the needle-like "antenna" transmitting every word Kelly spoke. He continued with me, "Each word you speak, each breath you sigh, Your eye trance-mits to the Eye in the Sky." Kelly believed it, which locked her into silence. Leahy's secret was safe -- for the moment.

While I was literally out of my mind from intense pain, Leahy utilized the opportunity to program me with what he said was financial information to deliver to Byrd. This required no "personality" therefore the shattered fragments Leahy had deliberately shifted me into when raping Kelly would be ideal to "computer-eyes" his message. He told me that my body was a conduit to link him up to the Eye in the Sky, where he was transmitting the information for storage until such time as Byrd accessed it. "Only the tiniest little prick can access the computer-eyesd' storage bank," Leahy said, laughing at his own double meaning mockery of Byrd's penis size.

This was not the first time Leahy transferred apparently sensitive U.S. government intelligence information to Byrd through me. I had photographically recorded numbers in my mind's "computer banks" ever since Leahy prepared me for the task some months before at White Sands Missile Base in New Mexico. It was there in the TOP SECRET mind control area of the base that Leahy subjected me to extreme tortures and high tech programming. Combining purposes as usual, Leahy was saying, "Funding will continue to be approved as long as [mind control] Projects such as this continue to receive your full attention." I was treated like a lab animal with no apparent regard for whether I lived or died. I was put in an electrified metal walled and floored cell, referred to by some as the woodpecker grid, which provided inescapable physical torture.

In spite of his tortures, intelligence, high tech methodism, and sophisticated mind manipulations, Senator Leahy failed to cover his "secrets" -- including his sexual abuse of Kelly. He did succeed, however, in causing Kelly and me to be hospitalized from his torturous abuses upon our return to Tennessee. I had suffered excruciating pain and irreparable damage to my right eye, while Kelly psychosomatically suffered respiratory failure due to his extreme traumas. The physical manifestations of the psychological devastation reeked on us by Senator Leahy failed to raise questions from outsiders as to the cause.

Equally worthy of mention, are numerous other high profile perpetrators that Kelly and I had exposure to over the years. These individuals, in spite of the CIA's "need-to-know" M.O. of maintaining "the left hand does not know what the right hand is doing," were in positions to be knowledgeable of Kelly's and my victimizations. All of them accessed our programming either for drug distribution, banking/message delivery, mind control demonstrations, or, most often, for their perverse sexual gratification.

These too numerous individuals and events are significant chapters in my life who, in the interest of time and space, will be fully exposed in a forthcoming book. Rather than point a finger at these individuals for reasons of "vengeance" (there is none comparable), they must be publicly identified for all our sakes and, above all, for our children's sakes. Therefore, a list of perpe-Traitors has been compiled and strategically distributed for posterity, as well as to prevent these individuals from interfering in any Congressional hearings[2] that should be forthcoming as a result of this exposure.

---

[1] Black LL Bean Swiss Army Knives were a coded indicator of White House level operations. Red LL Bean Swiss Army Knives, and regular Swiss Army Knives were a standard CIA indicator with which I was also familiar.

[2] Please support us in this effort by writing your Congressmen.

CHAPTER 31

THE KING AND EYE

Saudi Arabia threaded in and out of most operations in which I was involved, primarily due to their purchase and routing of weapons, drugs, and blond-haired, blue-eyed programmed children. According to George Bush's claims, Saudi Arabia was in essence a controlled financial arm of the United States. Saudi Arabian King Fahd and his Ambassador to the U.S., Prince Bandar, provided a front for the unconstitutional and criminal covert operations of the U.S. This included the arming of Iraq and the Nicaraguan Contras; U.S. involvement in the Bank of Credit and Commerce International (B.C.C.I.) scandal; and funding of the Black Budget through purchase of our nation's children to be used as sex slaves and camel jockeys. Since the U.S. "won" control of the drug industries through the so-called Drug Wars, Saudi Arabia played an integral role in distribution. It was my experience that Bush's claim of having Saudi Arabian King Fahd as his puppet was, in fact, reality. It was only natural that criminal diplomatic relations with Mexico interface with Saudi Arabia under the circumstances. After all, King Fahd and Mexican President Miguel de la Madrid were active members of George Bush's elite "Neighborhood" in the New World Order. Before I left Washington, D.C., it was "my duty as a [programmed] American Patriot" to participate in initiating the King and Eye branch of Operation Greenbacks for Wetbacks.

While plans were being finalized for a clandestine 3:00 A.M. meeting at L'Enfante Hotel which I would be attending, I was rushed around D.C. gathering last minute messages and information. I had no choice in leaving Kelly at Bush's Residence Office where Houston had dropped us off earlier in the day for my initial briefing. Congressman Guy VanderJagt was in Bush's office along with Dick Cheney when we arrived. Before taking Kelly upstairs to the residence area, VanderJagt told Bush his story about taking my virginity when I was a small child. He recommended Bush do the same to Kelly before someone else "beat him to it." Bush laughed and replied, "What makes you think I haven't?"[1]

VanderJagt took Kelly by the hand and led her upstairs while Bush and Cheney began giving me my instructions. Bush joked about working "grave yard" in the "shadows" for "the White House night shift" of the King and Eye operation. Cheney began my instructions with the usual threat to Kelly's life, and was interrupted by a phone call ordering me over to the White House. The whole time I was gone, I experienced a sensation of panic and dread at having had to leave Kelly at Bush's. Although I could not think to reason, the Shasta experience had left me with an incomprehensible subconscious fear for Kelly's life that was compounded by Cheney's most recent threats. I was apprehensive when I was returned to Bush's house late that evening for completion of my instructions. A party was underway, and I was dismayed to see the place so crowded yet void of children.

As I made my way through the crowd, Cheney saw me and started across the room towards me. I spotted VanderJagt nearby, who had been drinking excessively, and anxiously asked him where Kelly was. He said, "Upstairs sleeping. George is expecting you." I wanted desperately to go to Kelly, but Cheney, who was drunk as usual, had reached me by that time.

214

"Walk this way," Cheney slurred. He imitated the Oz Scarecrow's walk as he led me through the middle of the crowd to Bush's office. Bush was busy behind his desk, and his tension was apparent. He said, "Phil Habib is doing a number on his highness's [Fahd's] head. I want you to do a number on his 'dick'."

"Please," Dick Cheney groaned at the term. "That means give him a Royal fucking. Wear him out. You're going on a magic carpet ride tonight, little Genie, down through the rabbit hole, through the mirror and we'll meet you on the other side."

"Good. He'd better have a smile on his face when we walk in [to the 3:00A.M. meeting]," Bush told me as I went out the door. "If you do your part right, he will."

I was escorted to L'Enfante hotel where I was to be prostituted to King Fahd. I had been exposed to him sexually before, but this was my first time with him and his five young girls. Physical likeness characteristics strongly suggested that these Saudi Arabian girls were his own children. Their ages ranged from approximately ten to twenty years old. Indicating Genie-in-the- Bottle programming, of which Fahd was familiar, I bowed and said, "Your wish is my command." Fahd's first wish was for information, which I told him I would deliver later at the meeting. Fahd "disrobed" as his girls removed my dress. Then they "prepared" me as ordered by "washing me" with their tongues, while the youngest briefly performed oral sex on him. The girls were ordered aside while I proceeded to sexually gratify Fahd according to his instruction and those I had received earlier from Cheney and Bush. When I finished doing "my part" in the name of "Diplomatic Relations," Habib was at the door to escort me out. I was to meet with Fahd again at 3:00 A.M. in Habib's suite.

As I stepped out the door, Habib was impatiently hopping up and down like he was energized from cocaine. Using his role as White Rabbit, he said in Wonderland cryptic, "We're late! We're late! For a very important date!" He led me downstairs to the entrance of the hotel, where Bush and Cheney had just walked in looking ridiculously conspicuous in their trenchcoats.

Bush immediately ordered Habib, "Call in" and gestured to the phone across the lobby. Habib turned and hurried for the phone. Cheney dashed up the stairs, leaving me alone with Bush. Bush said, referring to Habib, "Don't you love to see the wabbit hop?"

When Cheney returned a moment later, my (identified) Secret Service escort led me to the boutique area of the hotel to wait while the meeting in Habib's suite got under way. I had endured water deprivation for some time, which my escort noted as we sat near a fountain. He told me his orders were, "You can lead a whore to water, but you can't let her drink." He teased me further, stating that he knew I could "suck the humps of a thousand camels dry." At last, he took me on to the meeting in Habib's room, where Bush, Cheney, Fahd, and Habib were in the midst of discussion.

Bush accessed the messages and bank transaction details I was programmed with at Shasta, and ordered me to relay an account of my meeting with de la Madrid and subsequent opening of the Juarez border. The complexities of this meeting, compounded by my being privy only to certain parts, should not be documented here out of context. I do know that Bush was setting the stage for implementing the New World Order, using Mexico and Saudi Arabia's roles for cover and for further expansion of U.S. covert criminal activity. This included the arming of Iraq with weapons and chemical warfare capabilities. The message Reagan had me programmed with earlier that day was further evidence of this. I delivered Reagan's message to King Fahd as ordered:

"Greetings to King Fahd from President Reagan. The negotiations you are about to embark on are not only critical to the world peace process, but may solidify U.S.-Saudi relations beyond your wildest expectations. You have my word that what appears to be the building up of forces in Iraq is but a mirage in the whirlwind. And when this operation is completed and the dust finally settles, you will see that the sands have shifted in time, running out on our adversaries and shifting all power and control to our unified effort. United we stand to conquer all in the name of world peace and world order, and I am confident that together we can not fail. The more Saddam destroys is that much less for us to do and deal with when we implement the Order. In the meantime, we all have much to gain and not a moment to lose."

It was raining by the time I was escorted back to Bush's residence where Houston was waiting to take Kelly and me back to Tennessee.

---

[1] The Alaska state appointed child sexual abuse physician's exam and photos corroborate that, for once, Bush may have told the truth.

CHAPTER 32

A PLACE TO RUN, NO NEED TO HIDE

Alex Houston had maintained his capacitor distributing business cover throughout the years, routinely changing company names and customers. By summer's end in 1987, Houston had stumbled onto a legitimate sales inquiry from the Peoples Republic of China. Unable to profitably manage a legal business, he took on a partner whom he said checked out to have a curious but inconclusive association in U.S. Intelligence. This partner was Mark Phillips. Houston had forbid me from meeting Mark until his background check was completed and his allegiances understood. As much as he was intrigued with Mark's past, Houston was enthralled with his propensity for conducting international business. In exchange for Mark's cooperation, Houston and he formed a legal corporation. Mark Phillips became President and CEO of Uniphayse. It wasn't long thereafter that he won Houston's confidence through repeated professional successes, and Houston permitted me to meet him.

I sensed right away that Mark was very different from the other men I encountered routinely. He treated me as though I were a person, and his eyes revealed no sexual interest in me at all. Instead of discussing world domination, slavery, pornography, drugs, and genocide like the other men I knew, he introduced me to the raccoons he had years ago rescued from certain death and then tamed. I was deeply impressed with how his "wild" pets loved and trusted him. I could not think to trust, ask for help, or even question at the time what it was that made Mark different.

In the fall of 1987, Kelly was enrolled in Nashville, Tennessee's St. Pius Catholic School. Her unusual behaviors were addressed in school counseling, but their causes and/or origins were never addressed. Kelly still laughs at the absurdity of being counseled to vent her "anger" by scribbling the source of her anger on a piece of paper and then jumping on it. With her "anger" being caused by extreme physical and psychological tortures and sexual abuse, it could not be so simplistically relieved. Houston had forbidden Kelly to display emotion, and had so conditioned her. Once, when he savagely beat her for laughing, I huddled in a corner holding her for hours. That did not positively affect her enormous nurturing needs any more than jumping on a piece of paper. With tears streaming down her face, she opened her bedroom curtains and cried out to what she believed was "Bush's Eye in the Sky." "Why do you hate me? Why do you hate me so much, world, when I love you? I want to die now. I can't take it any more."

That, as evidenced by the near death asthma attack she endured, further proved that Houston's tortures were too much for a seven-year-old child to co- exist with. In retrospect, that remaining part of her mind that could question why her existence was too horrible to comprehend was locked away. And so it goes in the "life" of a mind controlled slave.

In December 1987, my 30th birthday launched the final countdown to my death. Houston was in regular contact with Michael Danté (as telephone receipts prove), and arrangements were finalized for Kelly and me to be transferred to California. There, I was supposed to be burned alive in a snuff pornography film and Kelly would become the property of Dante'. But first, I had orders to conclude my part in Operation Greenbacks for Wetbacks by meeting with de la Madrid. Houston had booked a New Year's NCL cruise to Mexico for all three of us.

Kelly and I were walking among the Mexican pyramid ruins in Tulum, when Houston pointed out an iguana lizard sunning itself on a rock near the parking lot. As Kelly and I approached the iguana, two Mexican Secret Servicemen emerged from a dark blue Mercedes. They used the keys, codes, and triggers to our programming that had been provided them to hypnotically create the illusion that the iguana was trance-forming into de la Madrid. This control technique was to build an amnesic block to ensure against memory recall.

In reality, we were transported by automobile to de la Madrid's tacky museum-style house nearby. There, Kelly and I were taken into his all too familiar bedroom by a uniformed matronly woman. De la Madrid's bed was a king size waterbed set in a dark wood canopy frame. This time the bedspread was a plush black-blood red, which de la Madrid pointed out to Kelly as he set her on the bed. It was my experience that de la Madrid's bed was in itself a NASA technology adventure.

Mounted inside of the canopy was a movie screen where de la Madrid viewed porn videos and/or NASA provided films. From his bed I saw replicas of the NASA Goldstar multiscreen monitors that were routinely used in "experimental" mind-control conditioning. By filming the actual NASA multiscreen grouped monitors, the resultant video provided the illusion of seeing a Goldstar multiscreen when shown on a (single) screen such as was built into de la Madrid's bed canopy. For example, once when I was in his bed, the same light blue sky with moving clouds was depicted on the monitor screens that NASA had used to lock-in my programming "Somewhere in Time," de la Madrid showed on his canopy movie screen. He further enhanced the effect by having me hypnotically "float/drift" on his waterbed which he had covered with a spread of similar light blue sky with clouds print. My previous NASA programming was easily accessed "Somewhere in Time" through this simple, but nevertheless complex visual triggering method. The pornography shown was of me from previous taping, alternating with a built-in video camera projecting our sex acts onto the screen as they occurred.

This time de la Madrid said, "Let us end where we began...," referring to my witnessing the rape of my daughter in Shasta. He ordered me to undress and recline against the headboard of his bed. At the foot of the bed, he began pulling Kelly's jeans off as he said, "You gave birth to her, just as you gave birth to the border agreement, and now your role is through on both counts. The tears she will shed as you burn cannot extinguish the flames of passion you have passed on to her. Your intense sexuality has been regenerated in her, and this hormonal experiment in genetics will successfully evolve for generations to come. Your role is complete. And thanks to my friends in Washington, NASA has perfected the formula and given birth to the technology of mirrored procreation using recreated bloodlines. The only detectable difference makes the blood run cold. Reptilian. See for yourself."

De la Madrid gestured up toward the canopy screen, where the NASA created video of my "giving birth" to the lizard was depicted. By this time, the NASA provided designer drug for mind control, "Tranquility," had been administered and was kicking in full force. My eyes were hypnotically fixed on the video as he began performing oral sex on my daughter. She, too, was rendered helplessly defenseless by the drug and

218

quietly complied with his every demand. Using specific commands, de la Madrid ordered me to spread my legs and display the

vaginal mutilation carving. He positioned himself over Kelly's face, smothering her with his penis while he performed oral sex on my carving. When at last we were returned to the NCL cruise ship, Kelly and I were vomiting sick from de la Madrid's abuse and the high voltage trauma that followed. An unusually large shipment of cocaine and heroin had been loaded, which was transferred into the walls of our custom built motor home once we docked at Key Biscayne, Florida. Houston supposedly stayed aboard ship for the next week of his engagement, while I drove the motor home full of drugs and my sick daughter to Houston's farm where we resided in Tennessee.

By the time Houston returned to Tennessee from his NCL cruise, Ken Riley had already emptied the motor home and dispersed the drugs as previously planned. The only business Houston had to attend was implementing the final phase of trance-ferring Kelly and me to Danté and being updated on Mark Phillips' latest successes.

Houston immediately began programming me to not take anything but Kelly's and my clothes when sent to Danté. At the same time, Mark Phillips and I had reached a level of communication that was new to me. Although I had no conscious understanding of what he was saying, the truths he spoke resounded throughout the depths of my being. For instance, when he showed me his "Back to the Future" Delorean sports car, he wisely cryptically stated, "Sometimes you have to know where you've been in order to know where you're going."

Just before Kelly and I were to leave for California, Mark asked me to help him force Houston out of business by providing him with the files on suspected (corporate) criminal activity that Houston kept hidden at our house. Not only did I gladly do so, but "somehow" I was able to ask for help in return. I asked him to help Kelly and me get away from Houston before I was killed and Kelly was sentenced to a fate worse than death. Mark assured me that he would help.

The day Houston intended for Kelly and me to be transferred to Dante', I felt a strange compulsion to telephone Mark and notify him. That morning, Houston drove to Mark's office believing he was going to meet with him later that day. But Mark had brought a team of movers to the house, and rescued Kelly and me. He had brilliantly intercepted us as we were being passed to our intended destination! Mark even understood Kelly's and my need to rescue our farm pets from Houston's abuse. He not only found good homes for our livestock, but he had arranged for them to be loaded and transferred during our frantic rush to move out of Houston's house. Within two hours, Mark safely moved Kelly, me, our pets and livestock to freedom. Despite brilliant orchestration, pandemonium broke out when it was discovered that Kelly and I had been intercepted and detoured from our intended demise.

"Wake up, sleeping beauty," Mark said as he gently roused me with a cup of fresh coffee. "Welcome to a new day."

My eyes opened. I had never experienced such kindness before, and it seemed like a whole new world to me. Mark presented me with a beautiful watch, which he strapped on my wrist. Noting my wonder and surprise, he explained, "Now you will always know that I gave you the time of day."

The time of day? No one had ever given me their time before. They only took mine. And I never wore a watch before. I did not even know what month or year it was, let alone the time of day. I had no concept of time, which Mark explained I must always monitor from that moment on.

"You say someone is trying to kill you. Why?" Mark asked. I could not think to answer. I was totally amnesic. All three of us were now in grave jeopardy, literally dodging bullets while I desperately sought the answers. How could I have requested help when I did not even know who and/or what I was running from? Somewhere inside were the answers, and I intended to uncover them all. Fast. Now there were three lives on the line.

Mark understood that safety was tantamount to memory recovery. At the same time, none of us could be safe until I could recall who and what we were up against. Mark quickly sold everything he owned, including his DeLorean, retaining only basic necessities. He also sold the motor home which had been awarded me in my divorce from Alex Houston. Using these funds, Mark took Kelly and me to the peaceful wilderness of Alaska.

February 4, 1988 marked the beginning of life for Kelly and me, free from our mind controlled existence. It also marked the beginning of a new kind of survival as we embarked on "The Most Dangerous Game" of international proportions. Despite death threats and attempts, intimidation and cover-ups, we have survived these past seven years by refusing to keep secrets[1] -- which is in itself "another story".

---

[1] As quickly as the accuracy of my deprogramming notes were corroborated and/or verified, abstracts of various experiences and identification of abusers were vastly disseminated. Those who read these abstracts over the years, literally watched me gain piece/peace of mind (reintegrate.)

CHAPTER 33

EPILOGUE

Absolute mind control was the only existence we knew until Mark Phillips rescued my then 8-year old daughter, Kelly, and me directly from the CIA/DIA's MK Ultra Project Monarch in 1988. Through a series of carefully orchestrated events, Mark cleverly maneuvered our mind control handler, Alex Houston, into a position of "trust" that provided him the latitude to lift us free of our existence unscathed. When my "owner," U.S. Senator Robert C. Byrd, and other so-called leaders of our country involved in the Project realized the problem Alex Houston's bumbling had created, Mark took us to the safety of Alaska where we began remembering that which we were supposed to forget.

The safety and serenity of Alaska provided an atmosphere conducive to deprogramming, despite the pandemonium that ensued. Mark Phillips was the first man who not only did not abuse us, but cared for our welfare and well being. His patient, gentle manner was therapeutic, while his propensity for handling weapons and apparent intellect kept us safe against all odds. Through his noble actions, Mark taught Kelly and me that the world of human interaction in which we had existed for so long was contrary to most human behavior. We learned that goodness does exist on this earth, and that there were those in Washington, D.C. who refused to tolerate the mind control atrocities they witnessed us and others enduring.

As my eyes opened and I woke up to reality, I became enraged. Enraged for the traumas inflicted on my daughter. Enraged for a lifetime of abuse at the hands of our country's so-called "leaders." Enraged that the American public had no idea as to who and what was/is running their country. Mark helped me refocus my rage in a productive direction when he told me, "The best revenge is total recovery."

I began recovering at the rate of 18 hours a day through intensive therapy destined to restore my memory and, ultimately, my mind. I learned the ins and outs of my own mind and recorded my memories in a journal. The stack of journals grew as over a decade of White House/Pentagon level abuse flooded my mind and intruded on my thoughts. Pictures from my past flashed across my mind as neuron pathways opened in my brain. I was regaining access to my own mind and control over my future by recovering memory of my past.

Best of all, I was falling deeply in love with Mark Phillips. Why wouldn't I fall in love? He rescued my daughter and me from certain demise, restored my free will, was helping me recover in total safety, and was the polar opposite of my abusers. He treated me with love, respect, and thoughtful consideration. Equally as important, Mark proved to be an ideal father figure to Kelly. He provided her with unconditional love and deep understanding. Through him, Kelly caught a glimpse of how kind men could be -- and how good life could be. I had long since ceased to hope that such a man even existed.

The love factor in my recovery is considerable. Not only did Mark Phillips save my life, but now I had a reason to live it! The love we share kept me going at times... like when Kelly was institutionalized in 1989 for homicidal/suicidal behavior. The loving relationship that Mark shared with Kelly during our short year together as a family was sufficient to arm her with the strength to survive her ensuing ordeal as a victim of the so-called mental health and <u>criminal</u> "justice" system.

Kelly, until she turned 18, remained a political prisoner in the custody of the State of Tennessee where she was denied qualified therapy for the MK Ultra Project Monarch mind control abuses she endured. The State of Tennessee, under the politically powerful influence of Kelly's abusers, was in violation of numerous laws and basic civil rights in their determined efforts to keep Kelly from qualified therapy and the family she loves.

While many of those in positions to make a difference in Kelly's case operate on a "Need to Know" basis rather than deliberately conspire with the bad guys, a closer look into Kelly's case history should raise serious questions in their minds. Questions like; "What could a child have to do with the so- called "National Security" of our country?" The Juvenile court judge presiding over Kelly's case closed the doors to the media and onlookers for "reasons of National Security" while gross and blatant violations of laws and rights ensued. For over three long years, Kelly and I have been denied our right to an unbiased attorney while court appointed advocates and so-called "guardians" join forces with attorneys paid off by my pedophile father. My own court appointed "attorney," who doubles for the Juvenile Court judge when he takes a day off, has yet to represent my interest. My interest is in Kelly's well being and future -- and if she will have a future at all.

While Kelly is still amnesic with regard to most of her past, she is deliberately denied therapeutic access to her past, due to who and what she will recall. I am denied access to Kelly for fear she would be triggered into remembering by my mere presence. As for my deliberately "triggering" Kelly to remember what she was supposed to forget, as her abusers fear, it has been my experience that recovery must come from the inside out. Not from outside input. I want no less for Kelly than the piece/peace of mind I have gained through qualified rehabilitation. Which raises the questions: Why has the Juvenile court prohibited us from saying the name "George Bush?" Why is the "Wizard of Oz" a taboo subject for Kelly while the State of Tennessee provides her with Stephen King horror novels? Why are Kelly and I forbidden by the court to say the words "President," "politics," "New World Order," and "mind control?"

In an attempt by State employees to "normalize" our relationship, Kelly and I are forbidden to discuss the past, my immediate efforts to affect her dire and desperate situation, or future plans as a family.

Most appalling and unjust in Kelly's view is the State of Tennessee's refusal to allow her any contact whatsoever with Mark Phillips. While I am hindered from having private conversations with my daughter due to court ordered supervision and censorship, Kelly is denied the right to even wave to Mark across the parking lot. Considering that, like me, Mark has never been named as an abuser, declared unfit, or violated any court orders, the question must be asked: Why does the State of Tennessee go to such lengths to ban all communication between Kelly and the man who rescued her and taught her the meaning of unconditional love?

Kelly has asked these questions for years to no avail. The State of Tennessee refuses to even acknowledge her request for "an unbiased attorney who will represent her interests instead of those of the State." Kelly's pleas for an attorney to represent her go no farther than the deaf ears of the assigned state social worker "managing" her case. This social worker is operating on a "Need to Know" basis that has no basis, and she "Needs to Know" that she, along with the State of Tennessee, will be held accountable in the event that Kelly hurts someone or herself.

Kelly's frustrations have mounted beyond her ability to cope. I applaud Kelly for her determined but weakened efforts to stay in control of her own mind despite being denied qualified rehabilitation for the devastating results of Project Monarch mind control abuses. Kelly's daily attempts to accomplish the impossible by psychoLOGICALLY managing her psychiatric disorder is proportionate to her high intellect and willful determination. But it is not enough to fend off the Psychological Warfare that has been waged against her through CIA Damage Containment practices designed to keep her contained in amnesic silence. She needs help. She needs a collective voice.

Kelly can be helped through public outcry and through abolishment of the 1947 National Security Act (and 1984 Reagan Amendment to same) that has destroyed the true security of our once great nation. You can write to your Congressmen and Senators demanding that the so-called "National Security" act be reclaimed. Do it today. Thank you.

UPDATE…………..   Now that Kelly is 18

Fall 1998: Despite public outcry that grew to include a wide variety of international rights organizations, with numerous documents / letters directed to Tennessee's Governor(s), many of which were copied to me, Kelly has yet to be granted her right to qualified technological rehabilitation for the proven U.S. Government sponsored MK Ultra mind control abuses she endured since birth. Those few criminals in control of our country, our information, and subsequently our "criminal" justice system refuse to provide the known, but nevertheless classified, technological antidote for a problem they won't admit exists. In view of over 70,000 (declassified) documents, evidences, videos, medical records, affidavits, and government insider testimony proving the reality of the MK Ultra mind control abuses Kelly and I endured that are part of what Mark Phillips and I accumulated over the years, it is absolutely inexcusable that cover-up continues. Or, as the only "judge" Andy Shookhoff, thus far involved in this case said in a 1993 Nashville, Tennessee Juvenile Court hearing, "laws do not apply in this case for reasons of national security." After a decade of cover-up, Kelly was released, untreated, from the custody of the State of Tennessee. In the interim she is waiting, in a safe environment, for the rehabilitation she so desperately deserves.

VICTIM OF THE SYSTEM
-TIMELINE-

February 4, 1988: Mark Phillips rescued Kelly and me from our tortured mind control existence as slaves of the U.S. Defense Intelligence Agency/ Central Intelligence Agency's MK Ultra Project Monarch. Totally dissociative and amnesic, we fled from our CIA operative mind control handler, Alex Houston, my "owner" U.S. Senator Robert C. Byrd, Kelly's primary abuser George Bush, and the criminal covert "black budget" activity funding operation(s) in which we were forced to participate on national and international levels. We escaped this Pandora's Box of horrors with enough secrets to expose criminal and perverse activity on the highest levels of our government, but we have yet to escape the psychological warfare assault involving cover-up and intimidation tactics that continue to date.

March 1988: I swore out a series of three criminal warrants via the Nashville, TN Metropolitan Police Department on Alex Houston for threats and attempts on our lives. I sought further protection through Nashville's District Attorney's office, but was told by the D.A.'s Investigator Skip Sigmund that "until shots were fired" nothing could be done to protect me. Since Kelly and I were fleeing members of the U.S. Government, Intelligence, Military and Justice Department, "federal protection" was out of the question. Skip Sigmund, among others, suggested I leave town.

November 9, 1988: I was granted my divorce from Alex Houston in (proven 100% corrupt) Sumner County, TN. While still dissociative and programmed, Houston's attorney triggered (switched) me on the stand, and my own attorney, Jack Butler, refused to address the issues of mind control/abuse and cut a deal with his friend and Houston's mentor CIA operative "Reverend" Billy Roy Moore (of the Lord's Chapel/Marsha Trimble murder scandal). Subsequently, I was "freed" from my arranged/ programmed "marriage" to Alex Houston with little more than the clothes on my back. Jack Butler has retained to this day all evidences supplied him proving mind control/abuse.

December 9, 1988: With only a few hours notice, I was subpoenaed into court as Mark Phillips, Kelly and I were preparing to flee the state. Kelly's biological father and my first assigned trauma base handler (arranged by Byrd), Wayne Cox, an occult serial killer used professionally by the CIA whom Kelly had seen only three times in eight years, demanded she not leave the state. Dissociative and amnesic, I represented myself in 6th Circuit Court (there was no time to retain an attorney) against Cox, his mother, Alex Houston, and his/their attorney Bob Anderson, and plead my case to Judge Swiggart. I was granted the right to take Kelly out of state pending a two week visitation period with Cox in his home of Chatham, Louisiana. Amnesic, I could not remember why I feared Cox and for Kelly's life, and complied with the court order.

December 24, 1988: I telephoned Judge Swiggart at his residence to inform him that Kelly had reported ritual abuse (in a Mormon church at Winter Equinox/a high occult holiday Dec. 21) to me by telephone, and Cox informed me that I could not have Kelly back. Judge Swiggart said that due to the holidays, there was nothing he could do beyond suggesting I obtain local police backup to go in and retrieve her myself.

December 25, 1988: In a rather dramatic rescue, Mark Phillips and I successfully saved Kelly, but not before severe psychological damage had occurred. Kelly had witnessed and participated in human sacrifice and cannibalism, was drugged and sexually assaulted by Cox as is medically documented.

Mid January, 1989: We relocated to Chugiak, Alaska, 30 miles outside of Anchorage. Mark Phillips generously used his own resources until depleted to move us and keep us safe.

Spring 1989: Kelly's MK Ultra Project NASA produced programming had been disrupted by the traumas she endured while with Cox, and she began having flashes of memory which prompted her programmed respiratory failure. I took Kelly to Anchorage, Alaska pediatrician Dr. Lorrie Shepherd, who became gravely concerned over Kelly's lack of response to conventional medication. She recommended that Kelly see local child psychiatrist Dr. Pat Patrick, and that I immediately arrange to receive Medicaid benefits, as her therapy would be long term. She assisted with all the arrangements.

June 1989: Kelly's memory flashes began to trigger my own. She spoke of CIA covert operations run by U.S. Senator Robert C. Byrd pertaining to muling cocaine out of the Caribbean. Kelly went into respiratory failure as programmed to disrupt recalling/telling government "secrets", and was hospitalized in Intensive Care Unit of Anchorage's Humana Hospital. Psychiatrist Dr. Patrick was brought in on Kelly's case. After Kelly's release from Humana, she saw Dr. Patrick several times per week for therapy.

By August 1989: I was in intensive deprogramming with Mark Phillips, working an average of 18 hours per day in an effort to retrieve my memory and stabilize my mind quickly enough to affect Kelly's dire situation. Dr. Patrick had informed Mark and me that Kelly was suffering from Multiple Personality Disordered, now professionally termed Dissociative Identity Disordered. Within a month, I too realized that I was MPD/DID also. Because my initial abuse base was "simply" trauma rather than high tech (harmonics) like Kelly's, I soon went into fusion. Dr. Patrick informed us that Kelly exhibited symptoms of sexual/ritual abuses and advised we have her physically examined for same.

I reported to the Assistant District Attorney in Anchorage that Kelly's and my lives were in jeopardy and that I was recovering memory of political involvement for which we may require backup protection while reporting crimes to various local, state, and federal law enforcement agencies. I reported Kelly's abuse to the Anchorage Police Department (Jack Chapman, who tipped off our abusers and was later indicted/convicted in local scandal) and the Department of Human Services. Our Medicaid benefits/records were then sealed.

The federal crimes I remembered in detail were first validated and then reported to the Anchorage FBI's Ken Marischen (later found to be involved in the scandal with Jack Chapman) and resident Agent in Charge Joe

Hamblin. As a result, the FBI threatened Mark Phillips' life and liberty. Because I was still amnesic of my father's abuse/involvement, I contacted him pleading for financial assistance for Kelly's life threatening need. The FBI informed me that my father had filed "extortion" charges on me, and that they could lock me up. "Shocked" by the news, my memory began flooding into my conscious mind.

Alaska's US Customs Resident Agent in Charge, Max Kitchens, who was already aware of government/CIA involvement in cocaine operations, began investigating my/Kelly's allegations when I reported international crimes to him. He was informed by his Washington, DC supervisor to back off, as we were considered "the walking dead".

September 1989: Kelly's behavior had become violent. She exhibited homicidal/suicidal behavior, as she was writing out memories of mind control abuses; and her health was rapidly deteriorating. Mark Phillips' knowledge of government level mind control matters permitted Kelly a measure of temporary relief through LOGICALLY understanding the programming she had already remembered. However, due to Kelly's polyfragmentation (MPD/DID created in infancy through trauma before her base personality had developed) Kelly could not regain control over her own mind. Subsequently she was hospitalized at Humana Hospital again, then was transferred to Charter North Psychiatric Hospital via Dr. Patrick. Kelly told me that she needed help dealing with her homicidal urges, that they were programmed and rooted in the occult belief (reportedly instilled by Cox 12/88) that the "blood line"/family (me) must be murdered in order that she survive and the "voices in her head" cease. She cried and said she was "going to hibernate" until she received effective therapy, laid down her head and slept during the half hour drive to Charter North Hospital. I have not seen this soft, gentle side of Kelly since, and I look forward to the day when qualified therapy allows for her to be reintegrated and become whole.

September 11, 1989: Kelly had agreed to undergo physical exams (June 12) for the sexual abuse she remembered by Wayne Cox and Alex Houston in hopes justice would be served. Alaska State appointed expert Dr. Clinton Lillibridge confirmed Kelly's sexual abuse and took photographs as further proof/evidence. Dr. Lillibridge confirmed the abuse to Anchorage PD Jack Chapman and FBI Ken Marischen, and immediately informed me that a cover- up was underway. He assured me that should I "ever need his expert testimony in court, he would travel to any point in the United States to attest to her abuse" as it was "horrendous and should not be covered up".

Fall 1989: Cover-up and threats were reaching dangerous proportions, and Mark Phillips and I began arranging to leave Alaska. Knowing Kelly would require highly specialized care, I began an intensive search via telephone, mail and networking to locate a mental health physician knowledgeable of government/military mind control techniques/atrocities. Therapists involved in the infamous southern California McMartin case through newly formed organizations such as Believe the Children, in addition to reputable psychologists and psychiatrists familiar with mind control due to their own case loads, advised us that rehabilitative techniques were as classified as MK Ultra mind control records itself. Threats to their lives, liberties, and licenses compounded the dilemma of finding a therapist with both fortitude and integrity. Additionally, our finances had long since been depleted by moving, Kelly's medical needs, postage, phone bills resulting from our efforts, survival against all odds, and Kelly's Social Security benefits would not be granted until 1991 when SSI was extended by law to cover MPD/DID.

I wrote a pleading letter for assistance to Alaska's U. S. Senator Ted Stevens, who promptly responded by denying my request on Senator Byrd's Appropriations Committee stationary! I also contacted Nola Capp of Alaska's Violent Crimes Claims Commission, a federal organization that provides funding for the rehabilitation of victims of violent crimes. Nola Capp referred me to Tennessee's Claims Commissioner Richard Rucker

Commissioner Rucker began filing Kelly's/my claims before we left Alaska, as he had confirmed enough of Kelly's and my abuse to provide emergency funding. Commissioner Rucker worked diligently to assist me in arranging for Kelly's transfer from Charter North Hospital to a so-called dedicated psychiatric hospital specializing in treating dissociative disorders in Kentucky known as the Valley Institute of Psychiatry.

December 1989: U.S. Customs Resident Agent in Charge, Max Kitchens, unexpectedly visited Mark and me, visibly shaken, to inform us that our lives were in grave jeopardy. He explained that the "interest" in silencing me was beyond his ability to protect us from. Some of my primary abusers had arrived in Anchorage, and my father had joined forces with involved political and federal perpetrators to have me silenced. He had also joined with Wayne Cox to harass us through custody/paternal issues. I contacted Commissioner Rucker, who had not yet completed financial arrangements for Kelly, which prompted him to secure an emergency interim placement for Kelly at the aforementioned Valley Institute of Psychiatry in Owensboro, Kentucky.

January 1990: Mark Phillips and I had learned, through our network, of a so-called "Child's Rights Advocate" in Huntsville, Alabama, State District Attorney Bud Cramer (who soon became U.S. Congressman, setting precedent as the most junior member of Congressional Intelligence Oversight). Cramer invited us to Huntsville under "police protection" for the stated purpose of investigating/exposing local NASA and military involvement in MK Ultra mind control and its black budget criminal funding mechanisms. Under pressure, we temporarily relocated to Huntsville while Kelly was transferred to VIP in Kentucky. Commissioner Rucker provided Kelly and me with "emergency compensation" through Bud Cramer's office before our claim was shut down, reportedly by Byrd who is chairman of Senate Appropriations and oversees FBI Violent Crimes Compensation from his Washington DC "special"' office in the FBI building. Our lives were soon in grave jeopardy in Huntsville, and Bud Cramer, in association with the Huntsville Police Department, was actively involved in cover-up, intimidation, and CIA Damage Containment practices. The "Child's Advocacy" organization was an elaborate catch net of DID/MK Ultra victims, as public exposes further proved. We fled Huntsville back to Tennessee, where we would reside.

Spring 1990: Mark Phillips and I, upon the recommendation of sympathetic/concerned FBI agents, ensured our safety when reporting crimes to Tennessee's FBI through audio recording and having Nashville,

Tennessee U.S. Customs witness the interview. FBI agents Brad Garret and Phil Tuney attempted to "trigger" me into silence by using CIA codes, keys and triggers to my programming that were provided them, which to their amazement did not work. Tennessee Senator Sasser was caught in the FBI cover-up (proven) and the Tennessee Bureau of Investigation was used in an intimidation plot attempt as well. In the meantime, arrangements were back in order to obtain funding for Kelly's desperately needed therapy.

Summer 1990: Threats to our lives had again escalated, and Mark Phillips and I maintained our safety through vast dissemination of information to Time/Life, U.S. Senators and Congressmen, Tennessee legislators, victims' advocacy groups, supporters, and media which kept us alive since an untimely death could only confirm our reports. Valley Institute of Psychiatry informed me that Kelly's life was under threat from her father, Wayne Cox, my father and others, and that they did not have sufficient security to keep her safe. Also, they claimed they would have to release her from VIP due to increased federal pressure. Since finances were not yet available for obtaining qualified rehabilitation, I sought an attorney in order that Kelly not be turned into the Tennessee mental health system, as I believed her life there would be in serious peril.

July 1990: I had been advised that if Kelly could have Alex Houston arrested for child abuse, the state would be forced to release the remaining Violent Crimes Compensation to provide for her therapy. Believing this possible, I contacted Sumner County Sheriff Sutton and his Detective Jeff Paccino and reported Houston's abuse of Kelly *with documented medical and psychiatric proofs - only to have my life threatened*. I reported this to Sumner County's District Attorney Ray Whitley (who I later learned was Sutton's friend) and provided him with the evidences. He told me that "unless you have a videotape of Alex Houston having sex with the kid, there is nothing I can do." The evidences (documentation, videos, etc. from VIP) turned over to Ray Whitley were returned to me destroyed.

Tennessee State Legislator and Sumner County attorney Randy Stamps agreed to represent Kelly and me, until his life and that of his family were reportedly threatened by Sumner County Sheriff's officials. Representative Stamps, still fearing for his life, turned this information over to the Tennessee Bureau of Investigation, where cover-up was already underway. With no legal recourse, Kelly was turned out of VIP without having been rehabilitated.

Following the advice from a state victim's rights organization, I contacted U.S. District Attorney General Joe Brown's office to arrange for a meeting. Ray Whitley's wife Was Joe Brown's secretary, and we only endured further cover-up and threats.

Upon the advice of a concerned U.S. Senator, I contacted Tennessee Representative Ben West, who introduced a bill before the Legislature in Kelly's name. addressing the need for specialized care for sexual, ritual, and mind control abuses of children.

August 7, 1990: After only 72 hours since her release from V.I.P., Kelly's documented programmed respiratory failure (triggered by memory which surfaced naturally upon being reunited with me) resulted in her being admitted to Vanderbilt Hospital's Emergency Room where, again, she failed to respond to conventional medicines but responded instead to psychological intervention. Subsequently, it was ordered by Vanderbilt that Kelly be placed in the Tennessee Mental Health system.

Around midnight, and by police escort, Kelly was transferred to Tennessee Mental Health Institute for "evaluation" and referral. Exhausted, weary, and frightened, Kelly was viciously interrogated by Dr. Vassel until she vomited and collapsed. Irate over his insane line of questioning, such as " why are you crazy?" I defended Kelly and her dissociativeness and he threatened to lock me up. Kelly was transferred to Cumberland House, where I would not be permitted to see her for 48 hours.

August 9, 1990: When I finally saw Kelly at Cumberland House, they told me she had not moved from her bed since her arrival. She was sitting in her bed, not blinking, talking, etc. in a dilapidated room covered in satanic graffiti complete with blood smears on the wall, torn curtains, wrecked "furniture" and NO CARE! Appalled and horrified, I attempted to comfort Kelly while Mark Phillips photographed and scrubbed the blood from the wall. I met with Kelly's so-called resident psychiatrist, "Dr." Gabboy, who said that there was "no such thing as mind control or ritual abuse." I informed him that the pentagrams, 666, suicide, murder, and cannibalism graffiti on Kelly's walls and floor were indeed satanic. He argued that Cumberland House had never had any ritual abuse victims, until I told him we would see if the press agreed with him. They painted the rooms within 24 hours.

September 1990: I immediately and desperately sought resolution to Kelly's mental health predicament, and met with politically appointed Tennessee Commissioner of Mental Health Eric Taylor. He assured me that Kelly's dilemma could/would be resolved. Federal law stipulates that in order for a child to be transferred out of state (where supposedly qualified rehabilitation was available) a diagnosis to support the transfer must be obtained within the state. Since there was no one in Tennessee treating MPD/DID with classified military/NASA mind control programming in children, there was no one to diagnose her disorder. Commissioner Taylor gave the impossible task of locating a physician to diagnose Kelly to Department of Mental Health (DMH) worker Marsha Willis. Kelly remained UNTREATED at Cumberland House during the ensuing 8 month statewide "search" by Marsha Willis, who concluded what I knew all along-- that there was no one within the state who could diagnose or treat Kelly's MK Ultra mind control abuses.

March 1991: Marsha Willis and DMH attorneys met with me to "resolve" Kelly's dilemma by advising me to relinquish custody of Kelly to the Department of Human Services whereby the state would fund Kelly's transfer to qualified therapy. I was assured by them and Juvenile Court workers that Kelly would not become embroiled in a custody battle with Wayne Cox as he had been named/documented as an abuser by two institutions, if I simply made note of this fact, which I did.

April 2, 1991: Wayne Cox and his Nashville, Tennessee attorney Bob Anderson (admittedly paid by my father Earl O'Brien) filed abuse and neglect charges against me in Juvenile Court in an effort to regain control of Kelly.

As a result of Cox's allegations, Kelly and I were immediately denied visitation unless supervised. I never contributed to Kelly's abuse, but was unable to protect her from Cox and many others due to my own mind control abuse/existence. Kelly always understood this as she had witnessed me being tortured (documented). She and I share a close, open relationship, which is more conducive to two people who have endured great hardships together than a "normal" mother-daughter relationship -- but nevertheless is founded in love and respect. Kelly understood that we had/have much to overcome in order to receive her needed and deserved rehabilitation due to the political prominence of our abusers, and she resented having our mother-daughter conversations monitored, restricted and limited by court order.

April 3, 1991: I went back to see Tennessee DMH worker Marsha Willis, who informed me that she had had a visit and/or phone call by the feds from the Defense Intelligence Agency (DIA) and that "my life was in serious peril" if I kept talking about Kelly's and my abuse. Therefore, she would have nothing more to do with our case. This statement, like dozens of others, was covertly captured on audio tape! The DMH has since opposed me in Juvenile Court for two years.

April 1991 – April 1993: April 1991- April 1993: Violations of laws and civil rights, in conjunction with DIA's Psychological Warfare and the CIA's containment tactics, have been endured by Kelly and me both. Kelly is now a victim of the so-called Justice and Mental Health systems and still awaits qualified rehabilitation for the MK Ultra mind control abuses she has endured!

April 9, 1991: I was denied the right to defend myself in court, and could not afford an attorney. I was appointed a Legal Services (state paid) Attorney, but not until after Cox had intervened, and pressed false charges (with no evidence/documentation to back him), and restraining orders were placed against me. Plus, I was put on "probation" because I did not have a permanent address beyond the legal P.O. Box residency that Commissioner Rucker had established in order to protect me. Additionally, I met with DHS worker Ernest Fentress at the Juvenile Court, who was brought in by the state specially for this case from Sumner County, and he told me that "I would lose custody of Kelly" and that "she would be placed with abuser Wayne Cox." (This was before he even investigated our case.) He ordered that I undergo psychiatric and psychological testing, although I had never been named as an abuser, and that Cox should not.

Additionally, Judge Shookhoff ruled that all court proceedings would occur behind closed doors and ruled that the (sympathetic) press and local advocate Edith Hammons, President of Organized Victims of Violent Crime, leave the courtroom and not return. I was not permitted any support/witnesses on Kelly's and my behalf, and sat in court with "my" court-appointed attorney on one side of the room, while four attorneys, Cumberland House staff, DHS workers, etc. sat on the opposing side.

April 1993: None of the medical and psychiatric records obtained outside of the State of Tennessee were considered admissible in court. Thus, Kelly was to begin "counseling" in Tennessee with Janie Adams at Luton's Mental Health Center (who, along with Juvenile Court Judge Andy Shookhoff, is currently involved in scandal for labeling sexually abused children as sexual offenders and thus locking them up in detention rather than providing therapy). Janie Adams told us to report Kelly's sexual abuse to Metro Police or I would be the one prosecuted for the abuse Kelly's Tennessee based sex exams "might" prove. (I knew from experience that Metro Police Department was heavily involved in the very political corruption from which we escaped due to Nashville's cocaine business, as the ex-Police Chief Joe Casey, Mayor Richard Fulton, and soon to be convicted/imprisoned Sheriff Fate Thomas were present during a covert operations meeting involving drugs and arms shipments to Saudi Arabia!) We were referred to Homicide Detective Pat Postiglione, a close friend of Janie Adams and neighbor of Alex Houston's.

Kelly was taken to Metro General Hospital by Janie Adams. (I was forbidden to be there during her exam.) Kelly reports she was roughly examined (they tore her vagina) and declared her "NOT abused"! Kelly was then threatened under hypnosis (a lame attempt at hypnotic programming, documented) by Janie Adams and told she would die if she ever again said Alex Houston abused her. Janie Adams also claimed that Kelly was not sexually abused. Thanks to the forethought of Mark Phillips, I had obtained additional in-state medical records further proving her sexual abuse prior to Janie Adams teaming up with Metro P.D. in a classic cover-up.

Kelly was forbidden by Cumberland House social worker AKA "warehouse person" Charlene Johnson, in association with her friend/cohort Janie Adams, to ever discuss her past!

Kelly was punished when and if she did speak of her past, which is the worst "therapy" imaginable for a diagnosed dissociative! When Kelly ceased talking about her past as instructed because, as she says, "she had to live at Cumberland House", Cumberland House stated in court that Kelly was "not abused because otherwise she would talk about it"!

Kelly drew several graphic pictures depicting sexual abuse, including one of the torture dungeon at Youngstown, Ohio's "Charm School" (a sex slave training school overseen by U.S. Congressman Jim Traficant). These pictures, clearly depicting sexual abuse and mind control trauma, were rejected by the court as Janie Adams testified that "Kelly made it up."

At the same time, Metro Police threatened Mark Phillips' life. Pat Postiglione told me that former Mayor Richard Fulton and former Ambassador to France Joe Rodgers would "see to it that I was silenced" through threat to my life. Mark Phillips and I provided these covertly taped recorded threats to everyone we knew, sparking an investigation by Time/Life magazine.

April 15, 1991: Prominent Nashville gynecologist Dr. Richard Presley denounced the Metro scam-exam of Kelly, and reaffirmed her sexual abuse as well as documented my vaginal mutilation carving (carved for Senator Byrd's perversion). These reports were again ignored by the court.

Spring/early summer 1991: Commissioner Rucker arranged for me to meet with Governor McWherter's Legal Assistant Burnie Durham for resolution of Kelly's dilemma. Out of sheer desperation, I plead for help for Kelly. Burnie Durham told me Governor McWherter did not address such issues and therefore would not help. (I had been forced under MK Ultra to work on McWherter's initial campaign as he was being strategically moved into place for rubber stamping and implementation of Global Education, and therefore was not surprised at this response).

231

Time/Life arranged a meeting for Mark Phillips and me with DHS Manager Charles Wilson (currently involved in the same scandal with Luton's Janie Adams and Juvenile Court Judge Shookhoff), whom we did not realize at the time was part of a CIA containment effort. Mr. Wilson only assured me "Kelly would never receive therapy."

I filed charges against Cox for back child support of $21,000, which only resulted in further charges filed against me in 6th Circuit Court. Judge Thomas Brothers (currently indicted for cocaine conspiracy) violated laws and my rights to uphold Cox's charges and allow the Department of Mental Health to intercept any money that may be awarded.

April 22, 1991: I petitioned Juvenile Court to restrain Cox from having access to Kelly, as he had previously triggered her mind control programming (medically and psychologically documented) and openly threatened to do so again. Documentation from previous institutions, psychologists, psychiatrists and medical doctors, as well as Kelly's own testimony to the court, my testimony, etc. etc. etc., were all rejected by the court while Cox was granted unsupervised visitation with Kelly. Kelly and I both had explained how Cox would trigger Kelly, and I had documented in writing with medical records how he had previously triggered/activated Kelly's mind control programming, all to no avail. Social worker Charlene Johnson delivered a letter to Kelly from Cox which contained exactly the methods of triggering we had anticipated and predicted.

April 23, 1991: Despite Kelly's screams, tears and pleas for help and protection, Cox was granted visitation. Kelly reportedly confronted him with his abuses, including having witnessed his murdering, dismembering, and cannibalizing a human (as documented in previous institutions). Charlene Johnson reported that the meeting "went well." Cox's attorney, Bob Anderson, (who repeatedly had delivered sophisticated high level CIA triggers to me in court which, due to my deprogramming, failed) also had unsupervised time with Kelly. My attorney was refused visitation.

I witnessed the aftermath of Cox's visit with Kelly during my supervised visit overseen by Social Worker CeeCee Raiston. Kelly was screaming and crying, and asked CeeCee what she must do to be heard and thus be protected from her occult serial killer abuser Cox. She expressed confusion over being forced to visit him while not being permitted to see Mark Phillips who had rescued her, and why she had to have supervised visits with me. Kelly expressed confusion over the "reversal" of so-called justice. She asked, "Why am I locked up while my abusers remain free?"

When Kelly reported these abuses in court, she says she had believed that her "private meeting testimony" to Judge Shookhoff would bring about justice, when in fact she was only further punished by Charlene Johnson for having talked about her past with the Judge! Kelly sobbed uncontrollably at the loss of visitation with Mark Phillips, who she loves, respects, and has referred to as "dad" since our time in Alaska. To this date, Kelly still has not been able to speak with or have contact with Mark Phillips.

April 23 - March 7, 1991: Kelly (only 11 years old) lost over 10 lbs. in less than two weeks; she deteriorated psychologically to the pain of despondence, and her asthma, I which was deliberately triggered by Cox,

232

became so bad that she was taken to Vanderbilt Hospital by Cumberland House staff (without notification to me).

Summer 1991: I was constantly in and out of court, battling for Kelly's right to rehabilitation and to avoid further reprisals of charges against me. My father Earl O'Brien's vast wealth obtained when selling me and my brothers and sisters into the MK Ultra Project was being used against me, as well as sophisticated CIA codes, keys and triggers deliberately delivered by attorney Bob Anderson. Although these triggers were ineffective due to my deprogramming and reintegration, the blatant violations of laws and rights continued, including my being denied the right to speak/defend myself in court. I was again ordered by the court to undergo additional "evaluations" by psychiatrists and psychologists of DHS choice, and ordered to pay for Cox's scam psychological out-of-state evaluation of which I was permitted no input or choice. Cox's out-of-state evaluation being accepted by the court while hundreds of Kelly's out-of-state records were rejected added to the rapidly growing list of cover-up evidence.

Ernest Fentress of DHS, who was obviously working CIA damage containment, was caught blatantly spreading misinformation on Kelly to all state institutions, discrediting her need and preventing transfer, and leaving her at Cumberland House to withstand further abuses via Charlene Johnson. The Juvenile Court Judge dismissed Fentress from the case, while DHS promoted him. The dilemma created by Fentress' well orchestrated efforts hindered placement for Kelly.

Juvenile Court Judge Shookhoff ordered that Kelly be placed "temporarily" in the joint custody of DHS and myself for "purposes of obtaining funding necessary for her on-going residency (warehousing) at Cumberland House."

My psychological/psychiatric exams declared me sane, reintegrated, and substantiated my mind control victimization. Therefore, the opposition requested that I be tested again, which was granted. Obviously this was a set up, and federal efforts to silence me had increased dramatically. As always, I concealed a tape recorder in to my "psychiatric evaluation" session with Cynthia Turner Graham.

She immediately informed me that she did not require any information from me because she had been provided "everything she needed to know" from Ernest Fentress prior to his being taken from the case. Because of my recording, this "exam" on me was rejected by the court. Note: this criminal sham psychiatrist would soon be governor-appointed to become the next to serve as the Commissioner of Mental Health. I was instead told that I must undergo "counseling" and further examination in order to maintain any parental rights to Kelly at all (I have none anyway).

May - June 1991: I was contacted by the southeastern regional director of

U.S. Customs John Sullivan (George Bush's former division when he was head of CIA). This region includes Mexican and Caribbean operations. I was interviewed for over eight hours by agents sent to Nashville. They expressed concern for Kelly's plight and safety, as our lives were in increasing jeopardy from evidences substantiating my testimony that had "National Security" ramifications. These agents agreed to intervene on Kelly's behalf in legal proceedings.

These U.S. Customs agents received "the call" from Washington, DC which prevented their further involvement. Evidence substantiating criminal activity by then U.S. Attorney General Dick Thomburgh (one of my primary abusers) had corroborated a former FBI's similar allegations, creating serious internal departmental problems for Dick Thornburgh and his cocaine/white slavery operations. U.S. Customs' John Sullivan informed me that his boss, U.S. Customs Director Williarn Von Raab, was stepping down as head of U.S. Customs due to the criminal activity that was proliferating and being covered- up since Dick Thomburgh had to verify/approve all U.S. Customs internal investigations. Therefore, until we had a positive change of administration leadership, no help could be offered Kelly and her situation.

June 5, 1991: George Bush announced that Dick Thomburgh would be resigning for unstated reasons. Thomburgh's role in the Iran Contra cover-up scandal and more was so extensive that it could not be fully contained, and was aired on NBC's <u>A Current Affair</u> and through various newspapers.

I noted that any success obtained by me/Kelly was countered equally by our abusers through organized CIA intimidation and DIA psychological warfare tactics. Much was directed at Kelly, since they know nothing means more to me than her/her well being.

As a Result:

Kelly had been appointed a so-called "Guardian Ad-litem" Martha Child via the opposition, who told Kelly that the FBI had "cleared Cox of all charges" and that they said I was "insane" and that "Mark Phillips is a most dangerous man." (Most Dangerous Man is CIA cryptic term for being marked for imminent death.) I obtained proof and witnessed Martha Child and Charlene Johnson being paid off with my father's money for their participation. This evidence was not admissible in court.

Kelly and I were rarely permitted to see each other, being forced apart for months at a time including telephone communications.

Kelly was punished severely every time she spoke of her past abuse or current abuse by Charlene Johnson. This is documented.

I was denied access to Cumberland House records (despite several court orders) which included brain wave patterns, health deterioration, and documentation of efforts to trigger Kelly. A sympathetic worker did provide me access to some of Kelly's files to make copies.

Kelly said she was subjected to satanic/occult rituals at Cumberland House, referred to by staff members as "innocent candlelight séances."

Kelly was counseled by Charlene Johnson that her past "is not real." Cox maintained full access to Kelly.

Cumberland House testifies that Kelly is sane and therefore needs to be released to Cox's custody.

Cumberland House's testimony contradicted their previous statement, now saying that Kelly is INSANE, therefore can not testify in court.

234

Cumberland House representative testifies that there is "no such thing as mind control."

Cumberland House later testifies that Kelly can not see Mark Phillips "because he is an expert on mind control."

I am not permitted to comfort Kelly in any way, explain court proceedings, etc. Kelly expresses nightmarish confusion.

Kelly was involved in a Cumberland House van traffic accident, and was routinely hospitalized. She was denied the right to call me and notify me. She
secretly slipped me her hospital ID bracelet two weeks later.

July 29, 1991: I was denied the right to pursue prosecution of Charlene Johnson and Cumberland House, and therefore wrote an open letter for help.

Kelly wrote a few letters pleading for help, and was quickly denied further access to any outside communications, including with Edith Hammons/ Organized Victims of Violent Crime. Kelly was forbidden to make any telephone calls, or to send/receive mail.

September 13, 1991: Cox's out-of-state scam exam declares him "sane".

Summer 1991: A new organization, ICAM was assigned to Kelly's case as it had become so complex. This organization was supposedly a legal oversight committee dedicated to forcing justice in cover-up cases. An evaluation of Kelly was ordered by Nashville's reputed "best", Dr. Barry Nurcum (a CIA sponsored Australian national transplant), who had previously refused to treat Kelly on the grounds that he "was not qualified" when contacted in 1989 and again by DMH Marsha Willis in 1990. His report on Kelly's condition was inconclusive.

However, the ICAM manager had verified enough of my claims to understand Kelly's dire need for qualified therapy for the proven MK Ultra mind control abuses she endured. She was prepared to have Kelly transferred out-of-state to qualified therapy as quickly as arrangements could be made. My credibility out of Washington, DC and the Tennessee Legislature was impeccable, and this manager realized the magnitude of what Kelly and I were up against. She informed me that a Drs.' referral diagnosing even "the possibility that it looked like MPD/DID" was all that was required to finish the paperwork for Kelly's transfer. DHS dissolved the ICAM organization at this point.

January 1992: Dr. Barry Nurcum wrote a letter to the court stating that Kelly should be protected from Wayne Cox. This letter was rejected by Judge Shookhoff, as well as all other evidences including documentation of medical records proving the devastation that was wreaked on Kelly by Cox's deliberate triggering and trauma. The Judge ruled that the decision was "up to Cumberland House", and they lied and assured me in court that Kelly would not be subjected to Cox again. Mark Phillips was invited to converse with Dr. Nurcum and subsequently recorded him stating, "if you and Cathy don't shut up you will die".

Cox arrived in Nashville for depositions as necessary for 6th Circuit Court proceedings pertaining to back child support. At least the Assistant District Attorney, Scott Rosenburg, who was present at the deposition, was quickly convinced by Cox's testimony and actions that he was the abuser I said he was all along -- who was being protected by the CIA/US Government for the information he holds on MK Ultra Project Monarch and political abusers such as Senator Byrd.

Charlene Johnson allowed Cox access to Kelly at Cumberland House anyway, and forbid Kelly from telephoning me. Cox's abusive mother was also permitted access to Kelly.

Kelly screamed, cried, begged, pleaded, etc. to no avail, then collapsed in a heap on the floor from terror as documented in Cumberland House records that were 'accidentally' released to me by a compassionate worker. Charlene Johnson physically assaulted Kelly, shaking her violently and forcing her to stand at attention to visit with Cox. Kelly was later isolated in a padded cell for her lack of cooperation.

I again petitioned the court. Juvenile Court ruled that Cumberland House was unaccountable for their abuses of Kelly since I had no jurisdiction to press charges because Kelly was in joint custody whereby "one state agency cannot sue another". Charlene Johnson remains on the job at Cumberland House to this date. Cumberland House changed their logo to a child with Monarch Butterfly wings, with the initials R.I.P. written in bold lettering.

January 22, 1992: A new organization acquired by my attorney, OmniVision, took charge of oversight of Kelly's case. I was assured that OmniVisions would provide qualified therapy for Kelly, even out of state, as well as protection from Cox, IF I relinquished full custody of Kelly to DHS. I had no alternative considering that I had no parental rights anyway and Charlene Johnson was abusing Kelly so horribly. Before I made my decision, however, Judge Shookhoff ruled that Kelly be placed in full DHS custody.

January 1992: I was informed by Dr. Barry Nurcum that a diagnosis on Kelly would be obtained through a new-to-Nashville psychiatrist/psychologist who had studied mind control under U.S. Defense Department Psychiatrist Dr. Martin Orne. Considering that this highly credentialed physician could be with the opposition, I spent eight hours interviewing Dr. Mitchell to no avail. Dr. Mitchell took over Kelly's case under the condition that "her records remain confidential as was necessary for her safety."

Kelly was placed in a foster home by OmniVisions. I was not permitted to know who or where this foster home was. I was permitted, however, to see Kelly on a regular basis through Dr. Mitchell's office as quickly as arrangements could be made.

Court proceedings to arrange for Dr. Mitchell's confidentiality and my visitation dragged on for six months, during which time I rarely saw Kelly. I learned that she had been placed in foster care with the former Cumberland House worker who openly practiced witchcraft.

236

February 5, 1992: A restraining order by OmniVision through the Juvenile Court further forbade Kelly from writing letters for help or contacting supporters or victims' organizations, and restrained her from speaking of certain topics, including what little she recalled of her past.

March 8, 1992: I wrote a pleading letter to DHS to take accountability for the abuses and violations of rights Kelly was enduring. I wrote numerous letters pleading for help, and remained vigilant in my desperate efforts to obtain Kelly's much needed and deserved rehabilitation. I received a response from a supportive U.S. Senator recommending that I broaden my approach to the Tennessee legislature. Arrangements were made for me to speak as an invited guest before the Tennessee legislature and then Commissioner of the Department of Human Services, Grunow.

April 13, 1992: I spoke before the legislature, pleading for resolution of Kelly's dilemma. One of my former abusers, Tennessee State Senator Ray Albright, left the meeting while TN. Rep. McAfee promised to help and ordered Commissioner Grunow to provide him a report on Kelly's case. After the meeting, Commissioner Grunow growled in my face that "under no circumstances would Kelly ever receive any therapy." Our DHS caseworker, Denise Alexander, who had been supportive of Kelly and me, was reportedly pressured by Commissioner Grunow to such an extent that she quit her job rather than comply with his cover-up. She tearfully wished Kelly and me luck.

July 1992: Kelly was finally in therapy with Dr. Mitchell, and subsequently she and I were permitted a weekly visit in our "family therapy" session with his M.S.W. associate, Mr. Neiswender. Kelly and I were permitted to talk for the first time in two years. Kelly immediately expressed fear of Dr. Mitchell, and explained to Neiswender that she had no problems with me, but had horrible problems with her assigned foster "mother", occultist Melissa Thurmond. Kelly began expressing fear and anxiety, wore occult jewelry provided by Melissa, spoke of "full moon" campfire rituals/parties, and read occult literature. It was apparent to me that Kelly was again being subjected to occult trauma.

August 1992: Kelly's occult involvement through Melissa Thurmond caused her to switch into an occult persona and become violent. Melissa then literally dumped Kelly and her few belongings on the street curb near the YWCA and notified DHS. Kelly was institutionalized again for homicidal/suicidal behavior, this time at Vanderbilt where Dr. Barry Nurcum and Dr. William Mitchell would be working "on" her. OmniVision determined Kelly was no longer "fit for their program" and withdrew from her case, leaving DHS in full control.

Early September 1992: I had been forewarned by knowledgeable and cooperative members of the U.S. Intelligence Community that the Psychiatric section of Vanderbilt University subcontracted to the same corrupt faction of the U.S. Government that posed immense threat to Kelly. I was court ordered to attend family session at Vanderbilt, and experienced/witnessed that Kelly's mind and life were in grave danger there. I was further informed that an attempt was being made to silence Kelly through classified MK Ultra mind control means, and to expect that she may be re-programmed to request access to her abusers.

October 1992: I had been sufficiently prepared to deal with the trauma of seeing Kelly negatively programmed. She asked me "why don't I have memory flashes any more?" and said that she wanted to see Cox. Mr. Neiswender, who was supervising the visit, asked Kelly if she could remember anything- good or bad-- about Cox. She replied, "No." So I reminded her how our brain compartmentalizes memory of trauma too horrible to comprehend, and asked if, perhaps, this was why she had no memory of Cox. The logic restored her control over her own mind, without my having triggered memory which could have resulted in respiratory failure. Instead, Kelly decided that she would not see Cox after all, then told me that all she could remember about her past was .....

Mr. Neiswender literally fell off his chair with surprise, and told Kelly to tell Dr. Mitchell about this that evening. Kelly had remembered specific CIA codes and operations in the Caribbean, as well as being in and out of the Pentagon and White House, and told explicit sexual details involving George Bush.

Late October 1992: Court records show that Vanderbilt underwent a battle of allegiances between Kelly and government ties. I do not know who was on which side, but Kelly was reportedly subjected to "harmonics" in an effort to make her forget what she had just remembered. I was forbidden to see Kelly any more at Vanderbilt, and Mr. Neiswender "retired" immediately. I went to see Dr. Mitchell and Dr. Nurcum only to find locked doors and sealed lips.

During this same period of time, I was informed that information I had released pertaining to the North American Free trade Agreement was greatly endangering our lives, particularly as this was an election year. The NAFTA information I had tied directly to George Bush and my own memories of his brutal sexual abuse of Kelly. I had obtained further proof/corroboration of his pedophile activities, and arrangements were made for vast dissemination of information as well as a speaking circuit whereby "silencing" either of us would only prove us credible.

George Bush made five separate trips to Nashville in October, during the most important time of his re-election campaign, most of which were not nationally publicized, but are well documented.

I was told that the brain stem scarring damage done by the harmonics programming that Kelly reportedly endured during this time could be effectively treated and reversed if she was transferred to qualified rehabilitation immediately.

November 5, 1992: Mark Phillips and I spoke before a large group of state and federal law enforcement personnel outside Houston, Texas to release my well documented NAFTA information, a meeting which may well have saved our lives.

January 5, 1993: A new oversight organization, ACCT, took over management of Kelly's case. She was transferred to Charter Lakeside Psychiatric Hospital in Memphis, Tennessee without my being permitted any contact. It had been over four months since I last saw her at Vanderbilt. I was granted the light to attend an ACCT meeting and was allowed some input by one of their supervisors. The paperwork drawn up by ACCT states that Kelly, always an A-B student with far above average intelligence, now meets the criteria for certification as learning disabled since "her brain was allegedly damaged" at Vanderbilt hospital.

March 11, 1993: I received a supervised telephone call from Kelly under the direction of her new Charter Lakeside social worker, Abbot Jordan. This was my first time to speak with her since the incident at Vanderbilt. Kelly cried and told me that when she reported to Dr. Mitchell what she had recalled (about CIA operations and Bush), he forced her to sit in a chair for 48 hours with no food, water, or sleep prior to her forgetting everything she had told him.

Now Kelly is diagnosed "oppositional". Who could blame her? She is not at all the same child that I knew - and I knew every personality fragment and facet of her. All she knows is that her conscious focus has been eroded and that she is in desperate need of specialized, qualified rehabilitation. As always, I assure her "It's not over till we win."

March 17, 1993: I had been repeatedly denied my right to testify in court. A motion was pending, filed by Cox's attorney and charging that I should pay child support from the $3000 in back child support that was awarded me through 6th Circuit Court. The Assistant District Attorney, Scott Rosenburg, testified that this was not legal, and that the $3000 had already been spent obtaining further evidences for Kelly's case. The Judge said, "Laws do not apply in this case for reasons of National Security", and that I should pay child support unless there was a reason why I should not work. Cox's attorney Bob Anderson shouted that I should spend time in jail for having "spent the money" (which, in fact, I never saw). I was not permitted to testify that due to threats to my life and establish a routine under our circumstances. On March 17, 1993, Judge Shookhoff ruled that I should pay $25 a week for child support, retroactive to January 1993.

I was advised that this ruling (because I had no way of paying) could quickly result in termination of all parental rights (as if I have any) and jail time for contempt/failure to pay.

April 1, 1993: I spoke with Kelly, who still has no further memory of her past and has been seen by her court appointed physician at Charter Lakeside only one time. We are waiting on his determination that Kelly requires qualified rehabilitation for classified abuses.

September 1995: Mark and I had our well documented book entitled TRANCE Formation of America published, complete with irrefutable graphic details which are in themselves evidence to present to Congress, all factions of law enforcement including the FBI, CIA, DIA, DEA, TBI, NSA, etc., all major news media groups, national and international human rights advocates, both American Psychological and Psychiatric Associations, the National Institute of Mental Health, and more... to no avail. TRANCE thoroughly exposes many of the perpe-TRAITORS and their agenda replete with names, which raises the question "why haven't we been sued?" The obvious answer is that the same "National Security Act" that continues to block our access to all avenues of justice and public exposure also prevents these criminals from inevitably bringing mind control to light through court procedures, an opportunity we would welcome.

Meanwhile, as reported by both APAs, survivors of U.S. Government sponsored mind control began to surface all across our nation. The first to encounter the vast number of survivors were law enforcement and mental health professionals, and these professionals began to ask questions. in other countries,

answers are being provided through somewhat less controlled media, reflecting the CIA's involvement in Project MK Ultra human rights atrocities. A television documentary entitled The Sleep Room aired across Canada by the Canadian Broadcast Corp. in the spring of 1998. Dr. Martin Orne, an associate boasted by Dr. William Mitchell M.D., Ph.D. who thrust Kelly into Vanderbilt's cover-up attempt (re: p.14), is named as an accomplice to Dr. Ewing Cameron's MK Ultra 'experiments' in Montreal, Quebec. Additionally, it should be known that Dr. Cameron went on to found the American Psychiatric Association, which has helped to maintain America's mental health profession in the dark ages of information control.

Since the release of our Victim of the System timeline in 1991 a new organization was formed by concerned, prominent psychiatrists and psychologists entitled The International Society for the Study of Dissociation. This organization is dedicated to informing mental health practitioners worldwide of Dissociative Identity Disorder (DID), formerly inappropriately termed Multiple Personality Disorder (MPD), which is the basis for mind control. DID is professionally defined as "the mind's sane defense to trauma too horrible to comprehend" due to the elaborate coping mechanism of the brain's compartmentalizing memory of abuse so the rest of the mind ran function somewhat "normally." This compartmentalization results in what is known as repressed memory or amnesia enclosed within a traumatic event. The victim cannot think to bring to conscious mind the incomprehensible abuse, leaving the dissociative, emotionally shattered victim/survivor's personality highly suggestible with the subconscious easily led. Hence the reason DID victims become prime candidates, or "chosen ones" for mind control, as is/was the case with Kelly and me.

In order to heal from trauma-anchored repressed memory, the survivor must learn of their past from the inside out, not through outside input. As a recovered survivor, I reiterated this fact repeatedly to Tennessee Juvenile Court Judge Andy Shookhoff who imposed monitored censorship on Kelly's and my conversations (i.e. topics of our past, present efforts, future plans, and the words "mind control", "president", "Bush", etc.). I knew what was in Kelly's best interest, and his ignorance was glaring and obnoxious!

December 1995: After the publication and subsequent release of TRANCE, public outcry forced Judge Shookhoff to lift his five year gag order forbidding Kelly outside communications and mail. He sarcastically said to Kelly, "far be it for me to violate your Constitutional rights", as he mimicked the public plea. During the same hearing, he also ordered Kelly to read TRANCE to which she responded, "It's my Constitutional right to choose what I read." Representatives in attendance from Jabneel, her newly assigned Knoxville Christian based placement, then voiced their opposition to Judge Shookhoffs obvious lack of concern for Kelly's mental state. And while they admittedly did not understand mind control, they did recognize a glaring cover- up and vowed to stand by Kelly at all costs. And the costs were insurmountable.

July 1997: The doors of Jabneel were closed forever. Kelly reports that a team of federal officers flashing FBI identification, shackled some of the children for transport to other facilities while confiscating all records. Due to the volatility of Kelly's case and circumstances, arrangements were immediately made to transfer her to relative safety. From this disorganized "safehouse", Kelly was thrust into a nonrestrictive, unstructured lifestyle highly detrimental to her well being. And pursuit of her confiscated health and school records began in earnest and to no avail thus far.

Fall 1997: After years of conditioning through various institutional/warehouse placements instructing Kelly to "get along with her peers," including gang members, satanists, the violently dangerous, and mentally disturbed. Kelly attended a public high school. Her dissociative mind was highly suggestible and vulnerable to the same kind of 'peers' she had been forced to get along with the previous eight years. Her diagnosed DID rendered her defenseless, without conscious discernment, void of self awareness/self esteem, awareness that she was/is subject to reactivation of program(s), and in dire need of understanding. Kelly began a downward spiral from which she has yet to recover.

I was blocked by the State of Tennessee, who still had custody of Kelly, from having necessary contact with school officials and/or guidance personnel. Their glaring lack of understanding of Kelly's condition and plight was compounded by the fact that all of her past medical, mental health, and school records were being withheld by the FBI who had confiscated them. Kelly was unable to provide the school with pertinent information, of which she was still dissociative due to lack of therapy, and was subsequently told she could not/would not graduate with her class unless her records were provided.

We appealed to the Tennessee DHS, now re-titled the TN. Department of Children's Services, for relief. Instead, Kelly's so-called case worker Katie Finney who had blatantly covered up the reality of her needs for years, was being replaced by a new case worker, Fred Polacek, which delayed resolution indefinitely. In the meantime, Kelly's Tennessee state medical insurance failed to cover any and all needs, including hospitalizations, medication, and/or therapy. To compound this "felony," Kelly was told that her Social Security benefits, which had been established for her in 1989 in Alaska, had lapsed through negligence of the State of Tennessee and would no longer be available for her when she turned 18.

Still in the custody of the State of Tennessee, Kelly was maintained in limbo, unable to recall her past or progress toward her future. And her immediate health needs rendered her weak and sluggish. Her once high grade point average had plummeted. Where she once academically tested way beyond her grade level, she now was struggling to maintain sufficient focus on her schoolwork to complete it.

On a brighter note, Christian patriot singer and songwriter Gad Klang wrote a song of encouragement for Kelly using our family motto as its title "It's Not Over Till We Win," included it on his latest release, and it began getting airplay nationwide. Kelly's routine boxes of cards, letters, and gifts from supporters swelled to overflowing, yet her predicament remained unchanged. Still no medical relief, no qualified mental health therapy, no Social Security benefits, no school records, and her extensive case records were scattered among workers at the Tennessee Department of Children's Services, despite my persistent efforts to stimulate attention and action. My efforts were extremely hampered by the "legal" reminder that Kelly was not in my custody.

Kelly was ordered to take a menial job to pay for her basic necessities which were not being supplied by the State. Unable to focus at work any more than she could at school, Kelly was not able to meet the routine work demands placed on her.

September 20, 1997: Kelly took flight from her dilemma, fled her Knoxville placement, and was found sleeping 200 miles away under a bridge in the homeless section of Riverfront Park in Nashville. She had no medication, change of clothes, or food. She was immediately transported to the Dee Dee Wallace shelter for battered women and homeless children. I was still legally forbidden custody!!

Not one of Kelly's difficulties had been resolved by the state, and no relief was provided her beyond a roof over her head. She was sent back to a public school, where again ignorance of her severe mental disorder and lack of understanding was fueled by a lack of records. Kelly's and my communications dwindled due to imposed restrictions that permitted intermittent 10 minute phone calls and 2 hours a month visitation.

February 1998: As Kelly neared her 18th birthday, Mark and I took the necessary steps and precautions to safely solidify arrangements for her transfer to high tech, privately sponsored "classified" rehabilitation. Certain records and finances were needed to complete the effort, which I expected would finally be "legally" obtained upon Kelly's leaving State of Tennessee custody. I learned that there would be a three month "grace period" for transition from custody, which equated to a gray area of legalities and red tape.

February 19th, 1998: Kelly turned 18. The steps planned for obtaining her qualified rehabilitation began to precariously detour when Kelly disappeared on to the streets of Nashville TN for weeks at a time. Our efforts appeared undermined while Kelly reported traveling outside the state to such areas as Fort Campbell, Kentucky, a "former" mind control abuse base she and I both endured, with proofs. During her absence, her State imposed placement of Try- Angle House (Suzanne Boone, 3137 Long Blvd. Nashville, Tennessee 37203) claims to have "divvied up" her belongings, including personal clothing and her "hope chest" of sentimental letters and artifacts, never to be seen again.

Spring 1998: With no records provided or relief in sight through the State of Tennessee, Kelly was again told that she would not be able to graduate with her class. Highly intelligent, but nonetheless unable to focus, Kelly, now 18, dropped out of school and again took to the streets. Reaching out to help her was akin to squeezing a handful of sand, and the tears I shed were shared by Kelly who "couldn't help her self". Her voiced fears included that she "couldn't keep with the program" (what program??), and her "friends" she discussed were violent satanists and drug dealers.

Knowing that love is the most powerful healing force in the universe, I maintained communication with Kelly while Mark, again, solidified arrangements off shore to have her technologically deprogrammed in hopes she could eventually be in control of her own mind. Kelly

242

continuously disappeared at the most inopportune moments. Even Social Security was willing to proceed with an appeal on her case, if only Kelly could show up for an appointment as legal procedures demand. Those armed with government insider intelligence poised and ready to help Kelly recover her mind, became more and more wary of the apparent adverse influence on her mind while in the custody of the State of Tennessee. Lives were at risk. Lives of some individuals known to Mark were lost and subsequently, the "secret mental health recovery team" partially disbanded and moved their remaining operations to another country.

Summer 1998: Distraught with events, my own conflict with love and logic between Kelly and her programming reached overwhelming proportions. I planned/fantasized ways to whisk her away to safety while the CIA's orchestrated psychological warfare intensified on us all. The political volatility of our country could potentially increase with the international ramifications of human rights issues instigated by her plight and the proven facts contained within TRANCE. I was told once again that our lives were in grave jeopardy, with no chance of survival for any of us if Kelly and I reunited, due to her active programming. (The high tech manipulation of brainwaves that Kelly endured on various NASA and military installations during the early 1980's is as fresh today as when d was instilled. And technology has advanced light years since then with the utilization of computerization.) This living nightmare couldn't overpower love, which fueled my determination to ensure Kelly's mental and physical freedom, whether it would be with or without me.

Years of physical separation only strengthened the bond between us. Kelly and I share a profound depth of communication beyond the usual mother- daughter relationship. Knowing who and what we have experienced together, in addition to what we are currently up against, Kelly sometimes expresses a basic understanding with an appreciation for our relentless efforts. Her own insight into life seems highly evolved, and her innate spirit is strengthened with love. Yet she struggles with the reality of her trauma and highly technologically based U. S Government mind control programming that has been harmonically instilled to control her brains' function over her respiratory system (mine was digestive and circulatory) whereby she, like today's spies, would die before telling government secrets. When she and I are together, it naturally triggers memory of past experiences which often results in her suffering respiratory failure. This program must be diffused in order for Kelly to regain control over her own life by remembering her past and reclaiming control over her own mind. Psychologically, Kelly is at times aware and determined. Yet, this cannot overpower the harmonic manipulation of brain wave patterns formed in infancy prior to full development of her brain. Instead, she continues to suffer repeated hospitalizations.

What You **Need to Know** is that Kelly's plight extends beyond her to u.s. all. Current events including High-Frequency Active Auroral Research Project (HAARP), and hype and media 'spin' lend increasingly intensified demands that we-the-people **WAKE-UP to Reality**, arm our selves with knowledge, and legally and peacefully take back *our* country, *our* "criminal" justice system, and reinstate Constitutional values of freedom and justice for all.

243

By understanding Kelly's plight, we will understand our own. By helping her, we will help ourselves. By gaining insight, we all positively evolve into the next millennium a stronger, wiser, healthier, more spiritual and loving mankind. With consideration to this timeline, Mark and I, respectfully ask that

you become responsible leaders and support our effort to resolve this case -- once and FOR ALL. Please help u.s. starting today by increasing awareness through broadcasting this timeline, writing your Congressmen, and referring to the details in our book **TRANCE Formation of America**...

... for Kelly's sake ...

... the sake of your loved ones ...

... and the sake of humanity as we know it.

SILENCE EQUALS DEATH

The primary key to our survival is attributable to the vast and timely dissemination of corroborated, detailed testimony. For five consecutive years beginning in 1988, we personally presented testimony and supporting irrefutable evidences to all applicable county, state, and federal law enforcement agencies. This same testimony was hand delivered by a sympathetic U.S. Congressman from Tennessee, Bob Clement, to all concerned Washington, D.C. government agencies, and to certain members of the U.S. House of Representatives and Senate. We did not discriminate between 'good guys or bad guys'--everyone received the same voluminous packet.

The responses we eventually received were bland form letters and/or threats to our lives and liberty. The threats were verbally delivered by local officers of law enforcement agencies in Nashville, Tennessee. These threats, we knew, were "hollow" due to the large number of people we had notified who believed we could only be credible if we were murdered. This is a normal human response that we bet would protect our lives. It did and we won this first round.

Secondary to disseminating information for ensuring our survival was to determine once and for all, if, in fact, our constitutional system of justice had actually collapsed. The bitter truth revealed through this five year exercise proved justice is no longer available when the National Security Act is invoked.

The following list of individuals and organizations represents a fraction of the total number we contacted with testimony. We left no stone unturned. And we were stonewalled **For Reasons Of National Security**.

NATIONAL/INTERNATIONAL: Senate Select Committee on Ethics, Chief Council, Wilson Abney; Amnesty International Editor Ron Lajoie; Defense Investigative Service Counterintelligence Security, Maynard C. Anderson; Secretary of State James Baker IH; Permanent Select Committee on Intelligence U.S. Congressman Doug Bereuter; U.S. Congressman David E. Boinor; U.S. Senator David L. Boren; B.C.C.I. Investigator Jack Blum; President George Bush; Director US Department of Justice Jane Burnely; President Jimmy Carter; Chairman of the National Security Council; Secretary of Defense <u>Dick Cheney</u>; Government Accountability Project Executive Director Louis Clark; U.S. Congressman Bob Clement; Senate Select Committee on Intelligence U.S. Senator William S. Cohen; U.S. Congressman 1,arry Combest; I-I. Ross Perot c/o Ms. Barbara Connelly; U.S. Congressman Bud Cramer; U.S. Army Criminal Investigation Command Major General Eugene R. Cromartie; Director of White House Correspondents Association; Citizens for Decency Through Law, Inc.; National Federation for Decency; Public Affairs Section of the Pentagon; U.S. Senator Robert Dole; U.S. Congressman Ronald V. Dellums; U.S. Army Criminal Investigations Division Sim Dibble; Air Force Brigadere General Francis R. Dillon; U.S. Senator Albert Gore; C.I.A. Director Helms; Director National Security Agency; U.S. Senator Bob Dole; U.S. Senator Pete Domenici; Assistant U.S. Attorney General, Civil Rights Division, John R. Dunne;. Mr. Louis H. Dupart of Permanent Select Committee on Intelligence; U.S. Arms Control and Disarmament Agency, Intelligence Division of State Department Mr. Manfred Elmer; U.S. Army Criminal Investigations Division Colonel Terry Frey; Justice Department Cocaine Division Mr.

Charles J. Gutensohn; Justice Department Community Relations Ms. Grace Flores- Hughes; Permanent Select Committee on Intelligence Mr. Calvin Humphrey; U.S. Congressman Henry J. Hyde; U.S. Congressman Barbara Kennelly; Deputy Director of the C.I.A. Richard J. Kerr;U.S. Senator John F. Kerry; National Coalition Against Pornography President Jerry Kiah; U.S. D.O.J. Mr. Frederick W. Kramer; NORAD General Kutyna; FBI Special Agent Kenneth V. Lanning; U.S. D.O.J. Ms. Mary C. Lawton; U.S. Representative Dave McCurdy; Congress Watch Director Craig McDonald; Assistant Secretary of Defense Werner E. Michel; U. S. Senator George Michell; Manuel Noriega and Attorney Frank Rubino; U.S. Senator Sam Nunn; Chief Council Michael J. O'Neil; General Council L. Brit Snider; Human Rights Watch Ms. Susan Osnos; The Perot Group; U.N. Intelligence officer Herbert Quinde; U.S. Congressman John O. Rowland; U.S. D.O.J. Mr. Charles Saphos; U.S. Senator Sasser; FBI Director William Sessions; U.S. Mr. Michael Shakeen; U.S. D.O.J. Special Investigations Mr. Neal Sher; State Department Intelligence Division Mr. William Shepard; Enforcement Operations Associate Director Gerald Shur; Office of the Inspector General U.S. D.O.D. Mr. Morris B. Silverstein; General Council L. Britt Snider; Defense Intelligence Agency Director General Harry E. Soyster; U.S. Senator Ted Stevens; National Security Agency Director Vice Admiral William Studeman; U.S. Senator Don Sundquist; D.O.J. Director Ozell Sutton; U.S. Attorney General Dick Thornburgh; Mr. Pat Truman and Mr. Bob Shartez of Child Exploitation and Obscenity Section; U.S. Customs Director William Von Raab; Independent Council Lawrence Walsh; U.S. Senator Harris Wofford; C.I.A. Director William Webster.

ORGANIZATIONS and MEDIA: *ABC, NBC, CBS, CNN*; Alaska Violent Crimes Bureau; Albuquerque (N.M.) Journal and Tribune; Akron (Ohio) Beacon Journal; American Civil Liberties Union; American Psychiatric Association; America's Watch; Amnesty International; Arkansas Democrat; Association of National Security Alumni, Ms. Julianne McKinney; Atlanta Constitution, Cynthia Tucker; Baptist Sunday School Board; Baseball Commissioner John Dowd; Editor James L. Cavanaugh Behavioral Sciences and the Law; Ms. Beth Vargo, Believe the Children; Dale McCulley, Cavalcade Productions; Charlotte (N.C.) Observer; *Chicago Tribune*; Child Find, Roy Stephens; Covert Actions Publications Editor William Schapp; Criminal Justice Legal Foundation President Michael Rushford; Christic Institute Investigator Jim Garrison; Christic Institute Sister Sara Nelson; Citizens Against Pornography Executive Director Richard Enrico; Citizens for Decency Through Law; Citizens for Law and Order; Clarion (Jackson, Miss.) Ledger; Congress Watch; Covert Action; Crucial Concepts; Cult Watch Australia; Cynthia Kisser and Betty Neysmith, Cult Awareness Network; DeCamp Legal Services, John DeCamp; *Detroit Free Press*; The Economist Group; Government Accountability Project; *Grand Rapids (Mi.) Press*; U.S. Department of Health and Human Services Medicaid Director Christine Nye; Dale Griffis; Huntsville (Al.) Times; Illinois Department of Public Aid; Index on Censorship; Investigative Journalism Project President Anne B. Zill; Investigative Reporters and Editors Mr. Steve Weinberg; National Coalition Against Pornography Michael Gilstrap; National Rainbow Coalition Reverend Jesse Jackson; Mr. Hayes Johnson of the *Washington Post*; Justice Unlimited, Faith Donaldson; *Los Angeles Times* Bureau Chief lack Nelson; *Kansas City Star.*, The Lighthouse Project; Michigan

Protection and Advocacy Service Executive Director Elizabeth Bauer; Milwaukee Star President Jerrel Jones; Mormon Bishop Pace; Bill Moyers; NBC Steve Goldstein; National Association of Chiefs of Police, Chief of Staff Eugene R. Cromartie; National Center for the Prosecution of Child Abuse Mr. James Shine; National Committee for Prevention of Child Abuse Executive Director Judy Rhodes; National Consortium for Child Mental Health; The Nation Company; National Coalition Against Pornography President Jerry Kiah; National Federation for Decency; National Institute of Mental Health James Breiling; National Victim Center Director Linda Lowrance; The Nebraska Leadership Conference; The New Republic Editor Dorothy Wickandew; Oprah Winfrey; Organized Victims of Violent Crime President Edith Hammons; Orlando Centinal; Parents Protecting Children; People's Justice Center; Prime Time Producer Herb O'Connor; Tennessee Association of Trial Lawyers President Reese Bagwell; The Progressive, Reverand Pat Robertson of Christian Broadcasting Network; Rocky Mountain News; San Diego Tribune; San Francisco Chronicle; San Francisco Examiner, Linda Goldstein San José Mercury News; Society for Professional Journalists; Southern Exposure; Ms. Gloria Steinem; Tampa Tribune; Time/Life Civia Tamarkin; Gordan Thomas; Victims for Victims; Attorney Andrew Vachss; V.O.C.A.L.; V.O.I.C.E.S.; Washington Post Editor Bin Bradley; Winston-Salem (N.C.) Journal; Women Against Pornography.

STATE LAW: (ALABAMA) D.O.D. Intelligence Judy Langren, Agent Chris Haynes; Huntsville Police Department's Jeff Bennett and Chuck Crabtree, District Attorney Bud Cramer; (ALASKA) Anchorage Police Detective Jack Chapman; (ARKANSAS) Detective Kirk Rokoin, Polasld County Coroner Steve Nowysld; (KENTUCKY) Nicholasvffie Police Detective Melyin Price; (LOUISIANA) New Orleans Criminal Investigations Bureau Sgt. Joseph E. 1-lebert, Jr., Homicide Lt. Gary Pittman; (TENNESSEE) Governor Ned McWherter; Governor's Legal Council Burnie Durham; Former Ambassador to France Joe Rodgers; U.S. Attorney General Joe Brown; U.S. Assistant Attorney General Wendy Goggin; Commissioner of Mental Health Eric Taylor; Child Welfare Charles Wilson; Tennessee Senator Thelma Harper, Senator Doug Henry, Senator Hicks, Representative McAfee, Representative Randy Stamps, Representative Ben West; Tennessee Bureau of Investigation Director John Carney, Agent Andy Earl, Agent Bill Thompson; Goodlettsville Police Chief Fred Schott; Sumner County Attorney General Ray Whitley; District Attorney Charles Burson; Nashville Metro Police Chief Robert Kirschner, Deputy Chief Ross, Lieutenant Tommy Jacobs, Lieutenant Jim Binkley, Sergeant James A. Hickson, Homicide Captain Mickey Miller, Detective Terry McElroy, Detective Pat Postiglione; Sumner County Sheriff Sutton, Criminal Investigator Jeff Puccini; Williamson County District Attorney Joe Baugh; Franklin Police Chief Wisdom; Nashville District Attorney Torry Johnson; D.A. Criminal Investigator Skip Sigmond; Violent Crimes Claims Commissioner Richard Rucker; White House Police Department Lt. Ron Miller; (TEXAS) Montgomery County Sheriffs Department Noel Stanley, Constable Billy Colson, Lt. John McPhillips; Houston, Harris County Deputy David Rossi, Deputy Dave Hasten; Milwaukee Wisconsin Chief of Police. FBI ALASKA: Special Agent in Charge Joe Hamblin, Special Agent Ken Marischen; FBI MISSISSIPPI: Special Agent Uuis Grever, Special Agent Pat McGlennen; FBI NEVADA: Special Agent Roger Young; FBI TENNESSEE Special

Agent in Charge Ben Purser, Special Agent Phil Tuney, Special Agent Brad Garrett; U.S. CUSTOMS ALASKA, Resident Agent m Charge Max Kitchens; U.S. CUSTOMS FLORIDA: Resident Agent in Charge John Sullivan, Detective Howard Rudolph, Detective Jack DeVaney; U.S. CUSTOMS TENNESSEE: Resident Agent in Charge Ed Walker, Special Agent Lou Bock; U.S. CUSTOMS Internal Affairs Director Ken McMillan.

Chiseled deep into the polished granite stone walls of the entrance to the U.S. Department of Justice in Washington, D.C. are the words 'The Price for Freedom is Eternal Vigilance'. This statement supports our belief that all American patriots and her allies must be aware that this particular criminal activity is being protected **For Reasons Of National Security.**

REFERENCE LIST

1. *The Oxford Companion to the Mind* by Richard L. Gregory; published by Oxford University Press, 1987, ISBN#: 0-19-866124-X
2. *Psychiatry and the CIA: Victims of Mind Control* by Harvey Weinstein; published by Wash. D.C.; American Psychiatric Press ISBN#: 90-707
3. *Journey Into Madness The True Story of Secret CIA Mind Control and Medical Abuse* by Gordon Thomas; published by N.Y. Bantam Books, 1989, ISBN#: 0553053574
4. *The Search for the "Manchurian Candidate": The CIA and Mind Control* by John D. Marks; published by N.Y. Times Books, 1979, ISBN#: 0812907736
5. *The Secret Team: The CIA and it's Allies in Control of the United States and the World* by Fletcher Prouty; published by Englewood Cliffs, N.J. Prentice-Hall, 1973, ISBN#: 0137981732
6. *The Nazi Doctors: Medical Killing and the Psychology of Genocide*; published by N.Y. Basic Books, 1986
7. *Secret Agenda: The United States Government/ Nazi Scientists and Operation Paperclip* by Linda Hunt; published by N.Y. St. Martin's Press, 1991
8. *Mind Control in the United States* by Steven Jacobson; published by Critique Publishing, 1985, ISBN#: 0-911485-00-7
9. *Clinical and Experimental Hypnosis in Medicine, Dentistry, and Psychology* by William S. Kroger, M.D.; published by J.B. Lippincott Company, 1977, ISBN#: 0-397-50377-6
10. *Hypnotherapy* by Milton J. Erickson and Ernest L. Rossi; published by Irvington Publishers, Inc., 1979, ISBN#: 0-470^{a}26595-7
11. *The Osiris Complex: Case Studies in Multiple Personality Disorder* by Colin Ross, M.D.; published by University of Toronto Press Inc., 1994, ISBN#: 0-8020-7358-1
12. *Trance Formations: Neuro-Linguistic Programming and the Structure of Hypnosis* by John Grinder and Richard Bandler; published by Real People Press, 1981, ISBN#: 0-911226-23-0
13. *Reframing: Neuro-Linguistic Programming and the Transformation of Meaning* by Richard Bandler and John Grinder; published by Real People Press, 1982, ISBN#: 0-911226-25-7

Abstracts, Journals, and Papers

14. *Human Rights Law Journal: Freedom of the Mind as an International Human Rights Issue* by Dr. Alan Scheflin; published by N.P. Engel, 1982
15. *In Through the Out Door: Subliminal Persuasion* by Eric Lander; Omni, February 1981
16. *Not What You Read, But How You Read It* by Junichi Kikuchi; Business Japan, July 1990
17. *Behavioral Modification Programs: Federal Bureau of Prisons* by U.S. Congress, House, Committee on the Judiciary
18. *Biomedical and Behavior Research* by U.S. Congress, Senate, Committee on Labor and Public Welfare, 1975

19. *Project MK Ultra: The CIA's Program of Research in Behavioral Modification* by U.S. Congress, Senate, Select Committee on Intelligence, 1977
20. *The Mind Control Papers* by Los Angeles Editors of Freedom, 1980
21. *The Mind Fields* by Kathleen McAuliffe, Omni, February 1985
22. *Brain Triggers: Biochemistry and Behavior* by Joanne Ellison Rodgers, Science Digest, January 1983
23. *Old Familiar Voices: Research on How the Brain Recognizes Familiar Voices* by Diana Can Lancker, Psychology Today, Nov. 1987
24. *Cells of Babel: Individual Nerve Cells can Manufacture Different Transmitter Chemicals and Thereby Speak Simultaneously in Various Languages of the Brain* by Julie Ann Miller, Science News, December 1992
25. *Brains Memory Chemicals* by Science News, April 1980
26. *New Maps of the Human Brain* by Ann Gibbons, Science, July 1990
27. *Sex and the Split Brain* by Carol Johmann, Omni, August 1983
28. *Molecules of Memory* by Geoffrey Montgomery, Discover, Dec. 1989
29. *Info Accumulating on How Brain Hears* by Charles Marwick, JAMA, June, 1989
30. *Mind In Motion: Neurologists Try to Unlock the Secrets of Language* by Geoffrey Montgomery, Discover, March 1989
31. *Brain Circuits and Functions of the Mind* by Colwyn Trearthen and Charles Gross, Science, September 1990
32. *Another Signaling System in Brain* by R. Weiss, Science News, January 1990
33. *Pain Perception Research: On and Off Cells in the Brain* by Frederick Golden, Discover, August 1990
34. *Charts of the Soul: Brain Chemistry and Behavior* by Judith Hooper, Omni, March 1983
35. *Relationship of Most Disorders to Violence* by J.J. Collins, J°Nerv-Ment-Dis, 1990
36. *Picture This: Discover Conscience/NASA* by Steven Scott Smith, Omni, October 1990
37. *Scientist in Search Of The Soul* by John Gliedman, Science Digest, July 1982

INDEX

251

Spread the Word and Raise Awareness on Truth that Makes us Free!

Pirated copies of all 3 titles by Cathy O'Brien with Mark Phillips are in circulation as a deliberate attempt to dilute and discredit their documented testimony. Therefore, to ensure the integrity of information received, order books direct from:

www.TRANCE-Formation.com
www.ForReasonsOfNationalSecurity.com

Books By The Authors:

TRANCE Formation of America by Cathy O'Brien with Mark Phillips

ACCESS DENIED For Reasons of National Security by Cathy O'Brien with Mark Phillips

PTSD: Time to Heal by Cathy O'Brien

Contact Cathy direct:
email: TRANCE008@hotmail.com
or write: Reality Marketing
      PO Box 868
      Guntersville, Alabama 35976 USA

Made in the USA
Monee, IL
16 October 2023

44240014R00154